# INTRODUCTION TO PROGRAMMING LANGUAGES

# INTRODUCTION TO PROGRAMMING LANGUAGES

HARRY KATZAN, JR.

ASSOCIATE PROFESSOR OF COMPUTER SCIENCE

PRATT INSTITUTE

First Edition

AUERBACH.
publishers

philadelphia
new york
london

AUERBACH Publishers Inc.
Philadelphia, Pa., 1973

**Library of Congress Cataloging in Publication Data**

Katzan, Harry.
 Introduction to programming languages.

 Include bibliographies.
 1. Programming languages (Electronic computers)
I. Title.
QA76.7.K39            001.6'424                73-9587
ISBN 0-87769-173-8
ISBN 0-87769-176-2  (pbk.)

# CONTENTS

## PART 3. THE FORTRAN LANGUAGE

# PREFACE

This book provides an introduction to programming languages; the viewpoint is that of the user. The three most widely used languages are covered: BASIC, FORTRAN, and COBOL. The languages form a continuum, by order of sophistication, and that is the manner in which they are presented. Introductory concepts are presented through the BASIC language and these concepts are extended systematically with FORTRAN and COBOL, respectively.

A programming language is the key link between man and the computer and has become a bona fide field of study. To a great extent, the growth of the computer industry is dependent on programming languages since they provide machine independence, they facilitate programming, and they provide a means of describing a process so that the information contained in it can be passed from generation to generation. The three languages covered in this book satisfy each of these needs.

The subject matter is covered in four parts. Part 1 presents introductory concepts necessary for the remainder of the book. Parts 2 through 4 present the BASIC, FORTRAN, and COBOL programming languages, respectively. The presentation has several distinct advantages:

1. The material is introductory and leads the reader from topic to topic and from language to language.
2. Three languages are covered in *one book*, eliminating the need for the reader to purchase three separate books (as is often the case).
3. Exercises are included with each chapter.
4. Each part is divided into reasonably sized chapters, appropriate for reading and class assignment
5. A liberal number of references is included.

6. The material is appropriate to both scientific computing and data processing.
7. A complete description of each language is given.

The book can be used as an undergraduate textbook and for professional development. As a text, it satisfies the needs of a "practically oriented" programming language course. As a professional development book, the material is appropriate for the problem solver (engineer, scientist, mathematician, analyst), for the professional programmer, and for the computer and/or data-processing manager.

It is a pleasure to acknowledge the assistance of my wife Margaret who typed the manuscript and provided a liberal amount of inspiration and moral support.

Harry Katzan, Jr.

# PART 1

## THE
## COMPUTER
## ENVIRONMENT

# 1

# AN OVERVIEW OF BASIC COMPUTING CONCEPTS

## 1.1 INTRODUCTION

The study of programming languages is one of the most popular topics in computer science and data processing. This is so for a variety of reasons. First, a programming language is the key interface between man and the computer. A computer is a precise instrument and an effective programming language relieves the drudgery of developing a computer program and verifying its correctness. Second, most programming languages are relatively machine independent so that a computer program written in a programming language can be run on several computers. Third, a programming language is designed to facilitate programming so that the time and costs required for synthesizing a program are decreased. Lastly, a program expressed in a programming language is a body of knowledge that can be passed from person to person and from generation to generation.

### Procedure-Oriented Languages

Programming languages, as presented in this book, are designed primarily to serve practical needs: that is, to aid in the preparation of computer programs for subsequent execution on a digital computer. These languages are frequently referred to as "higher-level" or "procedure-oriented" languages. The implications are twofold: (1) A program can be written, using any of these languages, without the user necessarily knowing the details of the computer on which the program is to be run; and (2) when writing a program in one of these languages, the user describes the steps to be performed by the computer as compared to the case in which a language is used to describe the problem to be solved. In short, while the user must state the steps to be followed in the execution of the computer pro-

3

gram, many of the details ordinarily associated with "machine-level" programming are eliminated. As an example of the significance of the preceding concepts, consider the following program, written in the BASIC language, that computes a table of even numbers less than or equal to 100 and their squares:

```
10  FOR I = 2 TO 100 STEP 2
20  PRINT I, I↑2
30  NEXT I
99  END
```

The statement numbered 10 marks the beginning of a series of statements that are to be executed repetitively while "I" successively takes on the values 2,4,6, ...,100. The statement numbered 20 specifies that the values "I" and "I squared" should be printed on the same line. In the case of "I squared," a numerical computation is required. (The character ↑ denotes exponentiation.) The statement numbered 30 specifies that the loop should be repeated for the next value of I. Lastly, the statement numbered 99 denotes the end of the program. Thus, when the program is executed, a single line is printed for each trip through the loop so that the output would look somewhat as follows:

```
 2    4
 4   16
 6   36
 8   64
10  100
12  144
```

and so forth.

### Other Computer Languages

Other types of computer languages exist. *Algorithmic languages* are used to describe a mathematical or logical procedure in an unambiguous manner. *Problem-defining languages* are used to state the characteristics of a problem without giving the steps to be followed in its solution. *Assembler language* is used to prepare a program using the specific instructions of the computer on which the program is to be run. *Job control language* is used to control the manner in which the computer system processes a given program or set of programs. In addition, many computer languages are classed as being scientifically oriented, commercially oriented, or multipurpose. One last major type of computer language is usually recognized. This type is known as a *problem-oriented language,* used to describe computer-oriented procedures for a particular class of applications. A "query" language for information retrieval applications might fall into this category.

### Overview

The three programming languages covered in this book are: BASIC, FORTRAN, and COBOL. Each language has specific characteristics of its own. The BASIC language is designed to be an easy-to-learn language for the problem solver, such as the scientist, business analyst, or student. BASIC is frequently used via computer terminals in a time-sharing environment. Of the three languages, BASIC is the easiest to learn and the most convenient to use.

The FORTRAN language is primarily designed for scientific applications and includes capabilities and flexibility not usually available with BASIC. FORTRAN is used for the full spectrum of scientifically oriented programming.

The COBOL language is designed for data-processing applications. COBOL is more readable than the other programming languages presented here, and is more oriented toward file-processing operations than numerical computations—as is the opposite case with BASIC and FORTRAN.

## 1.2 COMPUTER STRUCTURES

Modern digital computers are composed of four types of components: (1) the central processing unit; (2) main storage; (3) input/output data channels; and (4) input/output control units and devices. The structure of a typical computer system is depicted in Figure 1.1.

### Central Processing Unit

The *central processing unit,* often referred to as the CPU, performs data manipulation, data movement, and sequence and control functions and initiates all input/output operations. The operation of the CPU is controlled by computer instructions that are held in main storage along with the data on which the CPU operates. Instructions and data must be placed in main storage before they can be used by the CPU. The CPU operates by fetching an instruction from main

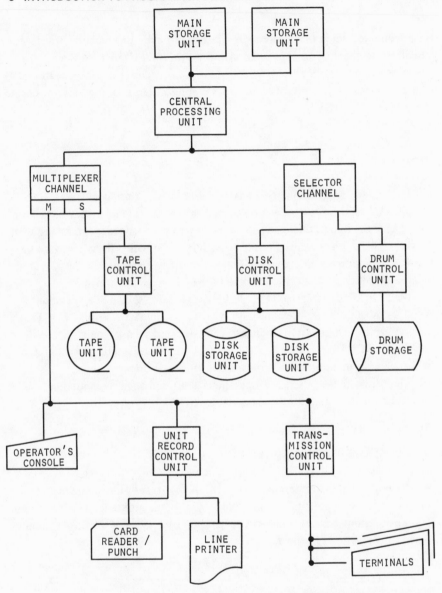

Fig. 1.1. Structure of a modern digital computer.

storage, decoding it, and then executing it. Computer instructions are normally executed sequentially and the CPU maintains a location counter to keep track of the main storage address of the next instruction to be executed. Different CPUs vary in several ways. The most obvious differences to the programmer are the instruction repertoire of the computer and the registers used for performing arithmetic. As far as registers are concerned, the most frequently used design philosophies are: (1) A single accumulator along with index registers for use during addressing; and (2) several floating-point and fixed-point registers of which the fixed-point registers can be used for addressing and for fixed-point arithmetic. The discussion returns to the CPU in subsequent paragraphs.

## Main Storage

*Main storage* is used to hold instructions and data while they are being used by the CPU. Usually, instructions and constant data values are placed in main storage by a loader program, discussed under section 1.6, "Operating Systems." Program data is read into main storage with input statements.

Main storage is frequently classed as to whether it is word oriented or byte oriented. A word is normally designed to hold an instruction or a numeric data item and occupies several storage bits—for example, 36 bits or 60 bits. Each word in main storage is assigned an address location and referencing that location normally provides access to a "word's worth" of information. In a byte-oriented computer, a standard unit of storage, such as an 8-bit byte, is defined. Each byte has an address location and words and instructions are composed of several contiguous bytes. Normally a byte location can hold a "character's worth" of information, whereas a word can hold several characters of information.

## Data Storage and Representation

Data can be represented in main storage in several ways:

1. As a string of characters corresponding to its external representation on a card, tape, or printed page
2. As a binary number stored in fixed-point or floating-point form
3. As a string of bits
4. As a decimal number stored in fixed-point or floating-point form
5. As implementation-defined program control values particular to a given programming language and a given computer

Figure 1.2 depicts character information as it is usually stored in byte-oriented and word-oriented computers. Each character assumes a coded form; for example, the letter A may be represented as 11000001 in an 8-bit byte and as 110001 in 6-bit character form. The most important difference is that byte organization

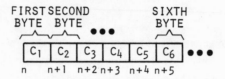

(a) BYTE-ORIENTED MAIN STORAGE

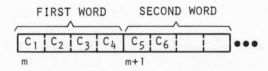

(b) WORD-ORIENTED MAIN STORAGE

Fig. 1.2. Character data (i.e., $C_1C_2C_3C_4C_5C_6$) read into byte-oriented (location $n$) and word-oriented (location $m$) storage.

allows the character to be addressed directly, whereas word organization does not.

Numeric data can be stored in character form, decimal form, or binary form. Character form is described in the preceding paragraph. One point should be obvious: eight bits, or even six, are not required to represent the digits 0-9. In fact, only four bits are needed. This fact allows a distinction to be made between the "zone" portion of a byte and the "digit" portion of the same byte. Consider the byte representation of the digits 0-9 given as follows:

| Digit | 8-bit Byte Representation | Zone Portion | Digit Portion |
|-------|---------------------------|--------------|---------------|
| 0 | 11110000 | 1111 | 0000 |
| 1 | 11110001 | 1111 | 0001 |
| 2 | 11110010 | 1111 | 0010 |
| 3 | 11110011 | 1111 | 0011 |
| 4 | 11110100 | 1111 | 0100 |
| 5 | 11110101 | 1111 | 0101 |
| 6 | 11110110 | 1111 | 0110 |
| 7 | 11110111 | 1111 | 0111 |
| 8 | 11111000 | 1111 | 1000 |
| 9 | 11111001 | 1111 | 1001 |

Obviously, the zones are not needed and are "stripped off" in some computers to give a decimal format. The process is referred to as "packing" and is depicted in Figure 1.3. Computers that recognize a *packed format* (also called *decimal format*) usually allow arithmetic computations to be performed directly on values stored in that form.

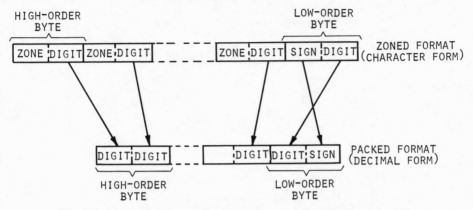

Fig. 1.3. Conversion from zoned format to packed (decimal) format.

Binary data can exist in fixed-point format or in floating-point format. *Fixed-point format,* depicted in Figure 1.4, usually requires that the relative location of the decimal point in the data value be maintained implicitly by the computer program. Figure 1.5 depicts a "nominal" process of converting a numeric value from external form to fixed-point binary form. Fixed-point numbers are discussed in Chapter 2. *Floating-point format* is used when it is desired to represent, in the computer, a class of values that range from large to small. Floating-point format is closely akin to scientific notation (also covered in Chapter 2), which includes a numeric sign, a fraction, and an exponent. As shown in Figure 1.6, the floating-point format includes one sign for the number itself. The exponent is usually biased by adding a number to it, such as 64, to avoid carrying an addi-

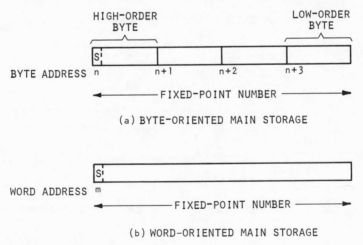

Fig. 1.4. Fixed-point binary numeric data in a byte-oriented and a word-oriented computer.

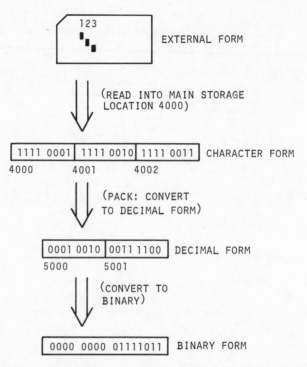

Fig. 1.5. Conversion of a numeric value from external form to fixed-point binary form.

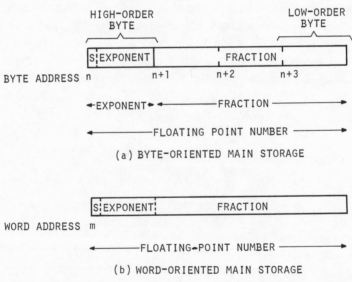

Fig. 1.6. Floating-point binary numeric data in a byte-oriented and word-oriented computer.

tional sign for the exponent along with the number. Floating-point format is often provided with different degrees of precision, such as short form, long form, and extended precision. In most cases, the size of the exponent field is kept at the same size and the fraction is extended to include additional bytes or words, as required. In some cases, floating-point values are stored in the decimal coded form, given previously, for convenience and for efficiency (obviously not related to computation). In almost all computers, however, floating-point values stored in a coded decimal form must be converted to binary form before floating-point arithmetic operations can be performed.

The manner in which bit strings and program control data is stored depends on the language and the computer. For example, a bit string can be stored as successive bits in a byte or as successive bytes. Similarly, truth values such as .TRUE. or .FALSE. (in the FORTRAN language) and event variables (to denote that a particular event has or has not occurred)—to name only two instances—are usually stored so as to facilitate compilation and provide efficient execution of the program.

Obviously, computer instructions are designed to operate on the various types of data. With word-oriented computers, the operand to an instruction is usually a computer word that is addressed directly. With byte-oriented computers, an operand is usually addressed by its high-order byte (that is, its leftmost byte) and the length of the operand is implicitly built into the instruction itself. In other words, some instructions are defined on bytes, others on short floating-point words, and so forth.

### Input/Output System

A *data channel* (see Figure 1.1, above) is effectively a small computer designed to transfer data between main storage and input/output control units and devices. The data channel allows the CPU to operate while input or output is taking place without requiring that incoming and outgoing data pass through the CPU. All the CPU does is to start an input/output operation on a given data channel, control unit, and device and pass the main storage address of a list of input/output commands to the data channel. The data channel uses the commands to control input/output operations. When the data channel has completed its work, it signals to the CPU by initiating an input/output interruption.

Normal CPU processing can be interrupted for other reasons: A hardware error is detected, a program fault is recognized, an external event takes place (such as when the interval timer runs down), or a program needs special attention. In all cases, however, interruptions are processed through a combination of hardware and software facilities. With a programming language, the user need not be concerned with the details of interruption processing. When an interruption occurs during the execution of a program, the condition is handled in one of two ways:

1. It is handled automatically by the operating system (see section 1.6 on "Operating Systems" in this chapter) as a default condition.
2. The programming language contains a special statement or a statement option that governs the action that should be taken when the interruption occurs.

Interruptions are considered in later chapters with respect to specific programming languages.

A *control unit* monitors the operation of one or more input/output devices. The control unit participates in data transfer operations, such as a "read" or a "write," and controls nondata operations, such as a tape rewind. *Input/output devices* serve to transfer data between the computer and the external world. For the purposes of this book, devices can be grouped into four classes: (1) unit record devices, (2) serial devices, (3) direct-access devices, and (4) miscellaneous devices. *Unit record devices* include the card reader, the line printer, and the card punch; a "block" of information transmitted between main storage and the device normally corresponds to a physical unit, such as a card or a line. *Serial devices* include magnetic tape and paper tape; these devices are characterized by the fact that information is stored serially and that access to the $i$th block requires that the unit pass over the $i - 1$th block. *Direct-access devices* include disk storage and drum storage; these devices, frequently referred to as rotating devices, are characterized by the fact that a block of information can be located directly, on the medium, prior to an input or output operation. *Miscellaneous devices* include data terminals, cathode ray tube (CRT) devices, audio-response units, and so on. Each device has characteristics of its own. The *terminal device* is frequently used in programming and has the general characteristics of a unit record device. More specifically, a terminal (as it is called) is a keyboard-driven unit used to transmit information between a computer and the terminal unit via telecommunications facilities. The user types the information on his device and it is transmitted to the transmission control unit of the computer. When the message is completed, the user presses RETURN or end-of-block (EOB) to indicate completion of the message. The process is reversed for output from the computer. Terminal devices vary greatly and range from typewriterlike units to CRT devices.

## 1.3  COMPUTER APPLICATIONS

Computer applications are usually classed by the function they perform, such as data analysis, realtime processing, payroll processing, and so forth. As a variation to the traditional approach, this section is concerned with what the computer does.

### Scientific Computing

In one class of applications, frequently associated with *scientific computing*, programs are designed to read a reasonably small amount of data into main storage, perform a relatively large amount of computation, and then output the results. The process of converting input data from external form to internal form is performed during the input operation so that data is held in main storage in a computational form. Similarly, the results are converted from internal form to a format suitable for printing, or whatever, during the output operation. This process is depicted in Figure 1.7. This is a cost-effective technique since a "large amount" of computation is performed and data is in a form suitable for computation. Programs written in BASIC or FORTRAN are usually placed in this category.

### Data Processing

In another class of applications, normally referred to as *data processing*, programs are designed to input and output large amounts of data and perform a small amount of computation. Applications where, for example, transaction records are matched against records from a master file naturally fall into this category. Thus, a relatively large amount of input (and perhaps output, as well)

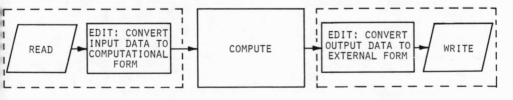

INPUT OPERATION        COMPUTE OPERATION        OUTPUT OPERATION

Fig. 1.7. The general flow of input, computation, and output in scientific computing.

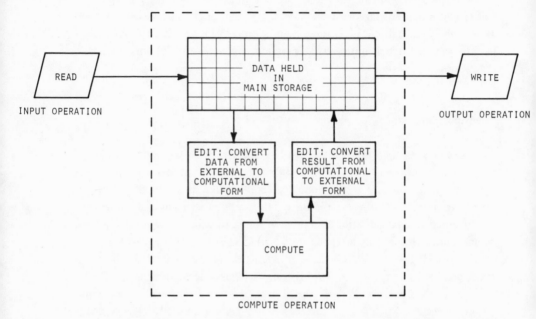

Fig. 1.8. The general flow of input, computation, and output in data processing.

precedes each unit of computation. This process is depicted in Figure 1.8. Input data is read directly into main storage in whatever form it was recorded. Before each unit of computation is performed, the operands are converted to a computational form. After computation, the results are converted to an external form and stored. During output, results are written directly from main storage to an output medium. Programs written in COBOL are usually placed in this category. For large amounts of computation, obviously, this is an inefficient way of doing business. On the other hand, the methods are efficient for file-processing operations.

### Information Management

The last class of applications is generally referred to as *information management.* This class is not characterized in any particular way except that a certain amount of computing is required during input and output operations. For example, the location of a data record may have to be computed or the "key" of a record may need to be matched against a set of keys that are maintained for storage and retrieval purposes. Programming languages that provide facilities for information management usually subordinate many of the details to the compiler or to a data management subsystem. Nevertheless, the necessary computer operations must be performed and should be considered in systems design and program development.

## 1.4 ALGORITHMS AND PROGRAMS

### The Concept of an Algorithm

Generally speaking, an *algorithm* is a set of procedures to be followed in solving any problem of a given kind. Procedures of this kind can be specified in a variety of ways ranging from concise mathematical formulation to description in a natural language, such as English. For example, a mathematical algorithm for computing the square root $r$ of a number $x$ is given as follows (where $\epsilon$ is a small value):

| Step | Instruction |
|------|-------------|
| 1 | Set $r$ equal to 1 |
| 2 | Compute $r = \frac{1}{2}\left(\frac{x}{r} + r\right)$ |
| 3 | If $|(r^2 - x)| < \epsilon$, then $r$ is the desired result; otherwise go to step 2 |

Similarly, a less formal algorithm for computing the greatest common divisor of two nonzero integers $A$ and $B$ is given as follows:

1. Compare the numbers $A$ and $B$; if they are equal, then each is the desired result.
2. If $B$ is larger than $A$, exchange their values so that $A$ always contains the larger value.
3. Compute $A - B$ and replace $A$ with the result. Continue with step 1.

Algorithms are frequently described with the use of flow diagrams[1] or decision tables.[2]

[1] Two references for flowcharting are: M. Bohl, *Flowcharting Techniques,* Chicago, Science Research Associates, Inc., 1971, and N. Chapin, *Flowcharts,* Philadelphia, Auerbach Publishers, Inc., 1971.

[2] Two references for decision tables are: H. Katzan, *Advanced Programming: Programming and Operating Systems,* New York, Van Nostrand Reinhold Co., 1970, and H. McDaniel, *An Introduction to Decision Logic Tables,* New York, John Wiley and Sons, Inc., 1968.

### The Concept of a Program

A *computer program* (usually referred to simply as a *program*) is a series of statements that specifies a computer representation of an algorithmic process. When the statements are executed (the manner in which this is done is covered next), the algorithm is performed. The "statements" are the key entity and always adhere to the specifications for a given language.

Informally, a statement is a series of characters punched on a card, recorded on disk or tape, or entered at a computer terminal. To be useful, however, a given statement must adhere to the *syntax* (rules) and utilize the *semantics* (operational meaning) of the language being used. Some examples of languages and programs are included in the following paragraphs.

### Assembler Language

As mentioned in an earlier section, assembler language is closely related to the machine language of the computer: operation codes, operands, and modifiers are simply represented by symbolic equivalents. Consider the assembler language program (listed as Program 1.1) that computes the greatest common divisor of numbers *A* and *B,* as described above. Each statement is written according to a format consisting of a "location" field, an "operation code" field, an "operand" field, and a "comments" field. The *location field* is used to reference the corresponding machine instruction or data field. The contents of the *operation code* and *operand* fields are used to construct machine instructions, to establish storage areas, and to specify program constants. Assembler language is not generally considered to be higher-level language.

### Higher-Level Language Concepts

As an example of a program in a higher-level language, consider an equivalent program in BASIC, given as Program 1.2. Each statement is identified by a line number that is prefixed to that statement by the user when the statement is entered into the computer. Otherwise, the statement is written in free format. A program is constructed by synthesizing a meaningful sequence of statements selected from the different statement types that make up the language. The implication, obviously, is that a programming language is a collection of different statement types that can be used to construct programs. This is precisely the case. The various languages differ in form (syntax), content (the different statement types that are available), and in the conventions used to construct state-

Program 1.1. Assembler Language Program Segment to Compute the Greatest Common Divisor of *A* and *B*

| Location | Operation Code | Operand | Comments |
|---|---|---|---|
| REPEAT | L | 5,A | Load register 5 with A. |
| | C | 5,B | Compare reg. 5 (i.e., A) with B. |
| | BE | DONE | Branch if equal to DONE. |
| | BH | OK | Branch if reg. 5 (i.e., A) is greater than B to OK. |
| | LR | 6,5 | Exchange A and B by placing A in register |
| | L | 5,B | 6, by loading reg. 5 with B, and then by |
| | ST | 6,B | placing the contents of reg. 6 (i.e., the old A) in B. |
| OK | S | 5,B | Subtract B from A. |
| | B | REPEAT | Branch to locate REPEAT to continue algorithm. |
| DONE | . . . | | (Program would continue here.) |
| A | DS | F | Storage for A. |
| B | DS | F | Storage for B. |

Program 1.2. BASIC Program Segment to Compute the Greatest Common Divisor of *A* and *B*

| Line No. | BASIC Statement |
|---|---|
| 10 | IF A=B THEN 80 |
| 20 | IF A>B THEN 60 |
| 30 | LET T=A |
| 40 | LET A=B |
| 50 | LET B=T |
| 60 | LET A=A−B |
| 70 | GO TO 10 |
| 80 | (continuation of program) |

Program 1.3. A Program Segment in the FORTRAN Language that Computes the Square Root of *X*

```
    E=.001
    R=1.0
2   R=.5*(X/R+R)
    IF(ABS(R**2−X).GE.E) GOTO 2
    ...
```

ments and programs. Program 1.3 depicts a sample program segment in the FORTRAN language that uses the square root algorithm given earlier.

**Program Structure**

Although the methods by which programs are actually executed on the computer have not been covered, it is safe to say, at this point, that a program can be viewed as a series of statements. It is also known, perhaps implicitly, that statements are executed sequentially until a statement is encountered that alters the sequence. Most computer programs are designed so that certain operational functions, such as the square root, are repeated frequently in the execution of the program. Thus, the machine instructions necessary for computing the square root (in this case) would be duplicated many times—an inefficient means of using valuable main storage. An alternate method and the one that is most frequently used is to include the square root function in the program only once as a "subprogram" and branch to it when needed. The process of using a "subprogram" is depicted conceptually in Figure 1.9. Thus, a program is effectively structured into a *main program* and possibly one or more *subprograms*. A main

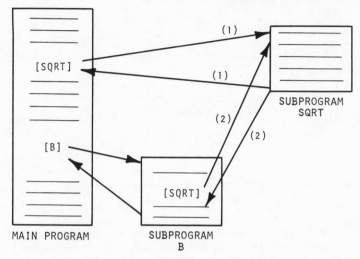

Fig. 1.9. Conceptual view of the process of structuring a program into a main program and one or more subprograms.

program can reference subprograms, a subprogram can reference other subprograms, and so forth. Considerably more is said later about subprograms. Subprograms are also utilized for standardization purposes and for programming efficiency.

## 1.5   LANGUAGE PROCESSORS

One of the key factors in the widespread use of programming languages is the fact that much of the detail ordinarily associated with "machine-level" programming is subordinated to another computer program, termed a "language processor." More specifically, a *language processor* is a program that accepts another program as input; the output of a language processor either is a translated version of the input program or a set of computed results.

### Terminology

A *language translator* is a language processor that produces an output program. Some terminology relevant to the use of language translators is shown in Figure 1.10. The program as expressed in assembler language or in a higher-level language is referred to as the *source program;* it is read into the language translator from cards, tape, a direct-access device, or from a terminal device via tele-

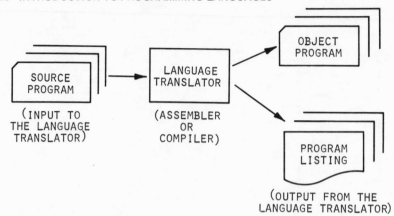

Fig. 1.10. The language translator accepts a source program as input and produces an object program and a program listing as output.

communications facilities. The output from the language translator is a translated version of the program, termed an *object program,* and a listing of the program. The object program is recorded on cards, tape, or a direct-access device for subsequent input to the computer for execution. Language translators come in two forms: assemblers and compilers.

### Assembler Programs

An *assembler program* (usually referred to simply as an *assembler*) converts a program written in assembler language to an equivalent program in machine language. The translation process is usually referred to as *assembly* or the *assembly process.* Assembly is usually performed in two passes over a source program. In the first pass, relative addresses are assigned to symbols in the location field. In the second pass over the source program, symbolic operation codes are replaced by internal machine codes and symbolic operands are replaced by corresponding addresses that were determined during pass one. The object program and the program listing are also produced during pass two. Various forms of error checking and analysis are performed during both passes.

### Compiler Programs

A *compiler program* (usually referred to simply as a *compiler*) converts a program written in a higher-level language to either machine language or to assembler language. In the second case, the resulting assembler language program must then

Program 1.4. Sample Assembler Language Statements that Would be Generated
for a Single Statement in a Higher-Level Language

| Higher-Level Language | Assembler Language | | |
|---|---|---|---|
| I=J*K+L | L | 6,J | (Load reg. 6 with J) |
| | M | 5,K | (Mult. regs. 5-6 by K) |
| | A | 6,L | (Add L to reg. 6) |
| | ST | 6,I | (Store reg. 6 in I) |

be processed by the assembler. Program 1.4 depicts sample assembler language statements that would be generated by a single statement in a higher-level language. In contradistinction to assembly where one machine instruction is usually generated for each assembler language source statement, the compiler usually generates several machine instructions for each source statement in a higher-level language. Compilation is generally considered to be more complicated than assembly since higher-level language structure tends to be more complex than assembler language structure. Although a compiler is necessarily dependent on the language being compiled, the following steps are usually involved:

1. The compiler reads the source program on a statement-by-statement basis and performs the following processing for each statement:
   (a) Lexical analysis to identify keywords, names, constants, punctuation characters, etc., is performed.
   (b) Syntactical analysis to identify the type of statement and determine that its structure is admissible is performed.
   (c) The constituents of that statement are placed in lists and tables to facilitate the generation of machine code and to allow a global analysis of the program.
2. A flow analysis of the program is performed to check for interstatement errors and to provide information on how machine registers should be assigned.
3. Program optimization is performed and machine instructions are generated.
4. An object program and a program listing are produced.

A compiler and an assembler have one important feature in common. That is, each has the complete source program at its disposal so that the various steps in the assembly and compilation processes can be executed at the discretion of the person designing the assembler or the compiler. Only after a source program has been completely analyzed by an assembler or compiler and an object program is produced is that object program actually executed.

### Interpreter Program

One type of language processor that allows program modification during execution is the interpreter. The *interpreter* is a language processor that executes a source program without producing an object program. An interpreter operates as follows:

1.  The interpreter reads the source program on a statement-by-statement basis and performs the following processing for each statement:
    (a)  The statement is scanned, identified, analyzed, and interpreted to determine the operations that should be performed.
    (b)  The required operations are executed by the interpreter and the intermediate results are retained.
2.  The next statement that is interpreted depends on the results of the statement just executed (such as in the case of a GO TO statement).

Although different interpreters vary in internal design,[3] the key point is that an object program is not produced and that all statements are not necessarily processed by the interpreter. The interpretive technique is frequently used with simple easy-to-use language (such as a desk calculator language) or in an operational environment (such as time sharing) where programs are not likely to be rerun many times.

### 1.6 OPERATING SYSTEMS

Although most programming languages are designed to be as machine independent as possible, a program is usually written in a programming language so that it can be executed on a computer and this ties it to the operating environment. A program is executed on a computer in one of three ways: (1) by using basic programming support; (2) with the aid of a control program; and (3) by using time-sharing facilities.

### Basic Programming Support

*Basic programming support* requires manual intervention by the user during the processing of his job and involves the following steps:

---

[3] Some interpreters convert a source program into an intermediate function language and then interpretively execute the statements in the intermediate form. One of the principal disadvantages of the interpretive technique is "slowness."

1. The computer program to be compiled is punched on cards or tape.
2. The compiler program is loaded into the computer.
3. The compiler program reads the program being compiled and produces a machine language program; it is punched into cards or tape.
4. The machine language program is loaded into the computer; it reads the user's data and produces computed results, as programmed.

The basic programming environment is depicted in Figure 1.11. Between each of the steps shown there and listed above, manual intervention by the user or a computer operator is required. If more than one source program needs to be compiled (for example, for a main program and a subprogram), then the compilation step is repeated as many times as necessary.

### Control Programs

The disadvantages of the basic programming environment are obvious: (1) The manual intervention between the steps of a job is wasteful of computer time; and (2) the mode of operation presents operational difficulties and the methods required for the scheduling of computer time are cumbersome. The solution to the problem is to have computer programs perform the job scheduling and provide automatic job-to-job transition. A set of operating programs such as this is known as a *control program* or an *operating system.* Although operating systems vary widely between installations and computer vendors, there are four types of facilities (or routines) that are usually provided:

1. *System management* routines control the operation of the computer system and provide a logical interface between the hardware and the

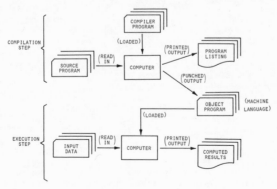

Fig. 1.11. Basic programming environment.

remainder of the software system. System management routines monitor hardware functions, perform actual input/output operations, schedule jobs for execution, control peripheral input/output devices, allocate main storage, and handle abnormal conditions that arise during computation.

2. *Job management* routines provide a logical interface between a job (processing program) and the system management routines. Job management routines control and monitor the execution of a job, read control cards, and handle job terminations.

3. *Data management* routines provide a software interface between processing programs and external storage. Data management routines control data transfer operations, maintain catalogs and libraries, manage input/output device assignment, and allocate space on mass storage de-

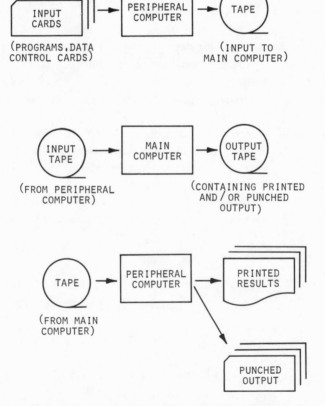

Fig. 1.12. Use of a peripheral computer with an early batch-processing operating system.

vices. Even though data management is generally concerned with input and output, it uses system management functions for that purpose so that all input and output is managed on a system-wide basis.

4. *User service* routines comprise utility programs, necessary for using a computer system, and service programs that facilitate the programming process. Utility programs include disk initialization, core dumps, card-to-tape, diagnostics, etc. Service programs perform sort/merge, editing, loading, and many other similar functions.

Early operating systems used a concept known as *batching* or *batch processing* whereby a collection of jobs was submitted to the main computer on a magnetic tape. The main computer was controlled by an operating system and input cards were placed on tape by a peripheral computer. Output from the main computer was also on tape and that output tape was later printed and/or punched by another (or the same) peripheral computer. The process is depicted in Figure 1.12. An obvious question is, "How are different jobs separated on the input tape and how does the user inform the operating system of the processing that he wants performed?" The answer is, with control cards. The term *control cards* collectively refers to a set of statements designed to supply control information to the operating system. A sample input deck setup is given in Figure 1.13. The

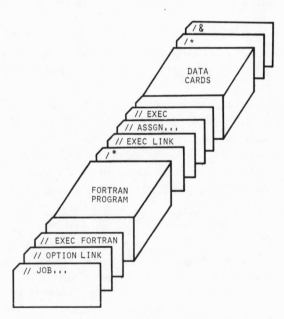

Fig. 1.13. Sample deck setup showing representative set of control cards.

control cards are read by the Job Management routines of the operating system and the processing performed is dependent on the card read. Four major types of statements are identified:

1.  The JOB card begins each job, establishes the job as a unit of work for the system, and provides accounting and control information.
2.  The EXEC card specifies that a particular program is to be loaded into the computer and scheduled for execution. Causing a program to be loaded also implicitly requests that subprograms used by that program also be loaded.
3.  The OPTION card provides information to the operating system and to an executing program.
4.  The ASSGN card serves to specify input and output requirements and to assign logical data files to physical devices.

Most operating systems also accept a variety of other control cards of lesser importance, that signify end of data, comments, end of job, and so forth.

### Multiprogramming

Early operating systems were characterized by the fact that jobs were loaded into main storage and executed on a sequential basis. In spite of automatic job-to-job transition, input/output systems, and so on, normal delays in the processing of a job caused the CPU to "wait" for short periods of time on an intermittent basis and resulted in ineffective use of main storage. Modern operating systems (see Figure 1.14) utilize a technique known as *multiprogramming* to allow several jobs to share the resources of the computer system and to allow card reading, printing, and punching to proceed concurrently with system operation. In a multiprogramming system, the scheduler program is designed to give control of the central processing unit to another program when the executing program encounters a *natural wait*—such as when waiting for an input operation. Thus, the more expensive units in the system are fully utilized. Input jobs are maintained in a queue on direct-access storage and output is maintained in a similar queue on the same or another device. When the operating system needs another job to process, it is selected from the input queue on either a sequential or priority basis. This technique is also regarded as batch processing; however, the jobs are batched in an input queue by the operating system instead of on a tape by the system operator.

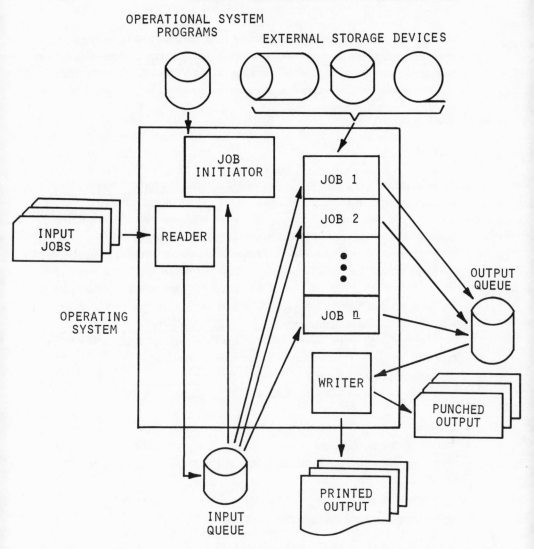

Fig. 1.14. Modern operating system environment.

## Remote Job Entry/Remote Job Output

By definition, batch processing causes delays. First, a user's job must be transported to the central computer and entered into the system. Next, the job must wait in the input queue until its turn for processing. Lastly, the output queue must be printed or punched and the results are sent back to the originator. A recent technique known as *remote job entry* allows a job to be transported from a remote location to the central computer over ordinary telephone lines. An analo-gous facility, known as *remote job output,* provides a means of sending results back to the originator over telephone lines. The user (or originator) in this case must have an appropriate terminal device in his work area to send and receive in-formation from the central computer.

### Time Sharing

Although remote job entry/output solves, in some cases, the problem of trans-porting programs and data to and from the central computer, the scheduling bot-tleneck at the computer still causes delays—especially when small one-shot pro-grams are involved. Another technique, known as *time sharing,* allows the user at a remote location to enter into a conversation with the computer (figuratively speaking) using, again, a terminal device and telephone lines. In a time-sharing system, however, computer time is scheduled differently. When time sharing, each user is given a short burst (called a *time slice*) of computer time on a peri-odic basis. The switching between programs, by the computer, is sufficiently fast that the user is given the illusion that he has the computer to himself—whereas, in reality, he is sharing it with many other users. Time sharing is most frequently used during program development, by problem solvers, such as analysts, scien-tists, or engineers, or to enter or retrieve information from the system on a de-mand basis.

Three well-established techniques have been introduced: basic programming, control programs (with multiprogramming and remote job entry/output varia-tions), and time sharing. Most users will utilize one of these techniques when running a job on the computer.

### 1.7 DATA AND STORAGE STRUCTURES

Usually, a distinction is made between data held in main storage and data that has been placed on a storage medium external to the computer, such as magnetic tape or disk. However, the distinction is more one of convenience and tradition than one of necessity. An attempt is made here to present the subject matter in-dependently of the physical devices involved.

### Storage Structures

Because the various methods used to store data are well known, most readers rarely think about the subject—much less the terminology used to describe it.

The basic unit of storage is a *bit,* which is a commonly used acronym for "*b*inary dig*it.*" Information is stored as combinations of bits in most computers since the physical representation of an "on" or "off" state is relatively simple to implement in hardware and provides for efficiency of storage.

In main storage, as mentioned previously, bits are grouped to form *bytes* or words. In a byte-oriented computer, bytes are grouped to form words; in a word-oriented computer, subdivisions of a word (such as 6 bits) are interpreted as characters, when necessary. On an external storage medium, information is stored as bits arranged in a characteristic manner. For example, bits are stored as lateral rows on tape, as columns on a card, or serially in tracks on a disk surface. In most cases, some sort of correspondence is made between a grouping of bits in main storage and a grouping of bits on the external media; for example, a byte or character in main storage usually corresponds to a column of a card or a lateral row in tape. A *block* is a unit of transfer between main storage and an external device. A block consists of several bytes or words, as specified in the count field of an input/output command controlling the data transfer operation. The contents of a block are governed by a user's program and by the data management routines of the operating system. Frequently, the bits that comprise a block are transformed by an algorithm implemented in hardware to achieve compatibility between the physical components involved. As an example, an 8-bit byte in main storage is transformed to a 12-bit card column by the control unit of the card punch.

## Storage Organization

Storage structures can be organized using four basic methods: consecutive organization, linked organization, keyed organization, and regional organization. *Consecutive organization* requires that an allocation of storage occupies contiguous storage positions. As depicted in Figure 1.15, arrays held in main storage and blocks placed on magnetic tape are common examples of storage structures that are organized consecutively. Storage structures can also be organized consecutively on direct-access media by assigning contiguous tracks or cylinders.

*Linked organization* permits distinct data elements (called *nodes*) to occupy discontiguous locations; a node includes pointers to preceding and/or succeeding data elements to facilitate storage access. In main storage, a node consists of several contiguous bytes or words and the pointer value is a main storage address. On direct-access storage, a node (usually called a data record, in this case) exists as a block that includes cylinder/head pointers to other blocks. Linked organization is also depicted in Figure 1.15.

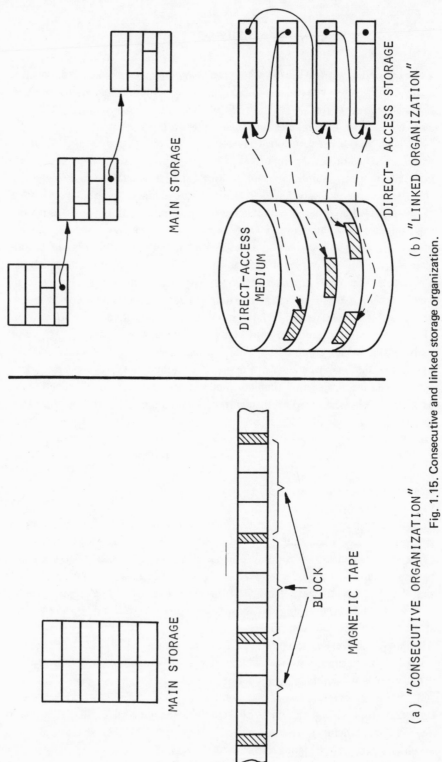

MAIN STORAGE

MAIN STORAGE

DIRECT-ACCESS MEDIUM

DIRECT-ACCESS STORAGE

(b) "LINKED ORGANIZATION"

BLOCK

MAGNETIC TAPE

(a) "CONSECUTIVE ORGANIZATION"

Fig. 1.15. Consecutive and linked storage organization.

30

*Keyed organization* is a method of storage organization in which data is located by means of a data key that is a part of the information being stored (for example, part of a data record) or is maintained as a separate data area distinct from the data record. In keyed organization, data is retrieved by key value—either by direct search or with the aid of a table of keys that points to associated data. Keyed organization is most frequently used with direct-access storage devices in which tables of keys effectively point to the various locations of data on the storage media. Keyed organization is suggested by Figure 1.16.

With *regional organization,* a region of storage is located by name, index, or key. After a region is identified and located, data are accessed as though that region were organized consecutively. In many cases, regional organization is used to partition a storage space that is allocated consecutively, such as a "library" of programs in object module format. The library is organized by program name; once a program is located in that library, it is accessed sequentially. Regional organization is also depicted in Figure 1.16.

## Storage Access

The modern theory of data structure and organization recognizes the distinction between storage organization and storage access. The significance of the concepts will be more meaningful later in the book and full comprehension, at least of the underlying implications, is not required at this point. However, it is important to use appropriate terminology, and for that reason this section is included as part of the text.

Two methods of storage access are usually identified: sequential and direct. *Sequential access* denotes that data elements are referenced in an order dependent on the order in which the data elements are physically stored. Card decks, tape files, and simple lists held in main storage are usually accessed sequentially. However, a linked list or a keyed data file can also be accessed sequentially by following the pointers or by referencing the keys in order.

*Direct access* denotes that a data item is referenced without having to reference preceding information. Direct access can be implemented in several ways:

1. The cylinder/head number of a data item on direct-access storage or the main storage address of a data item in main storage is known and that physical address can be used to reference the item desired.
2. A key is matched against a table that provides the physical location of the data item.
3. One or more mathematical operations are performed on the key giving

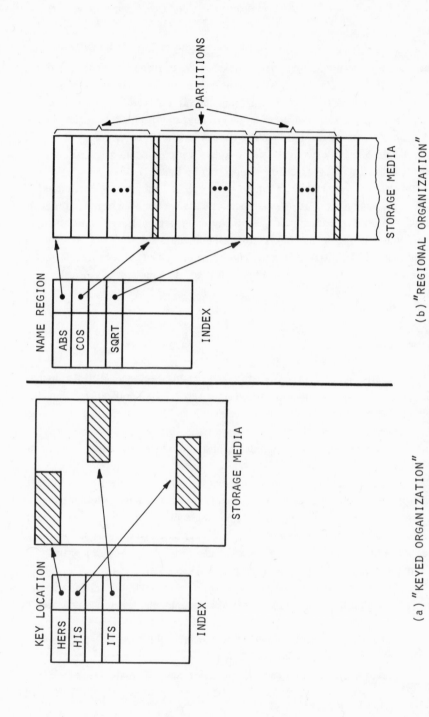

(a) "KEYED ORGANIZATION"

(b) "REGIONAL ORGANIZATION"

Fig. 1.16. Keyed and regional storage organization.

32

the relative location of the required data item in the storage structure.

4. The location of an element of an array organized consecutively is computed by using the starting location of the array, characteristics of the array, and subscript values. (The topic of "Arrays" is covered, as a special subject, in Chapter 2.)

The major point to be made is that storage access applies to both main storage and external storage and that two basic modes of operation (sequential and direct) are defined. Later, it will become obvious that a given programming language can provide an operational facility using combinations of storage organization and storage access.

## Data Management Structures

Thus far, the presentation of data and storage structures has been primarily independent of the manner in which the programmer would use them. This section is "user oriented" as is most of Chapter 2.

A *field* is a unit of storage that would lose its meaning if it were broken down further. Typical fields are a person's name or a number punched in a card. A character in either of the fields is simply part of the alphabet and has no meaning by itself.

In main storage, a group of consecutive fields that have some logical relationship to each other is termed a *data record*. Data records are frequently referred to as "logical records." A simple data record might be an employee's record on a personnel file. A group of related records is termed a *file;* hence the familiar terms "payroll file" or "personnel file."

When performing data manipulation and input/output operations, the user deals in fields, records, and files. However, the computer and the input/output system deal in blocks, as mentioned previously. What happens is that the data management routines of the operating system group several records to form a block, prior to the output operation. This process is referred to as *blocking*. On input, the process is reversed—termed *deblocking*. Thus, the user can visualize his file as a series of records. In reality, it is stored as a series of blocks, each of which can contain several data records.

The technique of using blocked records has two principal advantages: (1) It conserves space on the storage media; and (2) it contributes to efficient input/ output operations.

Three record formats are generally used: fixed-length records, variable-length records, and undefined-length records—as depicted in Figure 1.17. The size of a

(a) FIXED-LENGTH RECORDS

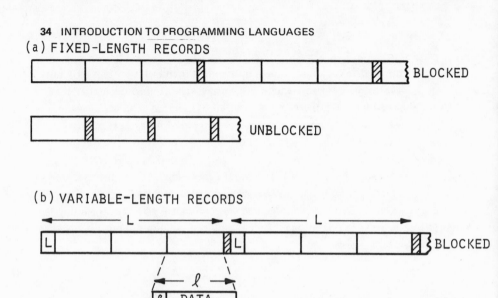

(b) VARIABLE-LENGTH RECORDS

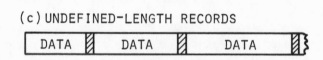

(c) UNDEFINED-LENGTH RECORDS

Fig. 1.17. Record formats.

*fixed-length record* is constant for all data records in a block, in addition the size of the block is also constant in size. Fixed-length records may be blocked or unblocked. In the former case, several data records comprise a block; in the latter case, a block is comprised of a single data record.

With *variable-length records,* the size of each data record and of the block may be variable in length. Moreover, the record format includes length fields for use by the data management routines.

*Undefined-length records* are established for cases in which the records to be processed do not meet the requirements of the preceding two types. When undefined-length records are used, it is the user's responsibility to perform blocking and deblocking, whereas with fixed-length and variable-length records, these functions are performed by data management routines.

The choice of a record format for a given application is a systems design problem and involves processing time and storage space. The characteristics of a data file are provided to the operating system with control cards or through facilities of a given programming language. Regardless of how the characteristics of a data file are specified, the blocking, deblocking, and housekeeping operations are normally transparent to the user through the use of a programming language.

## 1.8  COMMENTS ON THE OVERVIEW

The objective of the overview is to delineate the background that is needed to study programming languages effectively. The material is not intended to be a substitute for an introductory course covering basic computing concepts or for practical experience in the area. For readers who are unfamiliar with the topics covered, one of the following books is recommended: Awad [1], Bohl [3], or Davis [6]. For a slightly more advanced treatment of topics in the software and applications areas, Chapin [4], Flores [8], Katzan [11], and Pollack [16] are given. For a brief look at computer organization, Davis [7], Foster [10], Katzan [12], and Stone [17] are recommended. For information on information management and file processing, the reader is directed to Flores [9], Kent [13], and Meadow [15]. The above references are not exhaustive and are intended only as a sample of the many "good" references that are available.

To a limited degree, an effective programming language allows the user to develop programs with a minimum knowledge of computer technology. The BASIC language is a good example of this. As languages become more powerful, such as FORTRAN or COBOL, a more extensive background is needed to fully appreciate the advanced capabilities. Obviously, this is the practical approach to the study of programming languages. Toward that end, the reader is urged to constantly relate the facilities in a given programming language to the computer environment and to the applications for which the language is used.

## EXERCISES

1. Give three computer applications for which the use of a procedure-oriented language would be appropriate. Similarly, list three other applications for which the use of assembler language would be appropriate.
2. Select a typical scientific computer application. Give five attributes that characterize that type of application. Similarly, select a typical data-processing application. Give five attributes that characterize a data-processing application.

3. Distinguish between a CPU that uses a single accumulator and index registers and a CPU that uses multiple fixed and floating-point registers.
4. Distinguish between word-oriented main storage and byte-oriented main storage.
5. What is the essential difference between an input/output device and an input/output medium?
6. Why are data for scientific applications frequently stored in a computational form and data for data-processing applications frequently stored in an external form?
7. In what way is an ordinary kitchen recipe similar to an algorithm?
8. Give the advantages and disadvantages of each of the following techniques (use outside information if necessary):

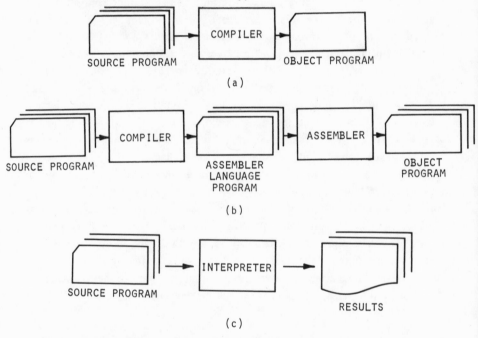

(a)

(b)

(c)

9. Give similarities and differences between batch processing with peripheral support and the use of a multiprogramming system.
10. Define the following terms:

| | |
|---|---|
| file | sequential access |
| block | direct access |
| logical record | consecutive organization |
| field | linked organization |
| record format | keyed organization |

## SELECTED READINGS

1.  Awad, E. M. *Business Data Processing.* Englewood Cliffs, N.J.: Prentice-Hall, Inc, 1971.
2.  Bohl, M. *Flowcharting Techniques.* Chicago: Science Research Associates, Inc., 1971.
3.  Bohl, M. *Information Processing.* Chicago: Science Research Associates, Inc., 1971.
4.  Chapin, N. *Computers: A Systems Approach.* New York: Van Nostrand Reinhold Co., 1971.
5.  Chapin, N. *Flowcharts.* Philadelphia: Auerbach Publishers, Inc., 1971.
6.  Davis, G. B. *Computer Data Processing.* New York: McGraw-Hill Book Company, 1969.
7.  Davis, G. B. *Introduction to Electronic Computers.* New York: McGraw-Hill Book Company, 1971.
8.  Flores, I. *Computer Software.* Englewood Cliffs, N.J.: Prentice-Hall, Inc., 1965.
9.  Flores, I. *Data Structure and Management.* Englewood Cliffs, N.J.: Prentice-Hall, Inc., 1970.
10. Foster, C. C. *Computer Architecture.* New York: Van Nostrand Reinhold Co., 1970.
11. Katzan, H. *Advanced Programming: Programming and Operating Systems.* New York: Van Nostrand Reinhold Co., 1970.
12. Katzan, H. *Computer Organization and the System/370.* New York: Van Nostrand Reinhold Co., 1971.
13. Kent, A. *Information Analysis and Retrieval.* New York: John Wiley and Sons, Inc., 1971.
14. McDaniel, H. *An Introduction to Decision Logic Tables.* New York: John Wiley and Sons, Inc., 1968.
15. Meadow, C. T. *The Analysis of Information Systems.* New York: John Wiley and Sons, Inc., 1967.
16. Pollack, B. W. (ed.). *Compiler Techniques.* Philadelphia: Auerbach Publishers, Inc., 1972.
17. Stone, H. S. *Introduction to Computer Organization and Data Structures.* New York: McGraw-Hill Book Company, 1972.

# 2

# FUNDAMENTALS
# OF PROGRAMMING
# LANGUAGES

## 2.1 INTRODUCTION

In Chapter 1, an overview of basic computing concepts was presented; it is oriented toward computer systems in the sense that aspects of the computer environment are emphasized. This chapter is oriented toward programming languages and associated topics. Knowledge of the material contained in this chapter is assumed throughout the remainder of the book.

### Alphabet

The characters that can be used to construct statements are termed the *alphabet* of the language (being used). Although there is much similarity between the alphabets of different languages, significant differences exist. It is important to realize that the user is actually dealing with codes when, for example, he enters the statement:

   A = B + C

The binary information that is transferred to the computer (via a punched card, via a terminal device, etc.) is used by the language processor and the manner in which it is displayed on a program listing is an operational convenience and not a requirement of the input process. Effectively, then, the user and the language processor enter into an "implicit agreement" as to the meaning of the various codes. In most cases, the characters are meaningful; for example, the + symbol usually denotes "plus," and so forth. Occasionally, they are not and many commercial programmers are familiar with having to interpret ▢ and % for ( and ), respectively.

Most programming languages use an alphabet that includes approximately 48 characters. The characters that comprise an alphabet are grouped into letters (such as A, B, and so forth), digits (such as 1, 2, and so forth), and special characters (such as +, *, %, and so forth). The size of the alphabet has very little to do with the computer since a 6-bit character permits 64 combinations ($2^6$) and an 8-bit byte permits 256 combinations ($2^8$). In many cases, however, the size of the alphabet is related to the number of printable characters on the card punch machine, the terminal device, or the line printer.

**Statements**

It is necessary to emphasize another important point. A program is composed of statements; but what constitutes a statement? Statements are punched on cards or typed in at the computer terminal. Different statements must be separated (or delimited) in some way and a convenient means of doing that is to start each statement on a new card or a new line. (This subject was mentioned briefly in Chapter 1.) In many programming languages, the end of a card (or line) denotes the end of a statement, unless a continuation is specified in some way, and a program is composed of a collection of data records (i.e., cards or lines).

In some other programming languages, a program is a string of characters formed by concatenating the data records that comprise the program. Each statement is terminated by a semicolon. Thus, a given data record may contain one or more statements or parts of statements.

In subsequent chapters, much of the discussion will concern statements and statement structure and very little is presented on the precise manner in which a statement is entered. This is because the statement is of prime concern and its means of representation is merely an operational convention.

## 2.2 DATA

In general, a computer program processes two types of data: problem data and control data. Problem data are associated with the computations performed by a program and include numeric data, logical data, and descriptive data. Control data, such as labels, addresses, and offsets, are used to control the execution of a program. Numeric data is of primary concern here since it comes in several forms.

## Fixed- and Floating-Point Data

In ordinary arithmetic, calculations are performed on numbers represented as sequences of decimal digits, possibly a decimal point, and possibly an algebraic sign. A number of this type is called a *fixed-point* or a *decimal* number. Thus, a fixed-point number $x$ can be represented by an expression of the form

$$x = n+0.d_1d_2d_3...$$

where $n$ is a signed or unsigned whole number and the $d_i$s are digits in the range 0-9. The following constants are regarded as fixed-point numbers:

| | |
|---|---|
| 7 | .00138 |
| −19 | −93000 |
| +54.137 | |

Obviously, it is not necessary that unneeded constituents be written—except as required by a particular programming language. A fixed-point number without a fraction is an *integer*. Integer arithmetic has some characteristic properties. When integers are added, subtracted, multiplied, or divided, the result is an integer (that is, a whole number). The same holds true for all arithmetic operations on integers. Thus, if the division of $a$ by $b$ is defined by

$$a = q \cdot b+r \text{ where } r < b$$

then the result is the quotient $q$ and the remainder $r$ is lost. Thus, when integer arithmetic is used, 5 divided by 2 (that is, 5/2) gives the result 2 and (3/2)*4 gives a result of 4. (The asterisk in the preceding expression denotes multiplication.)

Working with fixed-point numbers is not always convenient. For example, the evaluation of the expression

$$3000000 \times 150000000$$

is hindered by having to keep track of a large number of decimal places. Values of this type occur frequently in quantitative analysis and in computer applications. As a result, scientists and engineers use a simplified form known as *floating-point.*[1] The above example is expressed as

$$3 \times 10^6 \times 15 \times 10^7$$

---

[1] Also regarded as engineering or scientific notation.

which is easily evaluated to $45 \times 10^{13}$ using simple rules of arithmetic. In a floating-point number, the position of the decimal point is *not* fixed and is determined by the value of the exponent. In computer storage, the space occupied by a given number is fixed in size. Thus, floating-point notation is convenient for storing values that vary in magnitude from large to small, as mentioned previously.

### Characteristics of Fixed- and Floating-Point Data

When discussing data, an early distinction must be made between how it is written on the programmer's coding pad (or punched into cards)—called *source data*—and how it is stored in computer storage—called *stored data*. Thus, in the statement:

$$A = 10$$

the value 10 is source data. It is assigned to the variable $A$ when the statement is executed. $A$ is stored data.[2] A simple rule to follow is that when a data declaration[3] is made in a program, either explicitly or implicitly, it refers to how a data item is stored. A data constant, on the other hand, stands for itself and does not require additional specification. Source data is limited to a linear sequence of characters requiring that a means be established for recording the exponent of a floating-point number. The need is satisfied by the letter E, in a constant, that denotes a power of ten. The number $.31 \times 10^5$ would be keypunched as .31E5 and $1.43 \times 10^{-17}$ as 1.43E−17.

Stored data is another thing. The size of a specific numeric data item for a particular program is fixed when that program is compiled, regardless of whether the computer has a fixed word size or a variable word size and whether the number is stored in binary or in decimal form. The size of a data item is termed its *precision*. In general, the precision of distinct data items may differ depending on the needs of a particular application. Conceptually, a fixed-point number is stored as a sign followed by a fixed number of digits. The value −187.9, for example, might be stored as

$$\boxed{-}\boxed{0001879}$$

---

[2] Actually, the value 10 is also "stored." It assumes attributes determined by how it is written and, of course, the programming language involved.

[3] A data declaration, frequently called a *specification*, is made with a statement of a programming language. Statements of this type are DIM in the BASIC language, REAL in FORTRAN, integer in ALGOL, and the DECLARE statement in PL/I. COBOL utilizes a separate section of the program called the DATA DIVISION.

Usually, a decimal point is not stored and its implied position is compiled into the machine language program generated during compilation. The storage of a floating-point data item is slightly more involved. First, the number is stored as two parts: a fraction and an exponent. For example, the value $3 \times 10^6$ is stored with a fraction of .3 and an exponent of 7. Next, the exponent is biased by adding a positive value to it to eliminate the need for carrying two signs in a computer word. Lastly, the decimal point is implicitly assumed to be placed to the left of the leftmost digit of the fraction. Using a bias of 64, the value $-.3 \times 10^7$ is stored as

| $-$ | 71 | 30000 |
|-----|-----|-------|

and $.143 \times 10^{-11}$ as

| $+$ | 53 | 14300 |
|-----|-----|-------|

In either case, the digits could be binary or decimal. Actual implementation is dependent on a specific computer. With floating-point values, the precision of a number stored is a function of the size of the fraction field and the range is determined by the size of the exponent field.

### Complex, Logical, and Character Data

For scientific and engineering applications, numeric data can include an additional component—the *imaginary* part. A *complex number* of this type is stored as two numbers: the real part and the imaginary part. It follows that a number without an imaginary part is regarded as a *real number*.

Logical data which can assume either a *true* or a *false* value is usually stored in one of two forms: (1) As a sequence of one or more bits where the value 1 represents true and the value 0 represents false; and (2) as an implementation-defined pair of values not accessible to the programmer. Since truth values stored as bits are essentially numeric values, they are permitted in arithmetic computations in some programming languages.

Finally, character data can possess either a fixed or a variable length, in terms of characters, and its actual storage depends to some extent on the computer involved. A character constant is termed a *literal,* which is nothing more than a series of characters enclosed in quotation marks; that is, for example,

"TEA FOR TWO"

## Control Data

Control data is necessarily dependent on a particular programming language and/or the implementation of that language on a particular computer. It is not discussed further in this chapter.

## 2.3 VARIABLES AND IDENTIFIERS

### The Concept of a Variable

In mathematics, the name given to an unknown quantity is *variable.* For example, one might say, "Let $x$ equal the ... ." In actual practice, the concept is more general and enables principles to be developed independently of a particular problem. The term "variable," in contrast to the word "constant," implies a term that can assume a set of values; or in other words, that the value of a variable is not constant but is subject to change. The equation:

$$y = 3x^2 + 2x + 5$$

for example, defines a second-degree polynomial for all real values of $x$.

A variable is also used as a symbolic name in everyday discourse. Thus, variables such as $x$ or $y$ are frequently used to represent an unknown quantity or to help in explaining a complex idea for which ordinary language is inadequate.

### Identifiers

Symbolic names are frequently used in computing and are referred to as *identifiers*–obviously because a symbolic name identifies something. In the discussion of assembler language in Chapter 1, for example, programming was greatly facilitated by allowing meaningful names to be assigned to operations and operands. The concept is extended in higher-level languages such that symbolic names are used for a variety of reasons–hence the more general name of "identifier."

The most familiar type of identifier is used to name a data element that can change during the course of computation; it is termed a *variable* in line with the above discussion. Other identifiers are used to name statements (that is, statement identifiers), data files, "key" words, attributes, and many other entities. Sample identifiers are:

```
B2      READ
LET     END
FOR     TO
```

Thus, in the BASIC statement

FOR I = 1 TO N

the tokens FOR, I, TO, and N are identifiers and the number 1 is a constant. Of the four identifiers, FOR is a "statement identifier" that identifies a particular type of statement, I and N are variables, and TO is an identifier used as a "separator." The concept of an identifier is discussed further with respect to specific programming languages.

## 2.4 OPERATORS, EXPRESSIONS, AND REPLACEMENT

A computer can perform a variety of operational functions, known as computing or computation. Some of these functions are: (1) arithmetic and logical operations, (2) data movement, (3) sequence and control functions, and (4) input and output. Normally, these operational functions are available to a user through statements in a programming language and when the user desires to specify a particular type of operation, he uses the most appropriate statement for that purpose. Arithmetic and logical operations are particularly important since they are made available to the user in several ways (not necessarily in a single language) and are frequently used in several types of statements.

Assume that one desires to add the value of variable A to the value of variable B. This operation could be specified in several ways, such as

$$A+B \tag{1}$$

or

$$ADD \ A \ TO \ B \tag{2}$$

Method (1) is similar to ordinary mathematical notation and is the most frequently used method in programming. Method (2), which is similar to a COBOL statement, is less convenient when several mathematical operations need to be performed or when it is desired to include mathematical operations in one of the other statements in a programming language. As a means of specifying a standalone operation, however, method (2) has the advantages of being convenient, straightforward, and readable.

## Operators

In a programming language, a symbol that denotes a computational operation is known as an *operator*. Thus, in the statement

A+1

for example, + is an operator; the variable A and the constant 1 are *operands* to the operator. If A has the value 7, then A+1 has the value 8. More specifically, an operand is a quantity upon which an operation is performed; it can be either a variable or a constant. Some operations, such as addition and subtraction, require two operands and are written with the operator symbol separating the operands. The expression A+B, to use an earlier example, denotes that the value of variable B should be added to the value of variable A. (The example is, of course, abbreviated since there is no indication of what to do with the result.) An operator of this type is referred to as an *infix operator*. Operators that require a single operand, such as negation, are referred to as *prefix operators* and written with the operator preceding the operand. The expression −A, for example, computes the expression 0−A and is used to change the sign of A. If A=10, then −A equals −10.

In programming, operators are classed into four general categories:

1. *Arithmetic operators* such as + (for addition and identity), − (for subtraction and negation), * (for multiplication), / (for division), and ** (for exponentiation).
2. *Comparison operators* that compare two data items (also referred to as relational operators), that is,

    < for *less than*
    ≤ for *less than or equal to*
    = for *equal to*
    ≥ for *greater than or equal to*
    > for *greater than*
    ≠ for *not equal to*

3. *Logical operators* that determine the truth of one or more assertions, that is,

$\wedge$  for *and*

$\vee$  for *or*

$\sim$  for *not* (or complement)

4. *String operators* that operate on character strings; for example, the PL/I operator || denotes catenation.

The representations of some of these operators vary between programming languages; for example, the logical operator "and" is represented by .AND. in FORTRAN, AND in COBOL, and & in PL/I. However, the mathematical meaning of the operations is invariant. Table 2.1 gives a "semiformal" definition for each of the above operators.[4]

Table 2.1

Computational Operators

| | Operation | Type | Form | Definition (R = result) | Example ($\leftrightarrow$ denotes equivalence) |
|---|---|---|---|---|---|
| **ARITHMETIC OPERATORS** | Addition | Infix | A+B | R=A+B | $2+3\leftrightarrow5$ |
| | Subtraction | Infix | A−B | R=A−B | $6-4\leftrightarrow2$ |
| | Multiplication | Infix | A∗B | R=A×B | $4*3\leftrightarrow12$ |
| | Division | Infix | A/B | R=A÷B | $9/2\leftrightarrow4.5$ |
| | Exponentiation | Infix | A∗∗B | $R=A^B$ | $3**2\leftrightarrow9$ |
| | Negation | Prefix | −A | R=0−A | $-A\leftrightarrow-3$, where A=3 |
| | Identity | Prefix | +A | R=0+A | $+A\leftrightarrow-5$, where A=−5 |
| **LOGICAL OPERATORS** | And | Infix | Q∧T | R is true if Q and T are both true and is false otherwise. | $T\wedge Q\leftrightarrow$false $\Big\}$ |
| | Or | Infix | Q∨T | R is true if either Q or T is true and is false otherwise. | $T\vee Q\leftrightarrow$true ⎬ T = true and Q = false |
| | Not | Prefix | ∼Q | R is true if Q is false; R is false if Q is true. | $\sim T\leftrightarrow$false ⎠ |

---

[4]The PL/I language is not covered in this book. The reader is referred to reference [4].

Table 2.1 *(Continued)*

| | Operation | Type | Form | Definition (R = result) | Example (↔ denotes equivalence) |
|---|---|---|---|---|---|
| **COMPARISON OPERATORS** | Less than | Infix | A<B | R is true if A is less than B and is false otherwise. | 3<2↔false |
| | Less than or equal to | Infix | A≤B | R is true if A is less than or equal to B and is false otherwise. | 3≤3↔true |
| | Equal to | Infix | A=B | R is true if A is equal to B and is false otherwise. | 3=2↔false |
| | Not equal to | Infix | A≠B | R is true if A is not equal to B and is false otherwise. | 3≠2↔true |
| | Greater than or equal to | Infix | A≥B | R is true if A is greater than or equal to B and is false otherwise. | 2≥3↔false |
| | Greater than | Infix | A>B | R is true if A is greater than B and is false otherwise. | 3>2↔true |
| **STRING OPERATORS** | Catenation | Infix | C‖D | R is formed by catenating string D to string C. | "SOFT"‖"WARE" ↔"SOFTWARE" |

## Expressions

As in mathematics, operators and operands can be combined to form an expression denoting that a sequence of operations is to be performed. For example, A+B∗C means that the product of B and C is to be added to A. Implied here is the fact that computational operations are executed in a prescribed sequence and that operators possess a priority that determines the order in which the operations are executed. A simple priority scheme is:

| Priority | Operator |
|----------|----------|
| highest  | ** |
| ↓        | * or / |
| lowest   | + or − |

which means that ** is executed before * or /, and so forth. Thus, the expression 2+3*4 has the value 14. The programmer can use the priority of operators to his advantage. For example, the mathematical expression $ax^2 + b$ can be written in a programming language as A*X**2+B while maintaining the intended order of operations. In other cases, such as $(a + 1)^2/a + b$, it is necessary to depart from the established order of execution. This need is served with parentheses that can be used for grouping. Expressions within parentheses are executed before the operations of which they are a part. The above example can be written in a programming language as (A+1)**2/(A+B). Similarly, the expression (2+3)*4 has the value 20. The use of parentheses can be extended to as many levels of nesting as are required by a particular sequence of operations.

### Replacement and Data Movement

Expressions are permitted in some statements in a programming language because a computed value is frequently needed. For example, the following statement in the BASIC language:

IF A+B>13.5 THEN 510

directs the flow of program control to the statement numbered 510 if the value of the expression A+B is greater than 13.5. However, the most frequent use of the expression is to specify that a set of computations are to be performed and that the value of a variable is to be replaced with the result. Thus in the statement

A=B+C

the value of A is replaced with the *value* of the expression B+C. The "equivalence sign (=)" denotes replacement but does imply equivalence since values and not expressions are involved. Thus if B contains the value 10 and C contains the value 20, then execution of the statement A=B+C causes A to be replaced with the value 30; B and C retain their original values.

In mathematics, an identity, such as

$$(a + 1)(a + 2) = a^2 + 3a + 2$$

is commonly used. Statements of this type are strictly illegal in programming languages. The *assignment statement,* which is introduced above, takes the general form:

$$v = e$$

which means that the value of variable $v$ is replaced with the value of expression $e$, evaluated at the point of reference. The precise forms that $v$ and $e$ can assume are discussed later with respect to the different programming languages. In general, an expression $e$ can be a constant, a variable, or a meaningful combination of constants, variables, operations, and parentheses. All of the following are valid expressions:

| | |
|---|---|
| P | 2\*\*ML |
| 25 | (A1+B2)\*C3–D4 |
| I\*J | A\*B\*\*2–1 |
| DOG+CAT | (A) |

An assignment statement, such as:

NAME=C1

causes no computation to be performed[5] and simply replaces NAME with the value C1. (C1 retains its original value.) A comparable facility is provided in the COBOL language with a separate statement of the form:

MOVE C1 TO NAME.

Similarly, the statement

ADD A TO B.

given previously, is equivalent to the assignment statement:

B=B+A

[5] That is, in the sense discussed previously; conversion may be required.

In fact, the statement B=B+A means: "Add A to the current value of B and replace the old value of B with the result of the addition."

One of the objectives of the above discussion is to emphasize the fact that each of the programming languages has characteristics of its own; these characteristics are one of the reasons that a user would select a particular language in which to write his program. Admittedly, several other factors (such as availability of a language processor, efficiency, programming standards, and so forth) would normally be considered in the choice of language.

## 2.5 DATA ORGANIZATION

### Scalars

A single item of data is known as a *scalar*. Thus, a value like a person's age, the name of a part, or the result of a logical operation is considered to be a scalar regardless of its data type. It can be expressed as a constant or as a variable. It follows that a variable that names a scalar is known as a *scalar variable.*

### Arrays

In a great many cases, data take the form of a family of related data items. For example, a measurement taken at different locations at successive intervals might be recorded as follows:

| Location–Date | Temperature |
|---|---|
| New York–Jan. 1 | 29° |
| Miami–Jan. 1 | 69° |
| Chicago–Jan. 1 | 26° |
| Los Angeles–Jan. 1 | 60° |
| New York–March 31 | 41° |
| Miami–March 31 | 79° |
| Chicago–March 31 | 38° |
| Los Angeles–March 31 | 67° |
| New York–June 1 | 75° |
| Miami–June 1 | 92° |
| Chicago–June 1 | 80° |
| Los Angeles–June 1 | 88° |

Storing the information in the above form is indeed cumbersome and would occupy an excessive amount of storage. In this case, an array, such as the following:

|  | | *Date Index* | | |
|---|---|---|---|---|
| | TEMP | 1 | 2 | 3 |
| | 1 | 29 | 41 | 75 |
| *Location* | 2 | 69 | 79 | 92 |
| *Index* | 3 | 26 | 38 | 80 |
| | 4 | 60 | 67 | 88 |

*Matrix*

would be considerably more convenient. The temperature in Miami, which has a location index of 2, on March 31, which has a date index of 2, is easily retrieved as 79°. A key point is that only the array, as a whole, need be given a name—in this case TEMP. Ordinary vectors and matrices are stored in a similar fashion. In computing, the concept is extended to include $n$ dimensions—hence the more general name *array*. The process of retrieving an element of an array, termed *selection*, uses the name of the array and the relative position of the desired element in the array. Indexes used to select an element from an array are termed a subscript and can be expressed as constants, variables, or expressions. The established practice is to reduce an index to an integer before selection takes place. The number of indexes in a subscript must equal the number of dimensions in the array. Thus, TEMP(3,2), in the above example, would select the value 38. When writing a subscript, the indexes are separated by commas and the entire set of indexes are enclosed in parentheses following the array name. The convention is used since subscripts or superscripts in the usual sense are cumbersome to enter into the computer.

An array has several properties of interest. The array A, defined as:

$$\begin{matrix} a_{1,-2} & a_{1,-1} & a_{1,0} & a_{1,1} & a_{1,2} \\ a_{2,-2} & a_{2,-1} & a_{2,0} & a_{2,1} & a_{2,2} \\ a_{3,-2} & a_{3,-1} & a_{3,0} & a_{3,1} & a_{3,2} \\ a_{4,-2} & a_{4,-1} & a_{4,0} & a_{4,1} & a_{4,2} \end{matrix}$$

is used as an example. The first property is the *number of dimensions* of which A has 2. Each dimension is further characterized by a bounds and an extent. The *bounds* of a dimension are the beginning and ending index for that dimension and determine the manner in which elements are selected. The *extent* is the number of elements in a dimension—regardless of how they are referenced. Another property is homogeneity. *Homogeneity* refers to the fact that each element of an array must have the same data attributes. Thus, for example, the array must contain all fixed- or all floating-point numbers. Obviously, distinct values may differ. Later, it will become evident that an array may contain more complicated types of elements—such as a structure. The last property of an array is how it is stored. Two methods are in widespread use: row order and column order. *Row order,* also known as *index order* or *lexicographic order,* denotes that the elements of an array are stored in consecutive locations in computer main storage in a row-wise fashion. Row order is used in the PL/I language. *Column order* denotes that the elements of the array are stored in a column-wise fashion. The most popular programming language using column order is FORTRAN. Examples of both techniques for the array A, given above, are listed as follows:

| Row Order | Index | Column Order |
|---|---|---|
| A(1,-2) | 1 | A(1,-2) |
| A(1,-1) | 2 | A(2,-2) |
| A(1,0) | 3 | A(3,-2) |
| A(1,1) | 4 | A(4,-2) |
| A(1,2) | 5 | A(1,-1) |
| A(2,-2) | 6 | A(2,-1) |
| A(2,-1) | 7 | A(3,-1) |
| A(2,0) | 8 | A(4,-1) |
| A(2,1) | 9 | A(1,0) |
| A(2,2) | 10 | A(2,0) |
| A(3,-2) | 11 | A(3,0) |
| A(3,-1) | 12 | A(4,0) |
| A(3,0) | 13 | A(1,1) |
| A(3,1) | 14 | A(2,1) |
| A(3,2) | 15 | A(3,1) |
| A(4,-2) | 16 | A(4,1) |
| A(4,-1) | 17 | A(1,2) |
| A(4,0) | 18 | A(2,2) |
| A(4,1) | 19 | A(3,2) |
| A(4,2) | 20 | A(4,2) |

It is necessary to know how an array is stored in a given language for the following reason. Consider these statements in BASIC:

DIM A(13,4)                                                    (1)

MAT READ A                                                     (2)

Statement (1) defines a matrix with 13 rows and 4 columns. Statement (2) specifies that data is to be read from a data set into computer storage to occupy matrix A. Data must be placed in the data file in a prescribed sequence so that a value is placed in the intended matrix position. Therefore, the order in which the matrix elements are stored must be known or a specific "convention" must be established.[6] (In the case of the BASIC language, elements are assigned from the data file to the matrix by rows.)

## Structures

Many computer applications, such as data processing, use an aggregate of data in which individual data items do not necessarily have identical sizes or identical data types. A data aggregate of this type is known as a "structure," which is frequently associated with a data record. More specifically, a *structure* is a collection of variables (possibly of different types and sizes) organized in a hierarchy. A typical structure is specified as follows:

```
01   PAYDATA,
     02   EMPLOYNO SIZE IS 8 CLASS IS NUMERIC,
     02   NAME,
          03   FINIT SIZE IS 1 CLASS IS ALPHABETIC,
          03   MINIT SIZE IS 1 CLASS IS ALPHABETIC,
          03   LAST SIZE IS 15 CLASS IS ALPHABETIC,
     02   DEP SIZE IS 2 CLASS IS NUMERIC USAGE IS
          COMPUTATIONAL,
     02   RATE PICTURE IS 9999V99 USAGE IS COMPUTATIONAL,
     02   GROSS,
          03   PAY PICTURE IS 99999V99 USAGE IS
               COMPUTATIONAL,
          03   FEDTAX PICTURE IS 99999V99 USAGE IS
               COMPUTATIONAL,
          03   FICA PICTURE IS 999V99 USAGE IS
               COMPUTATIONAL,
          03   STATETAX PICTURE IS 9999V99 USAGE IS
               COMPUTATIONAL,
          03   CITYTAX PICTURE IS 999V99 USAGE IS
               COMPUTATIONAL.
```

[6]Actually, only a "convention" is necessary. However, the knowledge of how an array is stored is necessary when more than one programming language is used in the construction of a program. This topic is covered later.

and depicted as it would be stored in Figure 2.1. For some purposes, such as input and output, it is convenient to treat a data aggregate as a single unit, as in the following input statement in COBOL:

READ PAYFILE INTO PAYDATA AT END GO TO DONE.

In this case, the complete data record is read into the storage reserved for the structure named PAYDATA. In other cases, it is necessary to be able to reference specific data fields in the structure, such as the following statement which updates the gross pay:

ADD RATE TO PAY.

In a structure, the relative position of the data element in the hierarchy is specified with a level number, such as 01, 02, or 03. Data items with the same relative level number are at the same level in the hierarchy. Structures are presented in detail with the COBOL language discussion.

## 2.6 SYNTAX NOTATION

Most programmers recognize that the process of constructing a computer program is a creative act and that once a program is suitably encoded, it is as much a contribution to the world of knowledge as a poem, a mathematical formula, or an artist's sketch. In fact, computer programming is usually regarded as an art rather than a science. A computer program written in a programming language becomes a body of knowledge when a suitable description of that language is available that can be used to distinguish between a syntactically valid program and a syntactically invalid program and to determine the meaning of the pro-

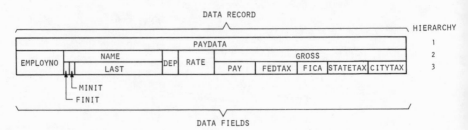

Fig. 2.1. Illustration of a typical hierarchic structure showing record and field levels.

gram. A *metalanguage* is used for this purpose and most programming languages utilize a descriptive technique of this kind.

### Backus-Naur Form

The first metalanguage to be used with any degree of regularity is *Backus-Naur Form* (BNF) developed for ALGOL 60.[7] Essentially, BNF includes three metasymbols from which definitions are formed:

| Symbol | Meaning |
|--------|---------|
| ::= | "Is defined to be" |
| \| | To be read as "or" |
| <> | Angular brackets that denote a name of a constituent rather than the constituent named. |

It follows that the formal structure of a programming language can be systematically constructed from basic symbols with definitions such as the following that are used to define a number:

```
<digit>::=0|1|2|3|4|5|6|7|8|9
<unsigned integer>::=<digit>|<unsigned integer><digit>
<integer>::=<unsigned integer>|+<unsigned integer>|
            -<unsigned integer>
<decimal fraction>::=.<unsigned integer>
<exponent part>::=₁₀<integer>
<decimal number>::=<unsigned integer>|<decimal fraction>|
                   <unsigned integer><decimal fraction>
<unsigned number>::=<decimal number>|<decimal number>
                    <exponent part>
<number>::=<unsigned number>|+<unsigned number>
           -<unsigned number>
```

Note that two constructions written in sequence are considered to be juxtaposed.

[7]P. Naur (ed.), "Revised Report on the Algorithmic Language ALGOL 60," *Communications of the ACM,* Vol. 6, No. 1 (January 1963).

### Extended Backus Notation

The most frequent use of a metalanguage is to describe a statement in a programming language in such a way that the reader can construct a valid instance of a particular statement. Thus, the metalanguage should utilize a notation outside of the programming language being described and should lend itself to use in the construction of valid statements by a user of the language described.

Through the years, the Backus-Naur Form, introduced above, gradually evolved to a notation known as *Extended Backus Notation,* which is more convenient for the kinds of programming languages covered in this book—namely BASIC, FORTRAN, and COBOL. It is utilized whenever appropriate to present complex material.

Extended Backus Notation employs seven rules and appropriate symbols, given as follows:

1. A *notation variable* names a constituent of a programming language. It takes one of two forms: (1) Lower-case letters, digits, and hyphens—beginning with a letter; for example:

   constant

   arithmetic-variable

   array-dimension-specification

   or (2) two or more words separated by hyphens where one word consists of lower-case letters and the others consist of upper-case letters; for example:

   DATA-statement

   MAT-READ-statement

   A notation variable represents information that must be supplied by the user and is defined formally or informally in preceding or adjacent text.

2. A *notation constant* stands for itself and is represented by capital letters or by special characters. A notation constant must be written as shown. For example, in the statement

   GOSUB statement-number

   NEXT arithmetic-variable

   the words GOSUB and NEXT are notation constants and must be written as indicated.

3. A *syntactical unit* is regarded as a notation variable, a notation constant, or a collection of notation variables, notation constants, and notation symbols enclosed in braces or brackets.

4. The *vertical bar* (|) is read "or" and indicates that a choice must be made between the item to the left of the bar and the item to the right of the bar. For example:

   character-reference|arithmetic-reference
   &PI|&E|&SQR2

5. A set of *braces* (⁅⁆) is used for grouping or to indicate that a choice is to be made among the syntactical units contained in the braces. For example:

   {+|−}
   {integer-constant|fixed-point-constant}

6. A set of *brackets* ([ ]) represents an option and the enclosed syntactical units can be omitted. For example:

   [+|−]
   alphabetic-character[numeric-character]

7. The *ellipsis* (a series of three periods) indicates that the preceding syntactic unit may be repeated one or more times. For example:

   DATA constant [,constant] ...
   REM [string character] ...

The syntax notation is further described by giving some examples from the various languages. The *FOR statement* in BASIC has the form:

FOR   arithmetic-variable = arithmetic-expression   TO
   arithmetic-expression   [STEP   arithmetic-expression]

An example of this FOR statement is:

FOR I = J TO M/2 STEP 2

The *computed GOTO statement* in FORTRAN has the form:

GOTO (statement-number [statement-number] ...),
   integer-scalar-variable

An example of the computed GOTO statement is:

GOTO (150,17,3000), I4B

The *MOVE statement* in COBOL has the form:

$$\text{MOVE} \left\{ \begin{array}{l} \text{data-name} \\ \text{literal} \\ \text{CORRESPONDING data-name} \end{array} \right\} \text{TO data-name [,data-name] ...}$$

An example of the MOVE statement is:

MOVE CORRESPONDING OLD-REC TO NEW-REC

The significance of the use of syntax notation will become apparent as the subject matter of the book unfolds.

## 2.7 COMMENTS ON FUNDAMENTALS

Here is why fundamentals are a necessary part of the study of programming languages. When discussing fundamentals, many questions are left open. For example, arrays were introduced as conceptual entities but were never tied down to the real world. Structures, operators, and expressions also fall into the same category—to name only a few. The manner in which the fundamental concepts are defined and implemented constitutes the difference between the various programming languages, and also can be used as a means of characterizing a given language.

As far as additional reading is concerned, bibliographic material is relatively scarce because most books on programming languages tell how to use a particular language rather than describe the characteristics and significance of that language. In many cases, the distinction between the two points of view is indeed a fine line and a personal judgment is necessary. However, particular languages are not ignored and references to a language are given when that language is covered in the book. For an overview of programming languages in general, the reader is directed to Higman [3], Sammet [4], and Sanderson [5]. Wegner [6] relates programming languages to computer organization and information structures, Galler and Perlis [1] give a more theoretical but a very readable treatment of the subject. The nature of programming languages is of international concern and the reader is directed to Genuys [2] for some different points of view on the subject.

## EXERCISES

1. Write the following numbers using floating-point notation:

| 1234.5 | −.000872 |
|--------|----------|
| .000163 | 300000 |
| −93.237 | .101 |

2. Store the floating-point numbers developed in exercise 1 using the following format:

| ± | XX | XXXXX |
|---|----|----|

   with a bias-64 exponent.
3. Give several explanations for the names "variable" and "identifier."
4. Classify the operators (infix or prefix) in the following expressions:

   | −A*B | A*(−B) |
   |------|--------|
   | 3.14*PT | A/(−B*C) |
   | (A+B*C)−1 | −13.4 |

5. Evaluate the following expressions, using the operator hierarchy given in the chapter, for the following values (A=10, B=5, C=2):

   (A+B*C)−1
   A/(B*C)
   (A+B*C−4)/2

6. Assume the following statements are executed in order:

   A=5
   B=(A+3)/2
   C=3*A**2−11*B+7

   What does variable C contain?

7. Given the matrix:

   $$A = \begin{pmatrix} -7 & 3 & 9 & 6 \\ 5 & 1 & 4 & 3 \\ 2 & 8 & 7 & 5 \end{pmatrix}$$

   where the row bounds are 1 and 3 and the column bounds are 1 and 4, give A(2,3), A(3,2), and A(1,2). Evaluate the following expressions:

$$2*A(3,3)**2 - 17$$
$$A(1,3) - 2*A(3,1) - A(2,2)$$

8. Store the matrix in exercise 7 in column order using fixed-point notation; floating-point notation.

9. Give two examples (i.e., instances) of a $<$sol$>$ defined as follows:

$$<\text{sil}>::=A|B|C|1|2|3$$
$$<\text{sal}>::=<\text{sil}>|<\text{sal}><\text{sil}>$$
$$<\text{sol}>::=<\text{sal}>|+<\text{sal}>|-<\text{sal}>$$

10. Classify the following assignment statements as being valid or invalid:

   a. $(X+1)(X+2)=Y$
   b. $Y=(X+1)(X+2)$
   c. DOG=CAT
   d. ZEB=2X
   e. TOM=A3+1
   f. $C4=3*F**2-3*W/4$
   g. $U=C**D$

For an invalid statement, give the reason(s) it is invalid.

## SELECTED READINGS

1. Galler, B. A., and A. J. Perlis. *A View of Programming Languages.* Reading, Mass.: Addison-Wesley Publishing Co., 1970.
2. Genuys, F. (ed.). *Programming Languages: A NATO Advanced Study Institute.* New York: Academic Press, 1968.
3. Higman, B. *A Comparative Study of Programming Languages.* New York: American Elsevier Publishing Co., 1967.
4. Sammet, J. E. *Programming Languages: History and Fundamentals.* Englewood Cliffs, N.J.: Prentice-Hall, Inc., 1969.
5. Sanderson, P. C. *Computer Languages.* New York: Philosophical Library Inc., 1970.
6. Wegner, P. *Programming Languages, Information Structures, and Machine Organization.* New York: McGraw-Hill Book Co., 1968.

# PART 2

## THE
## BASIC
## LANGUAGE

# 3

# BASIC LANGUAGE STRUCTURE

## 3.1 INTRODUCTION

The BASIC language achieves its greatest utility from the simple fact that it is easy to learn, easy to use, and easy to remember. (BASIC is an acronym for *B*eginner's *A*ll-purpose *S*ymbolic *I*nstruction *C*ode.) BASIC is particularly appropriate for the student or the problem solver who wants to utilize the advantages of computer processing without becoming a computer expert.

BASIC was originally developed at Dartmouth College under the direction of Professors John G. Kemeny and Thomas E. Kurtz. The project was supported by the National Science Foundation. BASIC has been under continuous development and several implementations of the language are currently available at universities, through computer-service companies, and in business concerns. Enhancements have been made to the original concept of BASIC such that one frequently hears of an "extended BASIC," "super BASIC," "advanced BASIC," and so forth. Occasionally, one even hears of a "basic BASIC."

The discussion of BASIC language serves two purposes in this book:

1. It prepares the reader for writing programs in the BASIC language.
2. It provides a "gentle" introduction to other computer languages.

This part of the book covers the original Dartmouth version of BASIC plus many of the subsequent extensions to the language, exclusive of file operations.[1] As yet, a BASIC standard has not been established such that variations exist between different implementations of the language. Any reader making extensive use of the language should consult the reference manual for the system he is using.

---

[1] The viewpoint of this book is pedagogical. File operations are introduced from different points of view through a variety of features in other languages.

## 3.2 THE INDIAN PROBLEM[2]

As an illustration of the manner in which BASIC can be used to solve a problem, consider the classic *Indian problem.* The problem is stated as follows: Manhattan Island was sold by the Indians to the settlers in 1626 for $24 worth of beads and trinkets. At a given interest rate, what is the island worth today? A "simple-minded" solution is presented as the following program:

```
10  LET P=24
20  LET R=.06
30  FOR Y=1627 TO 1973
40      LET P=P+P*R
50  NEXT Y
60  PRINT P
70  END
```

Output:

    1.44993E+10

where E denotes a base ten exponential multiplier. Thus 5E+2 is equal to 500. The statements numbered 10 and 20 assign the values 24 and .06 to the principal (P) and the interesι rate (R), respectively. The interest for a given year is computed as P*R and the principal at the end of a given year is computed as P+P*R. Statements 30 through 50 constitute a program loop; the principal is recomputed as the year (Y) advances from 1627 to 1973. After the loop is completed (that is, the number of iterations specified in statement 30 have been satisfied), the resultant principal (P) is printed in statement 60.

The PRINT statement can also be used to have several data items printed on the same output line by including those items in the PRINT statement, separated by commas. Thus if statement 60 read,

    60  PRINT "PRESENT VALUE OF MANHATTAN=",P

then the output would be,

    PRESENT VALUE OF MANHATTAN=    1.44993E+10

---

[2]To the reader who is being exposed to programming languages for the first time: It is not necessary that this section be read with complete comprehension. Only general concepts are required since all topics are covered in later sections.

Data items enclosed in quotes are printed as literals, whereas the *numerical value* of an expression is printed. (Recall that a variable is an expression.)

In the preceding program, the data of the problem was built into the program (that is, a beginning principal of 24 and a rate of .06). If the user desired to repeat the calculations for different interest rates, then he would have to build a set of data values with a DATA statement, such as:

   DATA .05,.06,.07,.08

and access the data set with a READ statement, such as:

   READ R

Thus, a program to compute the present value of Manhattan Island for different interest rates is given as follows:

```
10   DATA .05,.06,.07,.08
20   FOR I=1 TO 4
30       LET P=24
40       READ R
50       FOR Y = 1626 TO 1973
60           LET P = P+P*R
70       NEXT Y
80       PRINT "PRESENT VALUE OF MANHATTAN=",P
90   NEXT I
99   END
```

Output:

```
PRESENT VALUE OF MANHATTAN=    5.40628E+08
PRESENT VALUE OF MANHATTAN=    1.44993E+10
PRESENT VALUE OF MANHATTAN=    3.77035E+11
PRESENT VALUE OF MANHATTAN=    9.51162E+12
```

The program includes a nested FOR loop that has the form:

```
     ┌FOR...
     │   ...
     │   ┌FOR...
  A ─┤ B─┤   ...
     │   │   ...
     │   └NEXT...
     │   ...
     └NEXT...
```

The interpretation of the nested loops is as follows: For every iteration of loop A, loop B is executed from start to finish. (Thus, if A is executed *n* times and loop B is executed *m* times, then a given statement contained in loop B is executed $n \times m$ times.)

Several statements were used in the above examples:

>LET—assigns the value of an expression to a variable
>FOR—begins a program loop and specifies how many times it is executed
>NEXT—ends a program loop and tells the computer to return to the beginning of the loop for the next iteration
>PRINT—causes output data to be printed
>DATA—creates a set of data
>READ—causes data specified in a DATA statement to be accessed (i.e., read) and assigned to specified variables
>END—ends a BASIC program

Each of these statements is described in detail in Chapter 4.

Clearly, the examples presented in these sections are included to serve introductory purposes. Using the formula

$$A = P*(1+R)\uparrow N$$

the above program can be simplified as:

```
10   FOR R = .05 TO .08 STEP .01
20        PRINT 24*(1+R)↑347
30   NEXT R
40   END
```

## 3.3  CHARACTERS AND SYMBOLS

A computer program is essentially a coded form of an algorithm for solving a given problem on a computer. The program is developed using the alphabet, syntax, and semantics of a programming language; thus, a statement is encoded in the alphabet of the language using established conventions. It is necessary to distinguish between characters of the alphabet and symbols of the language. A *character of the alphabet* is an entity that has a representation internally and externally to the computer. The letter "A," for example, is a character of most language alphabets. The majority of characters have no meaning in their own right; for example, the letter "A" only has meaning through the language element of which it is a part, which may be a variable, a statement identifier, and so forth. Table 3.1 lists the BASIC alphabet, which consists of approximately 50-55 characters depending upon the equipment involved.

Table 3.1

Characters of the BASIC Alphabet

*Alphabetic Characters (26)*

A  B  C  D  E  F  G H  I  J  K  L  M  N  O  P  Q R  S  T  U  V  W  X  Y  Z

*Digits (10)*

0  1  2  3  4  5  6  7  8  9

*Special Characters (19)*

| *Name* | *Character* |
| --- | --- |
| Blank | (no visual representation) |
| Equal sign | = |
| Plus sign | + |
| Minus sign | − |
| Asterisk | * |
| Solidus (slash) | / |
| Up arrow | ↑ |
| Left parenthesis | ( |
| Right parenthesis | ) |
| Comma | , |
| Point or period | . |
| Single quotation mark (apostrophe) | ' |
| Double quotation mark | " |
| Semicolon | ; |
| Question mark | ? |
| "Less than" symbol | < |
| "Greater than" symbol | > |
| "Not equal" symbol | ≠ |
| Currency symbol (dollar sign) | $ |

A *symbol of the language* is a series of one or more characters that have been assigned a specific meaning. A symbol consisting of more than one symbol is termed a *composite symbol* that is assigned a meaning not inherent in the constituent characters themselves. Sample composite symbols are ** for exponentiation and $>=$ for "greater than or equal to". The symbols of the BASIC language are listed in Table 3.2. The characters listed are needed for language constructs. Additional characters that may exist in a given alphabet can be used in quotes as literal values.

Table 3.2

Symbols of the BASIC Language

| Symbol | Function | Alternate[a] |
|---|---|---|
| + | Addition or prefix + | |
| – | Subtraction or prefix – | |
| * | Multiplication | |
| / | Division | |
| ↑ | Exponentiation | ** |
| > | Greater than | GT |
| >= | Greater than or equal to | GE |
| = | Equal to (also see below) | |
| <> | Not equal to | ≠ or NE |
| < | Less than | LT |
| <= | Less than or equal to | LE |
| , | Separates elements of list or subscripts | |
| . | Decimal point | |
| ; | Separates elements of list | |
| = | Assignment symbol | |
| " | Used to enclose literals | ' |
| ( ) | Enclose lists or group expressions | |

[a]Some versions of BASIC use alternate composite symbols; frequently, the characters used are a function of the input devices available to the user.

In most implementations of BASIC, lower-case letters can be used interchangeably with upper-case letters. Spaces are ignored in BASIC, except in literals, so that they can be inserted by the user to promote easy reading.

## 3.4 DATA TYPES AND CONSTANT VALUES

Two types of data are permitted in BASIC: arithmetic data and character-string data. An *arithmetic data item* has a numeric value and is stored as either a fixed-point number or a floating-point number, depending on the magnitude and precision of the value and the manner in which the language is implemented on a given computer. An arithmetic data item is referenced through the use of a variable or a constant and may be generated as an intermediate result as part of a computational procedure. BASIC accepts arithmetic constants in three principal forms:

1.  As a constituent of a non-DATA statement, such as the number 5 in
    LET A=B+5
2.  As a constant in a DATA statement, such as
    DATA 25,-13.289,.734E-4
3.  In response to an input request (from an INPUT statement), such as
    ?-75,4.56

In general, the arithmetic constant is written in the usual fashion, that is, as a sequence of digits optionally preceded by a plus sign or minus sign and possibly containing a decimal point. (An arithmetic constant is specified in decimal and the user need not be concerned with how it is stored.) Sample arithmetic constants are -13.5, 12345, 1., +36, .01, -5, and 0. In addition, an arithmetic constant can be scaled by a power of ten by following the constant with the letter E followed by the power which must be expressed as either a positive or negative integer. Thus, the constant $x$E$y$ is equivalent to the expression $x \times 10^y$ in mathematics. To cite some examples, .12E-4 is equivalent to .000012, -3E2 is equivalent to -300, +1.234E3 is equivalent to 1234, and -1E+1 is equivalent to -10. The sign of an arithmetic constant is frequently omitted in expressions by applying elementary rules of arithmetic. Thus, instead of writing A+(-5), most users simply write A-5. Similarly, A-(-5) would ordinarily be written as A+5.

In an arithmetic constant, the E (if used) must be preceded by at least one digit. Thus, 1E2 is a valid constant where E2 is not.

A *character-string data item* is stored as a string of characters and can include any character recognized by the computer equipment. A character-string data item is referenced through the use of a variable or a constant. BASIC accepts character-string constants in three principal forms:

1.  As a constituent part of a non-DATA statement, such as
    LET F$ = "TEA FOR TWO"
    or
    IF P$ = "END" THEN 100
2.  As a constant in a DATA statement, such as
    DATA "BIG", "BAD"
3.  In response to an input request (from an INPUT statement), such as[3]
    ?"EACH HIS OWN"

[3] At least one version of BASIC allows the quotes to be omitted. In this case, the initial character of a character string must be alphabetic and a comma is used to separate distinct charter strings.

A character-string constant must be enclosed in single or double quotation marks. Any character within the quotes, including the blank character, is considered to be part of the character string. If the string is enclosed in single quotation marks, then a double quotation mark can be a character *in* the string and vice versa. The length of a character string is the number of characters between the enclosing quotation marks. If a string is enclosed in single quotation marks and it is desired to include a single quotation mark in that string, then the included quotation mark must be represented as two consecutive single quotation marks. The consecutive quotation marks are a lexical feature of the language and are stored as a single character. Sample character-string constants are:

| Character-String Constant | Length | Would Print As |
|---|---|---|
| "TEA FOR TWO" | 11 | TEA FOR TWO |
| '123.4' | 5 | 123.4 |
| ' "DARN IT" ' | 9 | "DARN IT" |
| 'DON' 'T' | 5 | DON'T |

Character-string data are frequently used for printing descriptive information and are occasionally referred to as "label data."

## 3.5 IDENTIFIERS

An *identifier* is a string of alphabetic or numeric characters, the first of which must be alphabetic. In BASIC, identifiers are used to name scalar variables, array variables, and user-defined functions, and also serve as keywords. A *keyword* is an identifier that is part of the language. Keywords are neither reserved words nor are they marked by a special symbol. In BASIC, keywords are used as:

1. *Statement identifiers,* such as READ in the statement
   READ A,B
   that specify the function a statement is to perform.
2. *Separating keywords,* such as THEN in the statement
   IF A=B THEN 500
   that separate constituent parts of a statement and make the language easier to interpret.
3. *Options,* such as STEP in the statement
   FOR I=3 TO N STEP J
   that augment a statement by affecting the manner in which it is executed.

4. *Built-in functions,* such as SIN in the statement

   LET S1 = 3*SIN(Y↑2)−1

   that specify computational procedures that are provided as part of the language.[4]

A *scalar arithmetic variable* identifier (also referred to as a simple variable) consists of a single letter or a single letter followed by a single digit. Thus, A, I, Z1, and K9 are valid simple variables while A10, DOG, and 3A are not. The initial value of a simple variable is zero and it can only be used to represent arithmetic data.

A *scalar character-string variable* identifier (also referred to as a simple character variable) consists of a single letter followed by a dollar sign (that is, the currency symbol). The maximum length of a character string that can be assigned to a character-string variable is 18. The initial value of a simple character variable is 18 blanks. Thus, A$, I$, and S$ are valid simple character variables while A1$, 5$, and IT$ are not.

Arrays and user-defined functions are introduced later in the book. An *arithmetic array* identifier consists of a single letter and a *character-string array* identifier consists of a single letter followed by a dollar sign. A *user-defined function* identifier consists of the letters "FN" followed by a single letter. Thus, FNE is a valid function identifier.

## 3.6  ARRAYS

An array is a collection of data items of the same type (that is, all arithmetic data items or all character-string data items) that is referenced by an array identifier. An *arithmetic array* can have either one or two dimensions and uses an identifier that consists of a single letter. An element of an array is referenced by giving the relative position of that element in the array. If the array has one dimension, then an element is referenced by appending a subscript enclosed in parentheses to the array name as follows:

   *a(e)*

where *a* is the array name and *e* is an expression evaluated at the point of reference. Thus, the array reference *a(e)* selects the *e*th element of array *a*. If the array has two dimensions, then an element is selected in a similar manner with an array reference of the form:

---

[4]In this case, the keyword SIN is used to identify a procedure that computes the trigonometric sine.

$$a(e_1, e_2)$$

where $a$ is the array name and $e_1$ and $e_2$ are expressions evaluated at the point of reference. Thus, the array reference $a(e_1, e_2)$ selects the element located in the $e_1$th row and the $e_2$th column of $a$. The following are valid array references: A(I), B(W4), C(P+1), C(I,J), E(T3/R+13,3*X↑2-1), F(A(2*Q)), and G(B(1),4). The last two examples depict subscripted subscripts. All elements of an arithmetic array are initially set to zero when the program is executed.

A *character-string array* (referred to as a character array) can have one dimension and uses an identifier that consists of a letter followed by a dollar sign. Each element of a character array can contain up to 18 characters and is initially set to 18 blanks when the program is executed. As with an arithmetic array, an element of an array is referenced by specifying the relative position of that element in the array with a construction of the form:

$$a\$(e)$$

where $a\$$ is the array name and $e$ is an expression evaluated at the point of reference. The following are valid array references: B\$(3), C\$(I), D\$(2*J-1) and D\$(A(K)).

The extent of an array can be declared implicitly or explicitly. An *explicit array declaration* is made through the use of the dimension (DIM) statement, which is used to give the extent of each dimension of the array. Thus, the statement

DIM P(3,4),Q(36),T\$(17)

defines a two-dimensional arithmetic array P with 3 rows and 4 columns, a one-dimensional arithmetic array Q with 36 elements, and a character array T\$ with 17 elements, each element of which can contain a character string of 18 characters. The lower bound for all array dimensions is one; the upper bound is the value declared with the DIM statement. The DIM statement is presented in Chapter 4.

An *implicit array declaration* is made when an array reference with either a single or a double subscript is made to an undeclared array. An array referenced in this way with a single subscript is assigned an extent of 10 with lower and upper bounds of 1 and 10, respectively. An array referenced in this way with a double subscript is assigned row and column extents of 10; each dimension has lower and upper bounds of 1 and 10, respectively.

The manner in which values are assigned to arrays is covered in subsequent sections. Two-dimensional arrays can also be used with statements specifically designed to operate on matrices. This topic is covered in Chapter 5.

## 3.7  OPERATORS AND EXPRESSIONS

Arithmetic and comparison operators are included as part of the BASIC language. Arithmetic operators are defined on arithmetic data and are classed as infix operators and prefix operators.[5] An *infix arithmetic operator* is used in the following manner:

operand {+|−|∗|/|↑} operand

where an operand is defined as an arithmetic constant, a function reference, an element of an arithmetic array, an expression enclosed in parentheses, or a subexpression that has been reduced to a numerical value. A *prefix arithmetic operator* is used in the following form:

{+|−} operand

where "operand" has the same definition as given earlier. The use of a prefix operator is restricted to the following cases:

1. As the leftmost character in an expression, provided that two operators do not appear in succession.
2. As the leftmost character in a subexpression enclosed in parentheses such that the prefix operator follows the left parenthesis.

An example of case 1 is −A+B↑C while an example of case 2 is A∗(−B↑(−3)). The result of an infix or prefix arithmetic operation is a numeric value.

An arithmetic expression can be an arithmetic variable, an element of an arithmetic array, a constant, a function reference, or a series of these constituents separated by infix operators and parentheses and possibly prefixed by prefix operators. Thus, any of the following are valid expressions in BASIC:

| | | |
|---|---|---|
| A1 | −(C1↑I−1) | −SQR(X↑3)−J |
| B+25 | SIN(X3) | ((Y+3)∗Y+16)∗Y−1 |

As stated previously, parentheses are used for grouping and expressions within parentheses are executed before the operations of which they are a part. When parentheses are not used in a given arithmetic expression, an operand may appear

---

[5] Also referred to as binary and unary operators, respectively, or dyadic and monadic operators, respectively.

as though it is an operand to two operators; that is, for example, the operand B in an expression such as:

A+B*C

In this case, operators are executed on a priority basis as governed by the following list:

| Operator | Priority |
|---|---|
| ↑ (that is, **) | Highest |
| prefix +, prefix − | |
| *,/ | ↓ |
| infix +, infix − | Lowest |

Thus, in the expression, A+B*C, the expression B*C is executed first and the result of that subexpression is added to A. Operators of the same priority are executed in a left-to-right order.

A *character expression* is a character variable, a character array member, or a literal (that is, a character constant).[6] Except when they are used in a PRINT statement, literals are handled in a special way:

1. If the literal contains less than 18 characters, it is padded on the right with blanks so that it can be stored as 18 characters.
2. If the literal contains more than 18 characters, it is truncated on the right so that its length is 18 characters.

(Literals in a PRINT statement are given a length determined by the enclosing quotation marks. No padding or truncation occurs.)

A *comparison expression* has the form:

operand {=|<>|>=|<=|>|<} operand

where the "operands" can be either arithmetic expressions or character expressions. (The operands cannot be mixed.) The result of a comparison expression is either a "true" value or a "false" value, which is used in the conditional IF statement. Thus, if A=10, B=15, C$="TEA", and D$="DOG", then the following valid comparison expressions given the indicated results:

---

[6] Some implementations of BASIC permit the catenation operation on character strings and use the plus sign for that purpose. Thus if A$="VOLKS" and B$="WAGEN", then A$+B$ yields the string "VOLKSWAGEN".

A=B yields the value "false"[7]
A↑2+A∗B>=B↑2 yields the value "true"
C$<>D$ yields the value "true"
(A+2.5)↑2>101.5 yields the value "true"
C$<D$ yields the value "false"[8]

In an arithmetic comparison expression, the arithmetic expressions that serve as operands to the comparison operation are evaluated first; then the comparison operation is performed.

## 3.8  STATEMENT STRUCTURE

BASIC is designed to be a terminal-oriented programming language and the structure of the language reflects that mode of operation. Each statement is prefixed with a *statement number* that serves two purposes:

1.  BASIC statements are executed in an order determined by the arithmetic value of the statement number.
2.  The statement number is used to reference another statement in statements such as:

   GOTO 500

in the first case, the statement number serves as a "line number," so that statements need not be entered in any specific order and to facilitate the insertion, deletion, and modification of statements.

The form of a BASIC statement is:

statement-number  [statement-identifier] [statement-body]

where "statement-number" is an unsigned integer,[9] "statement-identifier" is a keyword that identifies a particular type of statement, and "statement-body" is a series of characters that comprise the body of the statement. Sample statements are:

---

[7]Arithmetic comparisons use the arithmetic value of the operands.
[8]When BASIC (and as a matter of fact, any programming language) is implemented, a collating sequence among characters is defined. Frequently, the collating sequence is based on the numerical values of the bit representations of the characters.
[9]Usually, one to four decimal digits are permitted a statement number.

```
500   LET A=B+C*D
300   K3=16
783   GOTO 100
910   IF A>=B THEN 300
440   STOP
999   END
```

Thus, a statement is constructed from a statement identifier, a statement body, or both. Neither a statement identifier nor a statement body is required so that a blank line (except for the statement number) is permitted to improve readability and to serve as a point of reference in a program.

Only one statement is discussed in this section. A comment (that is, a remark) can be inserted anywhere in a program with a statement of the form:

```
statement-number REM [any-character] ...
```

For example, the following statements are comment lines:

```
350   REM THIS PROGRAM IS INCORRECT
890   REMARK FNG IS THE GAMMA FUNCTION
```

Comment lines are ignored by the BASIC language processor.


## 3.9  PROGRAM STRUCTURE

A program in the BASIC language is characterized by the fact that a complete program must be entered before any part of the program is executed and by the fact that it is usually transparent to the user whether the program is interpreted or it is compiled and executed. In general, the conventions apply regardless if the operational mode is time sharing or batch processing. The time-sharing mode is used as an example.

After the user identifies himself to the computer, the word "READY" is typed by the computer so that the user knows that the computer is ready to accept a command telling it what to do. (Obviously, commands differ between different implementations of the language.) Assume the user types the word NEW, telling the computer that he wishes to develop a new program, followed by the name of the new program. Another "READY" message is typed by the computer and the user can proceed to enter his program. (If the user had typed the word OLD followed by a program name, then the old program would be retrieved from direct-access storage for use by the terminal user.) The user enters information line by line. Statements preceded with a statement number are saved as a statement of the program. Statements without a line number are commands that cause the computer to take a specific action. The only restriction on a program is that it must end with an END statement; in other words, the highest numbered statement in a program must be the END statement.

When the user has entered his complete program, he normally enters a command to either RUN the program or to LIST the program. After the computer has performed a requested action, it types "READY" to inform the user that he can again enter either statements or commands.

The user can add or change a statement at any time by simply typing the statement number (of the line to be inserted or modified) followed by the new statement. When the program is run or listed, the statements are sorted by statement number and new statements replace old ones. A statement is deleted by typing its statement number with a blank line.

Once the execution of a program is started, the program executes until a STOP statement is executed, an END statement is reached, or a condition arises that prevents further execution. The following example depicts the preceding concepts:

```
Computer: READY
User:      NEW TRNGL
Computer: READY
User:      100  DATA 3,4,5,12,7,24
User:      200  READ B,H
User:      300  LET D=SQR(B↑2+H↑2)
User:      400  PRINT B,H,D
User:      500  GOTO 200
User:      999   END
User:      RUN
Computer: 3    4    5
Computer: 5   12   13
Computer: 7   24   25
Computer: OUT OF DATA IN LINE 200
Computer: READY
User:      150 PRINT "BASE", "HEIGHT","DIAG"
User:      RUN
Computer: BASE    HEIGHT    DIAG
Computer:   3         4         5
Computer:   5        12        13
```

Computer:    7        24        25
Computer: OUT OF DATA IN LINE 200
User:        LIST
Computer: 100 DATA 3,4,5,12,7,24
Computer: 150 PRINT "BASE", "HEIGHT", "DIAG"
Computer: 200 READ B,H
Computer: 300 LET D=SQR(B↑2+H↑2)
Computer: 400 PRINT B,H,D
Computer: 500 GOTO 200
Computer: 999 END
Computer: READY

Thus, the structure of a program in the BASIC language is inherent in the fact that it is a collection of statements ordered by statement number (that is, line number).

## EXERCISES

1. Study the "Indian program" given in section 3.2. Why is it necessary to include the following "program loop"?

    FOR Y=1627 TO 1973
        LET P=P+P*R
    NEXT Y

2. Distinguish between a "character" and a "symbol."
3. Can you think of any advantage that the use of the up arrow (↑) has for representing exponentiation over the use of the double asterisk (**)?
4. With regard to the use of exponential notation for writing constants, the following statement is made: "In an arithmetic constant, the E (if used) must be preceded by at least one digit." Why?
5. What function does the dollar sign ($) serve for naming character-string data items?
6. What is "label" data?
7. Give errors in the following BASIC statements:

    LET AB=16
    LET A3=K+10,000
    LET F$='DON'T'

REED A,B,C
DATA 4E–3.
LET A=W+3.12.3
LET K13= –3E–1

8. Interpretively execute the following program segments using the material given in the chapter:

LET A=3          DIM G(20)
LET B=6          PRINT G(7)+23
LET D=B/A+C
PRINT D

9. What is the only statement that must be present in a BASIC program?
10. How do you delete a statement in a BASIC program?
11. How do you replace a statement in a BASIC program?
12. In what order are the statements that comprise a BASIC program executed?
13. Which of the following expressions are invalid?

A+–B          (((34)))          T$(3)
+/A           A$<63            X(–4)
A(B(2))       –E+F             X+Y–1>13.4
D(E+1)        W(–I)            Q$+1

14. What is an "implicit array declaration"?
15. Give an example of a "character constant."

# PROGRAMMING IN BASIC

## 4.1  INTRODUCTION

The purpose of this chapter is to describe the various statements that comprise the core of the BASIC language. The statements are grouped by the functions they perform. For example, the first topic is input and output and statements relevant to that topic are presented. Other topics covered are: arithmetic statements, program control, the use of arrays, looping, and built-in functions. "Advanced BASIC" is presented in Chapter 5. The presentation of the BASIC language is descriptive in the sense that a description of the statements that comprise the language is of main concern and the "art of programming" is of secondary concern. Toward that end, the liberty is taken to use a statement, such as GOTO, in an example before it is "formally" presented. This approach is consistent with the necessity that the reader have at least a brief exposure to programming. The objective, of course, is to make the subject matter more meaningful and useful examples help in this respect by placing the presentation at a professional level.

## 4.2  INPUT AND OUTPUT

Input and output statements are used to enter data into the computer and to display results to the user. Five statement types are presented: PRINT, DATA, READ, RESTORE, and INPUT.

### The PRINT Statement

The PRINT statement is used to display results on the user's output unit, usually taken to be a terminal device. The form of the PRINT statement is:

```
PRINT [[,|;] [expression] ] [{,|;} [expression] ]...
```

where "expression" is an arithmetic or a character-string expression. The format of the PRINT statement denotes that the following cases are valid:

PRINT A     PRINT C,D1+3     PRINT H;I
PRINT 25     PRINT,E         PRINT J,K;L
PRINT 2∗B     PRINT F,,G       PRINT 'ABC';M

PRINT A,B,C,D,E     PRINT 2∗A↑3+4∗A+5
PRINT

The key point is that expressions must be separated by a separator that can be either a comma or a semicolon. In addition, variations such as beginning the list with a comma, eliding the expression between separators, or writing a PRINT statement without a statement body are also permitted by the syntax. Normally, the PRINT statement is used in a program somewhat as follows:

```
10 PRINT "3↑2=",3↑2
20 END
```

and a result such as:

```
3↑2=            9
```

is produced. The comma is used to separate the expressions. When it is desired to run the fields together, a semicolon is used as a separator, as in the following example:

```
10  PRINT  "3↑2=";3↑2
20  END
RUN

3↑2= 9

DONE
```

When a PRINT statement is completed, the carriage is normally moved up to the next line. The user can prevent the carriage from advancing by ending the PRINT statement with either a comma or a semicolon. The following example illustrates the latter point:

```
10 FOR I = 1 TO 5        10 FOR I = 1 TO 5
20      PRINT I          20      PRINT I;
30 NEXT I                30 NEXT I
40 END                   40 END
RUN                      RUN


1
2                         1   2   3   4   5
3
4                        DONE
5


DONE
```

More specifically, each print line is constructed from two types of print zones: full and packed. A *full-print zone* occupies 18 characters[1] and is used to form columns across the page. Thus, the page is divided, logically, into several columns, each 18 characters wide. When the comma is used as a delimiter, it simply advances a "position" pointer to the next full print zone. The size of a *packed-print zone* is determined by the size of the field to be printed; the magnitude and precision of an arithmetic value or the length of a character value govern the number of characters the field occupies.

The format for the PRINT statement also permits a "null" field, that is, one that does not contain a value. In other words, an expression of the form:

PRINT A,,B

would cause a column (that is, a full zone width) of the page to be skipped when the corresponding line is printed. A PRINT statement with no statement body simply advances the carriage one line. Thus, in the following example:

```
10 PRINT "FIRST LINE"
20 PRINT
30 PRINT "NEXT LINE"
40 END
RUN
```

FIRST LINE

---

[1] The width of the full-print zone varies between implementations of BASIC.

NEXT LINE

DONE

a line on the printed page is skipped as a result of the "null" print statement, whereas in the program

```
10 PRINT "FIRST LINE",
20 PRINT
30 PRINT "NEXT LINE"
40 END
RUN

FIRST LINE
NEXT LINE

DONE
```

the "null" PRINT statement is used to advance the carriage to the next line, since the preceding PRINT statement (that is, statement numbered 10) ends with a comma that prevents the carriage from being advanced.

## The DATA, READ, and RESTORE Statements

The DATA statement is used to create a data set, internal to the program, and has the form:

```
DATA constant [,constant]...
```

where "constant" is an arithmetic or character constant. All data specified in DATA statements are collected into a single data set; the order of the data constants is determined by the logical order of the DATA statements in the program. The internal data set can be accessed by the READ statement during the execution of a program. Actually, the DATA statement is a nonexecutable statement and the internal data set is created before the program is executed. Thus, DATA statements can be placed anywhere in a program. The logical order of DATA statements is determined by the relative magnitude of associated statement members.

The READ statement is used to initialize scalar and array variables and has the form:

```
    READ variable [,variable]...
```

where "variable" is an arithmetic or character scalar variable or a subscripted array variable. A pointer is associated with the internal data set constructed from
the DATA statements in a program. Initially, this pointer is set to the first value in
the data set. As READ statements are processed, successive values from the data
set are assigned to the variables in the READ statements. Logically, the values in
the data set are used up as READ statements are executed. Each value from the
data set must be the same type as the variable to which it is assigned. Thus, it is
the user's responsibility to insure that data values are sequenced in the required
order. If an attempt is made to "read" data when the data set is exhausted or the
type of a data value and the variable to which it is assigned do not agree, then a
READ error results and execution of the program is terminated. A READ error
also occurs when an attempt is made to "read" data when no DATA statement
exists in the program. Examples of the DATA and READ statements have been
given previously. The following example depicts the use of character-string constants, as well as arithmetic constants.

```
 5 PRINT "GRADE REPORT"
 6 PRINT
10 READ N$,T1,T2,T3
20 PRINT N$
30 PRINT "AVERAGE IS"; (T1+T2+T3)/3
35 PRINT
40 GOTO 10
50 DATA "R.ADAMS"
51 DATA 80,90,76
52 DATA "J.COTTON"
53 DATA 50,71,68
54 DATA "M.DODGER"
55 DATA 100,86,96
99 END
RUN


GRADE REPORT


R.ADAMS
AVERAGE IS 82
```

J.COTTON
AVERAGE IS 63

M. DODGER
AVERAGE IS 94

OUT OF DATA IN LINE 10

The RESTORE statement is used to reset the pointer to the first value in the data set constructed from the DATA statements in a program. The form of the RESTORE statement is:

| RESTORE |
| --- |

The RESTORE statement has no statement body. A program to demonstrate the use of the RESTORE statement is given as follows:

```
10 REM PROGRAM TO DEMONSTRATE USE OF THE RESTORE
   STATEMENT
20 READ A,B,C
30 PRINT "SUM="; A+B+C
40 RESTORE
50 READ A,B,C
60 PRINT "PRODUCT="; A*B*C
70 DATA 2,3,4
99 END
RUN

SUM= 9
PRODUCT= 24

DONE
```

Actually, the example is simply a demonstration since there is no need for the RESTORE statement, in this case, or the second READ statement.

### The INPUT Statement

In some cases, the data values to be used in a program are not known before-hand and must be entered on a dynamic basis. The INPUT statement allows the user to interact with an executing program and permits data values to be entered. The INPUT statement operates like the READ statement except that data is entered from the user's console on a dynamic basis instead of from an internal data set. The INPUT statement is placed in a program at the point that the data is needed. The computer types a question mark (?) and the execution of the program is suspended until the required data is entered. Since a program can include several INPUT statements, most users precede the INPUT statement with a PRINT statement identifying the data that should be entered. The form of the INPUT statement is:

> INPUT  variable[,variable]...

where "variable" is an arithmetic or character scalar variable or a subscripted array variable. The following example depicts the use of the INPUT statement:

```
10  PRINT "ENTER A,B"
20  INPUT A,B
30  PRINT "A+B=";A+B
40  PRINT "A*B=";A*B
50  GOTO 10
60  END
RUN


ENTER A,B
?  2,3
A+B=  5
A*B=  6
ENTER A,B
?3,4
A+B=  7
A*B=  12
?STOP
PROGRAM HALTED
```

The above program includes what is known as an *input loop;* in other words, program control is always directed to the statement numbered 10 and then to statement 20 (with the GOTO statement in line 50) to input new values for A and B. The user can terminate the loop by typing STOP instead of entering a data value.

## 4.3  ASSIGNMENT STATEMENTS

The assignment statement permits a data value to be assigned to a scalar variable, a subscripted array variable, or to an array. (Array assignment is covered with the matrix statements in Chapter 5.) This section covers the "simple" LET statement, the conventional assignment statement, and multiple replacement. Strictly speaking, each of these forms of scalar assignment is a specific instance of the generalized LET statement.

The general format for the LET statement is:

```
[LET] { {arithmetic-variable-[arithmetic-variable=]...
    arithmetic-expression } |{ character-variable=[character-variable=]...
    character-expression}}
```

The various alternatives inherent in this format are described in the following paragraphs.

### The Simple LET Statement

The LET statement has the form:

```
LET variable=expression
```

where "variable" is a scalar variable or a subscripted arithmetic array variable and "expression" is an arithmetic expression or "variable" is a scalar character-string variable or a subscripted character-string array variable and "expression" is a character-string expression. The statement means: "Replace the value of the variable with the value of the expression." The following examples depict valid LET statements:

```
LET  A=10
LET  B$= "TEA FOR TWO"
LET  C1=.00125  *A+3
LET  D(14)=191.8
LET  E$(I+1)="JOKER"
LET  P(K,3*J+1)=A*B(L-2)↑I
```

## The Conventional Assignment Statement

The use of the keyword LET in the assignment statement is a notational convenience and is not required by most language processors to recognize the assignment statement. In fact, the assignment statement has been defined, in some cases, as a statement without a statement identifier that contains the assignment symbol (=). The form of the conventional assignment statement is:

> variable=expression

where "variable" and "expression" are the same as defined above. Examples of valid assignment statements are:

    A=10
    B$="TEA FOR TWO"
    P(K,3*J+1)=A*B(L-2)↑I

and so forth.


## Multiple Replacement

One of the language features used to facilitate programming is to permit a single assignment statement to specify the replacement of two or more scalar variables or elements of an array. The format of an assignment statement that permits multiple replacement is given as follows:

> variable=[variable=]...= expression

where, again, "variable" and "expression" are the same as defined above. Thus, instead of writing successive statements, such as:

    T1 = A*B(3*J-14)↑(I-1)
    T2 = T1

the user is permitted to write:

    T1=T2=A*B(3*J-14)↑(I-1)

A statement that includes multiple replacement specifies that the expression is evaluated once and the value of the expression is assigned to variables that are placed to the left of the assignment symbol (=).

A variation to the format for multiple replacement is given as follows:

variable[,variable]... =expression

such that the statement includes a single assignment symbol (=). This form is a viable alternative to the above convention and has been used in some implementations of the language.

## 4.4  PROGRAM CONTROL

As was mentioned previously, statements in a program are executed sequentially until a statement is executed that alters the sequential flow of execution. Six statements are included in the BASIC language to control the manner in which a program is executed: GOTO, IF, END, STOP, FOR, and NEXT. The GOTO and IF statements are presented in this section and are used to alter the flow of program execution on an unconditional and on a conditional basis, respectively. The END and STOP statements are also covered briefly. The FOR and NEXT statements are used for looping and are described in a separate section.

### The GOTO Statement

The GOTO statement has the form:

```
GOTO statement-number
```

where "statement-number" must be the line number associated with a statement in the program. If the statement number used as the operand to the GOTO statement does not exist in the program, then the condition is recognized and continued execution of the program is not permitted.[2] Several examples of the GOTO statement are given in previous sections.

The *ON statement* is a variation to the GOTO statement that provides a many-way branch. The format of the ON/GOTO statement is:

---

[2]This is another case where the manner in which the language is implemented governs the specific action that is taken.

> ON arithmetic-expression GOTO statement-number
> [,statement-number]...

The "arithmetic-expression" is evaluated at the point of execution and its value determines the "statement-number" to which program control is directed. Thus, in the model statement

$$ON \ e \ GOTO \ s_1, s_2, ..., s_n$$

program control passes to the statement numbered $s_1$ if the value of $e$ is 1, to the statement numbered $s_2$ if the value of $e$ is 2, and so forth. For example, if Q contains the value 4, then the following ON statement

$$ON \ Q{-}1 \ GOTO \ 310,150,630,540,540$$

passes program control to the statement numbered 630.

### The IF Statement

The IF statement allows program control to be altered on a conditional basis, depending upon the value of a "conditional" expression. The format of the IF statement is:

> IF comparison-expression THEN statement-number

If the "comparison-expression" has the value "true" (in other words, the condition holds), then program control passes to the statement whose statement number is specified. If the statement to which control is branched is a nonexecutable statement (such as a DATA statement), then program control is passed to the first executable statement following the specified nonexecutable statement. If the "comparison-expression" is not "true" (in other words, the condition does not hold), then the execution of the program continues with the first executable statement that logically follows the IF statement.

It should be recalled that the comparison expression has the general form:

$$\{ \text{arithmetic-expression} \ \text{comparison-operator} \ \text{arithmetic-expression} \} \ | $$
$$\{ \text{character-expression} \ \text{comparison-operator} \ \text{character-expression} \}$$

so that a "complex" comparison expression, such as

$$A*Z\uparrow2+B*Z+C >= Y\uparrow(1/N)$$

is permitted.

The following example that computes the average of a list of values depicts the use of a simple IF statement, as well as an assignment statement, a GOTO statement, and a remark statement. The list is terminated when the value −999 is reached.

```
10  READ V
20  IF V=-999 THEN 70
30  REM S AND N ARE INITIALLY ZERO
40  S=S+V
50  N=N+1
60  GOTO 10
70  PRINT "AVERAGE IS"; S/N
80  DATA 24,42,68,50,-999
90  END
```

Output:

AVERAGE IS 46

Other examples of the IF statement are given in subsequent sections.

## The END and STOP Statements

Every program written in the BASIC language must end with the END statement, which has the following format:

```
END
```

The END statement serves two purposes:

1.  It denotes the logical end of the program, such that statements with statement numbers greater than that of the END statement are ignored by the BASIC language processor.
2.  It causes execution of a program to be terminated when program control flows to it.

The STOP statement, which takes the form:

```
STOP
```

causes execution of the program to be terminated. The STOP statement can be located anywhere in a program, making it unnecessary to branch to the END statement to terminate the execution of a program.

## 4.5 LOOPING

Many algorithms require that a sequence of steps be repeated. An algorithm of this type is usually programmed in one of two ways: (1) The program steps are duplicated the required number of times; and (2) the program is written so that the same program steps are executed iteratively. In complex programs or when the necessary number of iterations is not known beforehand, the second method is preferred.

### Introduction to Iterative Procedures

A series of statements to be executed repetitively is termed a *loop;* the statements that comprise the loop are termed the *body of the loop;* and one pass through the loop is termed an *iteration.* The number of iterations is governed by a *control variable* that usually operates as follows:

1. The control variable is set to an *initial value.*
2. The value of the control variable is compared against a limit value. If the limit value is exceeded, then the loop is not executed and the first executable statement following the body of the loop is executed. (This step is sometimes omitted.)
3. The body of the loop is executed.
4. The value of the control variable is incremented by a given value—frequently referred to as an *increment* or a *step.* (The obvious implication is that the program "steps" through the loop as the "control variable" assumes a set of values.)
5. The value of the control variable is compared against the limit value. If the limit value is exceeded, then the loop is terminated and execution continues with the first executable statement following the body of the loop. Otherwise, execution of the loop continues with step 3.

The following BASIC program depicts a simple loop:

```
 10  REM SUM OF EVEN INTEGERS <=N
 15  PRINT "ENTER N";
 20  INPUT N
 30  S=0
 40  I=2
 50  IF I>N THEN 90
 60  S=S+I
 70  I=I+2
 80  IF I<=N THEN 60
 90  PRINT "SUM=";S
100  PRINT
100  GOTO 15
110  END
RUN

ENTER N? 5
SUM= 6

ENTER N? 10
SUM= 30

ENTER N? 2
SUM= 2

ENTER N? 1
SUM= 0

ENTER N? STOP
PROGRAM HALTED
```

The program depicts each of the above steps. The statement numbered 40 initializes the control variable I (step 1). The statement numbered 50 tests the control variable I against the limit N (step 2). Statement 60 is the body of the loop (step 3). Statement 70 increments the control variable (step 4) with a "step value" of 2. Statement 80 tests the control variable against the limit (step 5); if the value of the control variable is less than or equal to the limit value, then program control is returned to the statement numbered 60 to repeat the loop.

Looping is a frequently used technique in computer programming such that special statements are defined to control the manner in which loops are executed.

### The FOR and NEXT Statements

Two statements are included in BASIC to facilitate the preparation of program loops. The FOR statement is used to start a loop; it specifies the control variable, its initial value, its limit value, and the step. The NEXT statement is used to close a loop; it specifies the control variable that should be "stepped." The previous loop written with the use of FOR and NEXT statements is given as follows:

```
10  REM SUM OF EVEN NUMBERS <=N
20  PRINT "ENTER N";
30  INPUT N
40  S=0
50  FOR I=2 TO N STEP 2
60      S=S+I
70  NEXT I
80  PRINT "SUM="; S
90  PRINT
100 GOTO 20
110 END
RUN

ENTER N? 5
SUM= 6

ENTER N? 10
SUM= 30

ENTER N? STOP
PROGRAM HALTED
```

The statements between the FOR and the NEXT statements comprise the body of the loop.

The format of the FOR statement is given as:

```
FOR arithmetic-variable = arithmetic-expression
    TO arithmetic-expression
    [STEP arithmetic-expression]
```

where "arithmetic-variable" must be a scalar variable and "arithmetic-expression" must be a scalar expression. If the STEP clause is omitted, it is assumed to be +1. The format of the NEXT statement is:

```
NEXT arithmetic-variable
```

where "arithmetic-variable" is the same scalar variable that is used in the corresponding FOR statement.

The FOR and NEXT statements are used in pairs to delineate a FOR loop. The FOR statement establishes the control variable and specifies the initial value, limit value, and step value. (The three values are referred to as *control parameters.*) The NEXT statement tells the computer to perform the next iteration. The control parameters are evaluated when the FOR statement is executed and cannot be changed in the body of the loop. *However, the value of the control variable can be modified from within the body of the loop.* FOR loops can be nested but must not overlap each other.

The execution of a FOR loop of the general form:

FOR v = expression-1 TO expression-2 STEP expression-3

.
.

.

Body of loop

.
.

.

NEXT v

is functionally equivalent to the following statements:

100  $e_1$ = expression-1
110  $e_2$ = expression-2
115  REM if STEP is omitted, expression-3 = +1
120  $e_3$ = expression-3
130  IF $e_3 < 0$ THEN 160
140  IF $e_1 > e_2$ THEN 260
150  GOTO 170
160  IF $e_1 < e_2$ THEN 260
170  $v = e_1$
180

.

Body of loop

.

.

.

```
200  v=v+e₃
210  IF e₃>=0 THEN 240
220  IF v<e₂ THEN 250
230  GOTO 180
240  IF v<=e₂ THEN 180
250  v=v-e₃
260  .
```

.

.

where $v$ is the control variable and $e_1$, $e_2$, and $e_3$ are dummy variables. The above expression completely describes the execution of the FOR/NEXT statements. The control parameters are evaluated and assigned to dummy variables. The control variable is first set to the initial value and is incremented by the increment value for each iteration. The value of the control variable is compared against the limit value to determine if the loop has been executed the required number of times. A transfer of program control out of the loop is permitted and a FOR loop is reinitialized each time program control passes through its FOR statement.

### Effective Use of the FOR and NEXT Statements

It is important to recognize that the use of a FOR/NEXT loop is a means of achieving control in a computer program. It can be used in some cases to eliminate the need for the GOTO statement, as shown in the following program that computes $n$ factorial:

```
10  FOR I = 1 TO 2 STEP 0
20      PRINT "ENTER N";
30      INPUT N
40      F=1
50      FOR J= 2 TO N
60          F=F*J
70      NEXT J
```

```
80      PRINT N;"FACTORIAL IS"; F
90      PRINT
100 NEXT I
110 END
RUN

ENTER N? 5
5 FACTORIAL IS 120

ENTER N? 7
7 FACTORIAL IS 5040

ENTER N? 1
1 FACTORIAL IS 1

ENTER N? STOP
PROGRAM HALTED
```

The above program depicts a nested loop (that is, a *double loop*, as it is frequently called). The outer loop is executed until a STOP is entered in response to the INPUT statement. The same effect could have been achieved with a FOR statement, such as:

FOR I = 1 TO 10000

where the loop is not expected to execute for the full 10,000 iterations but will be terminated by a special condition, as shown. In a similar fashion, a FOR loop can be used to count the number of times a series of statements is executed; for example:

```
10  DATA  8,10,7,20,15,0
20  REM COMPUTE AVERAGE AND NUMBER OF VALUES
30  FOR N = 1 TO 100
40      READ V
50      IF V=0 THEN 80
60      S=S+V
70  NEXT N
80  PRINT "AVERAGE  ="; S/N;"NUMBER OF VALUES  =";N
99  END
RUN
```

AVERAGE = 12   NUMBER OF VALUES = 5

The FOR statement, as defined above, allows several useful options, three of which are mentioned briefly:

1. There can be a nonintegral STEP.
2. There can be a negative STEP.
3. The value of the control variable can be changed in the FOR loop.

All three cases are described in the following example:

```
10 FOR D=2 TO –2 STEP –.5
20     IF D <> 0 THEN 40
30     D=–1
40     PRINT 1/D
50 NEXT D
60 END
RUN
```

```
0.5
0.666667
1
2
–1
–2
–1
–0.666667
–0.5
```

Other examples of the FOR loop are included in the next section on "arrays."


## 4.6  ARRAYS

Arrays are an important feature of most programming languages since a great many computer applications utilize the concept of a family of related data, referred to by a single name—the array identifier. The subject of arrays was briefly considered in Chapter 3; this section goes into more detail on how arrays are defined and used. First, a very brief review. An *arithmetic array* can have either one or two dimensions; an arithmetic array identifier must consist of a single letter.

A *character array* must have one dimension only; its identifier must consist of a single letter followed by a dollar sign ($).

### Implicitly Defined Arrays

An implicitly defined array is one that is used without being declared. A one-dimensional implicitly defined array has an extent of 10 with lower and upper subscript bounds of 1 and 10, respectively. A two-dimensional implicitly defined array has both row and column extents of 10; lower and subscript bounds, for each dimension, are also 1 and 10, respectively.

Implicitly defined arrays are allowed in BASIC for practical reasons:

1. "Small" arrays are frequently used, especially in an academic environment, and it is a convenience to be able to use an array of this type without having to define it. Also, by not having to specify the size of a "small" array, fewer characters have to be entered into the computer and the chances of making a simple mistake are lessened.
2. Computer storage is sufficiently large to easily handle the storage requirements of implicitly defined arrays.
3. For large arrays, which *do* have to be declared, storage must be managed judiciously.

As an example of a case where the use of an implicitly defined array would be useful, consider the generation of the first 10 Fibonacci numbers, where the $i$th Fibonacci number is defined as:

$$x_i = x_{i-1} + x_{i-2}, \text{ for } i > 2$$

The first two numbers in the sequence are: 1,1.

```
10  X(1)=X(2)=1
20  PRINT X(1);X(2);
30  FOR I=3 TO 10
40      X(I)=X(I-1)+X(I-2)
50      PRINT X(I);
60  NEXT I
99  END
RUN
```

    1  1  2  3  5  8  13  21  34  55

Another case might be to store and retrieve a parts list that takes the following form:

| Part Index | Part Name | Quantity | Unit Price |
|---|---|---|---|
| 1 | Plate ZR41T | 10 | .49 |
| 2 | Hinge J33 | 5 | 1.26 |
| 3 | .5x3 Bolt | 103 | .12 |
| 4 | Washer .5 Alum | 97 | .01 |
| 5 | Nut .5 Hex | 103 | .03 |
| 6 | PT 4001 T | 21 | .25 |

The program, which follows, first stores the "part name" as a string array and the "quantity" and "unit price" as a two-dimensional array; then, the user is allowed to input a part index and the computer prints out the name, quantity, and the value of the inventory.

```
10  REM ENTER INVENTORY DATA
20  READ N
30  FOR J= 1 TO N
40      READ P$(J),D(J,1),D(J,2)
50  NEXT J
60  REM RETRIEVE DATA
70  PRINT "ENTER PART INDEX";
80  INPUT I
85  IF I>N THEN 150
90  PRINT P$(I), "QUANTITY ="; D(I,1); "UNIT PRICE ="; D(J,2);
        "TOTAL VALUE ="; D(I,1)*D(I,2)
95  PRINT
100 GOTO 70
150 PRINT "INDEX ERROR"
151 GOTO 70
200 DATA 6
201 DATA "PLATE ZR41T",10,.49
202 DATA "HINGE J33",5,1.26
203 DATA ".5x3 BOLT",103,.12
204 DATA "WASHER .5 ALUM",97,.01
205 DATA "NUT .5 HEX",103,.03
206 DATA "PT 4001 T",21,.25
```

```
999  END
RUN
```

ENTER PART INDEX?    4
WASHER .5 ALUM    QUANTITY = 97    UNIT PRICE = 0.01
                 TOTAL VALUE = 0.97

ENTER PART INDEX?    7
INDEX ERROR
ENTER PART INDEX?    3
.5x3 BOLT                QUANTITY = 103   UNIT PRICE = 0.12
                 TOTAL VALUE = 15.36

ENTER PART INDEX?    STOP
PROGRAM HALTED

As mentioned in Chapter 3, the value of the elements of an implicitly defined arithmetic array are set initially to zero and the value of the elements of an implicitly defined character-string array are set initially to 18 blanks.

### Explicitly Defined Arrays

An array is explicitly dimensioned with the DIM statement that has the following form:

```
DIM array-specification[,array-specification]...
```

where "array-specification" is defined as:

```
{arithmetic-array-identifier(integer-constant[,integer,constant])}|
{character-array-identifier(integer-constant)}
```

where "integer-constant" must not be zero. The following example depicts valid array specifications:

DIM  A(17), B$(54), C(15,25), D(3,20), E(1000)

A one-dimensional array is specified as:

DIM $a(n)$

or

DIM $a\$(n)$

and has an extent of $n$ with lower and upper subscript bounds of 1 and $n$, respectively. An element of $a$ (or $a\$$) is selected by an array reference of the form $a(e)$ (or $a\$(e)$) where $e$ is an arithmetic expression that is evaluated at the point of reference and truncated to an integer. Similarly, a two-dimensional array is specified as

DIM $a(m,n)$

and has row and column extents of $m$ and $n$, respectively; the lower and upper subscript bounds for the row extent are 1 and $m$, respectively, and the lower and upper subscript bounds for the column extent are 1 and $n$, respectively. An element of $a$ is selected by an array reference of the form $a(e_1, e_2)$ where $e_1$ and $e_2$ are arithmetic expressions evaluated at the point of reference and truncated to integers.

The following example computes prime numbers using the Sieve of Eratosthenes. The program requests a number N and the program computes and prints the prime numbers less than or equal to N.

```
 10 DIM P(1000)
 20 PRINT "ENTER N";
 30 INPUT N
 40 IF N>1000 THEN 990
 50 FOR I= 2 TO N
 60     P(I)=I
 70 NEXT I
 80 L=SQR(N)
 90 FOR I= 2 TO L
100     IF P(I)=0 THEN 140
110     FOR J= I+I TO N STEP I
120         P(J)=0
130     NEXT J
140 NEXT I
150 PRINT
160 PRINT "PRIMES LESS THAN"; N
```

```
170  FOR I= 1 TO N
180       IF P(I)=0 THEN 200
190       PRINT P(I);
200  NEXT I
210  PRINT
220  GOTO 20
990  PRINT "TOO LARGE"
991  GOTO 20
999  END
RUN
```

ENTER N? 100

PRIMES LESS THAN 100

| 2 | 3 | 5 | 7 | 11 | 13 | 17 | 19 | 23 | 29 | 31 | 37 | 41 | 43 |
|---|---|---|---|----|----|----|----|----|----|----|----|----|----|
| 47 | 53 | 59 | 61 | 67 | 71 | 73 | 79 | 83 | 89 | 97 | | | |

ENTER N? 2000
TOO LARGE
ENTER N? 15

2   3   5   7   11   13

ENTER N? STOP
PROGRAM HALTED

The program also depicts nested FOR loops, and the variable control parameters that were promised in the preceding section.

As a final example of the use of one-dimensional arrays, the following program reads a list of numbers and sorts them in ascending order. The program utilizes an exchange technique, depicted as follows:

$$
\begin{array}{c}
1 \\
( \ 2 \ ) \\
3 \\
( \ 4 \ ) \\
5 \\
( \ 6 \ ) \\
7 \\
( \ 8 \ ) \\
9 \\
10 \ )
\end{array}
$$

The program initially sets a flag (F). When an exchange is made, F is set to 1. If both passes are made through the data without making an exchange, then the values are sorted and the program terminates. Otherwise, the process is repeated. The advantage of the exchange technique is that the process is efficient if the data is sorted or partially sorted beforehand. (A modified version of this program is given in a later section in which the GOSUB statement is presented.)

```
 10  DIM W(100)
 20  READ N
 30  IF N>100 THEN 990
 40  FOR I= 1 TO N
 50      READ W(I)
 60  NEXT I
 70  F=0
 80  FOR I= 1 TO N-1 STEP 2
 90      IF W(I) <=W(I+1) THEN 140
100      T=W(I)
110      W(I)=W(I+1)
120      W(I+1)=T
130      F=1
140  NEXT I
150  FOR I= 2 TO N-1 STEP 2
160      IF W(I) <=W(I+1) THEN 210
170      T=W(I)
180      W(I)=W(I+1)
190      W(I+1)=T
200      F=1
210  NEXT I
220  IF F<>0 THEN 70
230  PRINT "SORTED VALUES"
240  FOR I= 1 TO N
250      PRINT W(I);
260  NEXT I
270  STOP
500  DATA 12
501  DATA -7,3,9,6,5,1,4,3,8,0,2,7
990  PRINT "TOO MANY VALUES"
999  END
RUN
```

SORTED VALUES
–7  0  1  2  3  3  4  5  6  7  8  9

Two-dimensional arrays are defined and used in a similar fashion, as depicted in the following example. The program reads in a two-dimensional array and performs some elementary arithmetic operations.

```
10  DIM A(20,20)
20  REM READ IN ARRAY DIMENSIONS
30  READ M,N
40  REM READ IN ARRAY BY ROWS AND DISPLAY IT
45  PRINT "ORIGINAL ARRAY"
50  FOR I=1 TO M
60      FOR J= 1 TO N
70          READ A(I,J)
75          PRINT A(I,J);
80      NEXT J
85      PRINT
90  NEXT I
100 PRINT
110 REM REPLACE SECOND COLUMN WITH ONES
120 FOR I= 1 TO M
130     A(I,2)=1
140 NEXT I
150 REM DISPLAY ARRAY
160 PRINT "MODIFIED ARRAY"
170 FOR I= 1 TO M
180     FOR J= 1 TO N
190         PRINT A(I,J);
200     NEXT J
210     PRINT
220 NEXT I
230 PRINT
240 REM MULT EACH ELEMENT BY A(2,3) ADD DISPLAY IT
245 PRINT "ARRAY MULTIPLIED BY A(2,3)"
250 FOR I= 1 TO M
260     FOR J=1 TO N
270         A(I,J)= A(I,J)*A(2,3)
280         PRINT A(I,J);
290     NEXT J
```

```
300     PRINT
310 NEXT I
320 PRINT
500 DATA 3,4
501 DATA -7,3,9,6
502 DATA 5,1,4,3
503 DATA 8,0,2,7
999 END
RUN
```

ORIGINAL ARRAY

```
-7  3  9  6
 5  1  4  3
 8  0  2  7
```

MODIFIED ARRAY

```
-7  1  9  6
 5  1  4  3
 8  1  2  7
```

ARRAY MULTIPLIED BY A(2,3)

```
-28   4  36   24
 20   4  16   48
128  16  32  432
```

The results from multiplying the array by A(2,3) appear to be incorrect but are not as A(2,3) is modified partway through the computation. This example is also simplified in a later section.

## 4.7 FUNCTIONS

The computer is frequently used in applications that require the use of a mathematical function, such as the sine, cosine, or square root. In the computer, functions such as these are usually approximated to a given degree of accuracy with an algorithm such as the following series expansion for the trigonometric sine:

$$\sin x = x - \frac{x^3}{3!} + \frac{x^5}{5!} - \frac{x^7}{7!} + \dots$$

Two options exist:

1. Each user can program his own mathematical functions.
2. A set of frequently used functions can be provided as part of the programming language.

Usually, the second option is selected since not all users are versed in computer approximations and it is convenient *not* to have to bother with them. Moreover, they can be coded efficiently in assembler language and placed in a program library to be shared by all users.

## Built-in Functions

Functions that are supplied as part of the programming language are referred to as *built-in functions.* The form of a function reference is the function identifier[3] followed by an arithmetic expression in parentheses. The expression is evaluated at the point of reference and the specified function is applied to the value of the expression. The function returns a value that can be used as an operand in the expression. Thus, the expression 2+SQR(25) has the value 7, where SQR is the square root function.

The *function identifier* for built-in function is comprised of three letters that have mnemonic relationship to the function they name. The form of a function reference is:

```
function-identifier (arithmetic-expression)
```

where "function-identifier" is one of the mathematical functions defined in the implementation of the language. Table 4.1 lists the built-in functions included in the original Dartmouth version of BASIC. All of the functions listed in Table 4.1 take a single argument, although function references of the form:

```
function-identifier(arithmetic-expression[,arithmetic-expression] ...)
```

could easily be defined.

---

[3] That is, the name of the function.

Table 4.1

Built-in Functions

| Function Reference | Definition |
|---|---|
| SIN $(x)$ | Computes the sine of $x$ radians. |
| COS $(x)$ | Computes the cosine of $x$ radians. |
| TAN $(x)$ | Computes the tangent of $x$ radians. |
| ATN $(x)$ | Computes the arctangent in radians of the argument $x$; the result is in the range $-90°$ to $+90°$. |
| EXP $(x)$ | Computes the value of $e$ raised to the $x$ power; that is, $e^x$. |
| LOG $(x)$ | Computes the natural logarithm (that is, $\ln|x|$) of the absolute value of $x$. |
| ABS $(x)$ | Computes the absolute value of $x$ (that is, $|x|$). |
| SQR $(x)$ | Computes the square root of $x$, where $x \geq 0$. |
| INT $(x)$ | Computes the largest integer $\leq x$. |
| SGN $(x)$ | Returns the sign of $x$; if $x < 0$, then $\text{SGN}(x) = -1$; if $x = 0$, then $\text{SGN}(x) = 0$; and if $x > 0$, then $\text{SGN}(x) = +1$. |

The following list gives some mathematical expressions that include functions and their equivalent representation in BASIC:

| Mathematical Expression | BASIC Expression |
|---|---|
| $\sqrt{1 - \sin^2 x}$ | SQR(1–SIN(X)↑2) |
| $\cos 30°$ | COS(30*(3.14159/180)) or COS(3.14159/6) |
| $\sqrt{a^2 + b^2 - 2ab \cos c_1}$ | SQR(A↑2+B↑2–2*A*B*COS(C1)) |
| $\tan^{-1} (x/y)$ | ATN(X/Y) |
| $\dfrac{e^x - e^{-x}}{2}$ | (EXP(X)–EXP(–X))/2 |
| $(|x|)↑3$ | ABS(X)↑3 |

When a function reference is used as an operand, as in SIN(X)↑2 or ABS(X)↑3, the function is applied first and the result of the function is used in the arithmetic operation. In other words, a function reference has a higher priority than any of the arithmetic operators.

The BASIC language also contains four other types of functions:

1. Functions defined on matrices
2. Internal constants
3. Special functions
4. User-defined functions

Functions defined for use on matrices and user-defined functions are presented in Chapter 5. Internal constants and special functions are covered below.

### Internal Constants and Special Functions

An *internal constant* is a frequently used arithmetic value that is defined in the BASIC language. Three internal constants are frequently used: pi, *e*, and the square root of 2, and listed as follows:

| *Identifier* | *Approximate Value (short form)* |
|--------------|----------------------------------|
| &PI          | 3.14159                          |
| &E           | 2.71828                          |
| &SQR2        | 1.41421                          |

Internal constants, sometimes referred to as *figurative constants* in other programming languages, eliminate the need to remember and enter frequently used arithmetic values. An internal constant is treated as an ordinary operand.

A *special function* is a function that returns a value to the point of reference but does not necessarily require an argument. The random number generation function RND is an example of a special function that computes a random number in the interval 0 to 1. The form of the RND function is:

RND $[(x)]$

where $x$, if specified, is used to initialize the random number generator program. If $x$ is omitted, as it usually is, a random number is computed from the previous one generated. As an example, an expression simulating the roll of a die is given as: INT(6*RND+1). The objective in being able to initialize the random number generator is that computed results can be rerun *exactly*, a necessary feature in some simulation studies. Obviously, if the function RND is used without an argument and it has not been previously initialized, then it is programmed to initialize itself.

## 4.8 COMMENTS

Actually, the version of BASIC presented in this chapter is not patterned after any particular implementation of the language. Although the original Dartmouth system is mentioned a few times, the material presented here, as well as the current Dartmouth system, reflects a level of the language and its implementation that far surpasses the original version.

In addition, the author has taken the liberty to include definitions, such as the expansion of the FOR/NEXT statements or the description of the RND function, to facilitate an understanding of the language. There may be cases in which a particular implementation of the language deviates from the specifications given here. The key point, obviously, is that when studying a programming language, it is necessary to cover the meaning of a statement in addition to its structure. This fact is frequently overlooked with respect to "easy-to-learn-and-use" languages like BASIC.

The experienced reader has probably recognized a curious fact about BASIC. It is an ingenious collection of simple concepts and sophisticated techniques. For example, variable identifiers are restricted to either one or two characters; at the same time, a subscript can be any arithmetic expression. Similarly, blanks are ignored but separators such as THEN and STEP, which help reduce programming errors, are permitted. It appears as though rules, such as the following, were established for the design of "easy-to-learn-and-use" programming languages:

1. In general, language restrictions are established to facilitate learning and language implementation when the restriction is easily remembered, as in the case of the length of a variable identifier.
2. Language restrictions are not allowed that could result in simple mistakes, such as the order of control parameters in a FOR statement, or are hard to remember, such as the form of a subscript or a statement.
3. Regardless of language restrictions or operational conventions, the language allows no features that *could* be interpreted as being illogical by any user, regardless of his background.

Actually, it is not really important whether the designers of the BASIC language used guidelines such as these. The important point is that a language must be characterized in some way and in this case, the above rules partially fulfill that need. In everyday discourse, it is satisfactory to say that BASIC is a "simple" programming language; but among computer and data-processing specialists, a more definitive statement is usually required.

The next chapter covers some topics that are considered to be a part of "advanced" BASIC. Included is a discussion of subroutines, user-defined functions, and matrix operations.

## EXERCISES

1. Write a BASIC program to compute the product of the numbers 2E3, 173.89, −14.839, 63.1, and .123E−1 and print the result.
2. Write a BASIC program to evaluate the function:

$$y = \frac{e^{ax} - e^{-bx}}{2}$$

as $x$ ranges from 1 to 2 in steps of .01, for the following cases:

   (a) a=1, b=1
   (b) a=1, b=2
   (c) a=.5, b=1
   (d) a=.5, b=.5
   (e) a=.5, b=1.5

3. A depositor banks $10 per month. Interest is 6% per year compounded monthly. Write a BASIC program to compute the amount the depositor has in his account after 20 years.
4. Write a BASIC program that computes N! (that is, N factorial) and operates as follows: The computer requests that the user enter a number (N). After verifying that the number is a positive integer, the computer computes N!, prints it, and then requests another number. Error diagnostics should be printed if the number is not a positive integer.
5. Write a BASIC program to evaluate the polynomial $f(x) = 6x^2 + 4x + 7$ as $x$ takes on the values from 1 to 10 in steps of 0.1. Print the results as two columns with column headings.
6. Write a BASIC program that computes B and C for values of A that range from 0° to 360° in increments of 15°. B and C are defined as follows:

   B = 1−2 cos A
   C = 1+cos 2A−3 sin²A

Print the results in labeled columns. (1 radian = 180°/π)
7. Fill an array with 3 rows and 4 columns with the integers 1,2,...,12 by rows. Print the array.

8. Write a BASIC program to sum the numbers less than 100 that are divisible by 7.

9. Given several sets of data in the form:

    DATA $n, x_1, x_2, \ldots, x_n$

    write a BASIC program to compute the average and variance of the $x_i$s, where

    $$\text{Average} = \frac{\sum_{i-1}^{n} x_i}{n}$$

    $$\text{Variance} = \frac{\sum_{i-1}^{n} (\text{Average}-x_i)^2}{n-1}$$

    If $n=0$ the program terminates. Otherwise, the program should loop to read another set of data.

10. Given a set of numbers of the form:

    DATA $n, x_1, x_2, \ldots, x_n$

    (allow for at least 100 values), write a BASIC program that computes and prints the following:

    (a) Number of numbers in the list
    (b) Largest number
    (c) Smallest number
    (d) Number of numbers equal to 20
    (e) Number of numbers greater than 50 and less than 75

11. Given a set of pay records of the form:

    DATA employee-number, name, hours, hourly-rate, tax-rate

    such as:

    DATA 4439, "JOHN JONES", 45,2.10,0.18

    Write a BASIC program that computes the following values for each employee:

(a) Gross salary

(b) Tax

(c) Take-home pay

Produce the results as a payroll listing that gives for each employee (that is, each line of the listing): employee number, name, hours, gross salary, tax, and take-home pay. Label the columns. Pay time and one-half for hours over forty. Have the program terminate when a zero employee number is read.

12. Write a BASIC program that reads in an $m \times n$ matrix, by rows, and computes the following:

(a) The smallest value in each row

(b) The largest value in each column

A "saddle point" occurs if the maximum of the row minimums is the same element as the minimum of the column maximums. If this is the case, print out the message "SADDLE POINT" followed by the corresponding value. If no saddle point exists, print out the message "NO SADDLE POINT."

13. Write a BASIC program to read in the following table and sort the entries by key:

| Key | Value |
|-----|-------|
| 10 | −13.43 |
| 7 | 81.914 |
| 16 | −50.1 |
| 2 | 13964.2 |
| 9 | 63.173 |
| 24 | −.4E−2 |
| 11 | 0 |
| 6 | 2 |

14. Given the following one-dimensional array:

DIM A(50)

and the following data:

DATA $n, x_1, x_2, ..., x_n$

write a BASIC program that:

(a) Prints the values on one line
(b) Prints the values on successive lines
(c) Sums the elements of the array and prints the result
(d) Reverses and prints the elements of the array
(e) Deletes elements of the array with odd numbered indexes and prints the result
(f) Rotates the array left by two elements and prints result

15. Section 4.5 gives a general model for the execution of a FOR loop of the form:

```
FOR v = expression–1 TO expression–2 STEP expression–3
        .
        .
        .
        Body of loop
        .
        .
        .
    NEXT v
```

Flowchart the given statements that are functionally equivalent to the above skeleton.

16. Describe the operational characteristics of the following statement:

FOR I=1 TO 2 STEP 0

17. Distinguish between the operation of the following statements:

INPUT A
INPUT A;

18. Write a BASIC program that inputs $x$ in radians and computes:

$$\sin x = x - \frac{x^3}{3!} + \frac{x^5}{5!} - \frac{x^7}{7!} + \ldots$$

to three decimal places. (That is, if the next term in the series is less than .0005, then terminate the calculations.)

19. A magic square such as

| 8 | 1 | 6 |
|---|---|---|
| 3 | 5 | 7 |
| 4 | 9 | 2 |

can be constructed as follows:

The process always starts in the middle of the top row and numbers are inserted successively by progressing upward and to the right. If the top boundary is reached, continue again at the bottom. If the right boundary is reached, continue again at the left. If another element is reached (i.e., 3 to 1), drop down one row (i.e., 3 to 4) and continue. The method works for any magic square of order $n$, where $n$ is odd.

Write a BASIC program to compute a magic square of order $n$, where $n$ is entered from the terminal.

20. Using random numbers, simulate the game of *craps*. In the game of craps, a player rolls two dice. If the sum of the two faces on the first roll is 7 or 11, the player wins the amount bet. If the sum turns up 2, 3, or 12 on the first roll, the player loses. If the sum turns up 4, 5, 6, 8, 9, or 10, the player continues to roll until he turns up a 7 (he loses) or the same sum he turned up on the first roll (he wins). Use the random number function. Collect the sums as a vector and when the player's turn is over, list the sums.

# ADVANCED BASIC

## 5.1 INTRODUCTION

This chapter discusses three important topics: subroutines, user-defined functions, and matrix operations. Subroutines and functions are both subprograms in the sense that they are included once in a program and program control is passed to the subprogram whenever the execution of that particular process is needed. Thus, the user need not include identical statements at several places in his program and, also, the program requires less space in the computer. Computer execution time is essentially the same[1] in either case (that is, with or without using a subprogram) since the execution of the same number of computer instructions is necessary to compute the required procedure.

Many algorithms are defined on entire matrices so that the element-by-element manipulation of arrays is actually an inconvenience to the user and is a process that is susceptible to a variety of simple programming mistakes. In many applications, it is also customary to deal in matrices—such as a set of experimental observations or the coefficients of a set of equations. For use in these cases, the BASIC language includes several statements and a variety of operational procedures that allow the user to perform matrix operations.

## 5.2 SUBROUTINES

A *subroutine* is characterized by the fact that it is a procedure (that is, a series of statements) that can be "called" from anywhere in a program and by the fact

---

[1] Actually, the use of subprograms requires the execution of a few more computer instructions required to link to the subprogram and later to return to the point of invocation.

that *it does not return a value to the point of reference.* Thus, a subroutine cannot be used in an expression; in fact, the manner in which subroutines are used in BASIC prevents this from occurring.

### The GOSUB and RETURN Statements

In a BASIC program, a subroutine is a series of statements that performs an operational procedure that would be useful in several places in the program. A subroutine has the following structure:

```
10
20
30
 .
 .
 .
m     GOSUB 500   Causes program control to be transferred to
                    statement 500.
m+1   ____        Control returns to this point from subroutine.
 .
 .
 .
500   ____
501   ____        Subroutine
 .     ____
 .      .
 .      .
        .
n     RETURN      Causes program control to return to the statement
                    following the GOSUB.
```

A subroutine uses two statements: GOSUB and RETURN. GOSUB causes program control to be passed to the first statement of the subroutine and has the following format:

> GOSUB statement-number

The RETURN statement is part of the subroutine and causes program control to be returned to the first executable statement that logically follows the corresponding GOSUB statement. The form of the RETURN statement is:

```
 RETURN 
```

Rules governing the use of the GOSUB and RETURN statements are given after a brief example that includes a subroutine that rotates a one-dimensional array *n* places to the left, that is, toward the origin, and another that displays the array and an appropriate title.

```
10  FOR I= 1 TO 10
15      B(I)=I
20  NEXT I
25  REM DISPLAY LIST
27  T$= "ORIGINAL LIST"
30  GOSUB 300
35  REM ROTATE 1 PLACE
40  N= 1
45  GOSUB 400
50  REM DISPLAY LIST
51  T$= "ROTATE 1 PLACE"
55  GOSUB 300
60  REM ROTATE 2 PLACES
65  N= 2
70  GOSUB 400
75  REM DISPLAY LIST
77  T$= "ROTATE 2 PLACES"
80  GOSUB 300
90  STOP
299  REM PRINT SUBROUTINE
300  PRINT T$
301  FOR I= 1 TO N
302      PRINT B(I);
303  NEXT I
304  PRINT
305  RETURN
399  REM ROTATE SUBROUTINE
400  FOR J= 1 TO N
401      T = B(1)
402      FOR K= 2 TO 10
403          B(K-1)=B(K)
404      NEXT K
```

```
405      B(10)=T
406 NEXT J
407 RETURN
999 END
RUN
```

ORIGINAL LIST
1  2  3  4  5  6  7  8  9  10
ROTATE 1 PLACE
2  3  4  5  6  7  8  9  10  1
ROTATE 2 PLACES
4  5  6  7  8  9  10  1  2  3

A subroutine is frequently used in cases where a subprogram is needed that would return more than one value or no values at all.

### Execution of the GOSUB and RETURN Statements

The execution of the GOSUB statement causes program control to be transferred to the specified statement or, in the case of a nonexecutable statement, the first executable statement that logically follows the specified statement number. (Initially, GOSUB executes in the same way as a GOTO statement.) The GOSUB statement establishes a return path so that when the RETURN statement is executed, program control is passed back to the first executable statement that follows the GOSUB statement.

The execution of a RETURN statement is always associated with the last active GOSUB statement. (An active GOSUB statement is a GOSUB statement that has been executed without the execution of its complementary RETURN statement.) When no active GOSUB statement exists, the execution of a RETURN statement causes an error condition. A subroutine that could be entered with a GOSUB statement or "flowed into" might look something like the following:

```
        REM NULLIFY RETURN AND ENTER SUBROUTINE
        F9=0
        GOTO 705
        REM GOSUB ENTRY – USE GOSUB 700
700 F9=1
705 ____

 .      ____
 .
               Body of subroutine.
```

```
.  ____
750  IF F9=0 THEN 760
752  REM GOSUB RETURN
755  RETURN
757  REM NORMAL FLOW
760  ____
.  ____
.  ____
.
```

Subroutines of this type (that is, those that can be used with a statement such as GOSUB) have some characteristics that should be noted:

1. All variables used in the main part of the program are "global" in the sense that if they are used in the subroutine, they have the same value as in the main part of the program. This is logical since a single program is involved.
2. Program control can pass in and out of subroutines, at the discretion of the programmer, and the execution of subroutines can be nested, that is

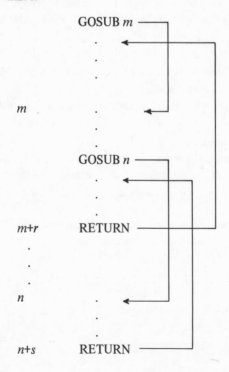

In other words, several active GOSUB statements can exist at the same time. (The only restriction is that at least one active GOSUB statement must exist when a RETURN statement is executed.)

## 5.3 USER-DEFINED FUNCTIONS

The intrinsic functions, covered earlier, represent a class of functions that are useful to a wide range of users. Not all functions that each user might want to use can be maintained on a system-wide basis. Therefore, the user is provided with the capability of defining his own functions. A user function is a function that is defined by the user and used in the same manner that an intrinsic function is used. Some common applications of user functions are to compute quantities such as:

$$\log_b x = \log(x)/\log(b)$$

$$\text{sind } a = \sin(a\pi/180)$$

$$\text{root}(a,b,c) = \frac{-b + \sqrt{b^2 - 4ac}}{2a}$$

or the evaluation of an equation such as

$$f(x) = ax^2 + bx + c$$

for any value of $x$. Other functions, such as the implementation of logical arithmetic or the factorial and square root functions ordinarily require a more lengthy definition but are equally useful once the function is defined.

User functions are usually defined for convenience or when the same expression is used several places in a program—perhaps with different data.

A user function identifier consists of three letters, the first two of which must be FN. Thus, up to 26 different functions (that is, FNA through FNZ) may be defined. A user function can have any number of arguments and always returns a value to the point of reference so that it can be used in an expression. In fact, a user function must be used in an expression since it would be meaningless to the left of a replacement sign (=).

Two kinds of user function can be defined: a single-line definition and a multiple-line definition.

### Single-Line User Functions

A single-line user function is defined with the DEF statement that has the following format:

```
DEF FN letter (scalar-variable [, scalar-variable]...)
    = expression
```

The following statements are valid single-line user function definitions:

DEF FNS (A) = SIN(A*&PI/180)

DEF FNL(V,B) = LOG(V)/LOG(B)

DEF FNR(A,B,C) = (-B+SQR(B↑2-4*A*C))/(2*A)

DEF FNX(X) = A*X↑2+B*X+C

The variables that are enclosed in parentheses following the function identifier are referred to as parameters. Actually, these parameters are "dummy variables" that are replaced, when the function is referenced, by the value of the expression that occupies the same relative position in the list of parameters. In general, there is no limit on the number of parameters; however, this again is dependent on the implementation of the language and some versions of BASIC allow only a single parameter. A function definition may appear anywhere in a program. Other variables that exist in the function definition assume the same values as in the remainder of the program; that is, they are "global variables." (See the preceding section on subroutines.)

The following program depicts the use of the FNS, FNR, and FNX functions defined earlier in this section:

```
 10  DEF FNS(A) = SIN(A*&PI/180)
 20  DEF FNR(A,B,C) = (-B+SQR(B↑2-4*A*C))/(2*A)
 30  DEF FNX(X) = A*X↑2+B*X+C
 40  PRINT "SIN"; FNS(30)
 50  Z1=-5
 60  Q=3
 70  PRINT "ROOT"; FNR(1,Z1,2*Q)
 80  A=1
 90  B=-5
100  C=6
110  PRINT "POLY";FNX(4)
```

```
999  END
RUN

SIN  0.5
ROOT  3
POLY  2
```

Another sample "one liner" is:

DEF FNR(X,N) = INT(X*10↑N+0.5)/10↑N

which rounds the argument X to N decimal places. It is used in a subsequent example.

The use of intrinsic and user functions is permitted in function definitions.

### Multiple-Line User Functions

All functions that a user might desire to define cannot be specified in a single statement. In fact, many functions, such as *factorial* and *square root*, usually require iterative procedures. A multiple-line user function definition has the following structure:

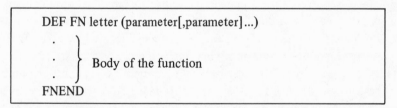

```
DEF FN letter (parameter[,parameter]...)
    .  ⎫
    .  ⎬  Body of the function
    .  ⎭
FNEND
```

where "FN letter" is the function identifier and "parameter" is a scalar variable. The function identifier must appear to the left of the equal sign in an assignment statement in the body of the function so that the function reference is assigned a value. As with intrinsic and single-line user functions, a "function reference" of a multiple-line user function takes the form:

```
function-identifier(argument[,argument]...)
```

where "argument" is an expression. (The number of arguments must agree with the number of parameters in the function definition.)

The following factorial function exhibits some of the preceding concepts:

```
 10  DEF FNF(K)
 20  FNF=1
 30  IF K<=1 THEN 70
 40  FOR I= 2 TO K
 50      FNF=FNF*I
 60  NEXT I
 70  FNEND
 80  FOR J= 1 TO 5
 90      PRINT J; "FACTORIAL="; FNF(J)
100  NEXT J
999  END
RUN

1 FACTORIAL= 1
2 FACTORIAL= 2
3 FACTORIAL= 6
4 FACTORIAL= 24
5 FACTORIAL= 120
```

As with single-line function definitions, a multiple-line function definition can appear anywhere in a program. The parameters in a function definition are dummy variables that are replaced at the point of reference by the value of the corresponding expression. Other variables, used in a function definition, assume their "global" values. A function definition (that is, the body of the function) can utilize other functions—either intrinsic or user defined. However, one function definition cannot be nested in another function definition.

The following program includes a defined function for computing the square root. The square root function uses the function that rounds a number to N decimal places given earlier in this section. (Obviously, there is no need for a square root function since one, that is, SQR, is provided with the BASIC language. The method of implementation, however, presents a useful technique.)

```
100  Z1=625
110  PRINT "SQ. ROOT OF";Z1;"=";FNS(Z1)
120  T=-20
130  A=2*FNS(ABS(T)+5)
140  PRINT "2*FNS(ABS(T)+5)=";A
150  PRINT "WHERE T=";T
310  DEF FNS(X)
315      IF X<0 THEN 380
```

```
320       E9=.005
330       FNS=1
340       FOR I9= 1 TO 1000
350            IF ABS(FNS↑2–X)<E9 THEN 400
360            FNS=FNS+.5*(X/FNS–FNS)
370       NEXT I9
380       PRINT "ERROR IN SQUARE ROOT"
390       STOP
400       FNS=FNR(FNS,2)
410  FNEND
500  DEF FNR(X,N)=INT(X*10↑N+0.5)/10↑N
999  END
RUN

SQ. ROOT OF 625 = 25
2*FNS(ABS(T)+5) = 10
WHERE T=–20
```

The final example of defined functions involves the implementation of logical operations in BASIC. A comparison operation is permitted in the IF statement; however, no "logical" data type exists so that comparison operators are not allowed in other statements. Assume that "true" is represented by the arithmetic value 1 and "false" by the value 0. User functions are presented for the "greater than" and the "and" functions. They are intended to provide additional insight into the nature of defined functions.

```
500  REM GREATER THAN FUNCTION
501  DEF FNG(A,B)
502       FNG=1
503       IF A>B THEN 505
504       FNG=0
505  FNEND
600  REM AND FUNCTION
601  DEF FNA(Q,R)
602       FNA=0
603       IF Q=0 THEN 606
604       IF R=0 THEN 606
605       FNA=1
606  FNEND
```

Thus, with the use of functions such as these, a user could construct a logical statement, such as the following:

$$P = FNA(FNG(A \uparrow 2-1,17.1),S)$$

where P and S are implicitly understood by the user to be variables restricted to the values 0 and 1.

## 5.4 VECTOR AND MATRIX OPERATIONS

When using vectors (that is, one-dimensional arrays) and matrices (that is, two-dimensional arrays), some sequences of statements occur frequently enough to be regarded as "super" operations. Procedures such as reading or printing a complete array, resetting an array to zero, or adding two matrices on an element-by-element basis fall into this category. It is also customary for mathematicians to manipulate vectors and matrices, and operations such as the matrix inverse or the matrix transpose are well known. The BASIC language includes several statements designed to operate on vectors and matrices; these statements, each of which begins with the prefix MAT, eliminate much of the detail ordinarily associated with array processing. Actually, each of the MAT statements can be programmed using a combination of statements introduced previously. However, the use of MAT statements has several distinct advantages:

1. They are a convenience and permit the user to think about his problem rather than the details of computer programming.
2. They shorten BASIC programs and the resultant computer program executes more efficiently than if the same operations were programmed using several BASIC statements.
3. Programming errors are reduced since much of the detail involved with array processing is eliminated.
4. Less typing is required to have the same function executed; this is an important consideration when programs are entered at a computer terminal.

Matrix operations are designed primarily for use with arithmetic arrays, as in ordinary mathematics. However, a limited capability is defined for use on character arrays. Character arrays are treated as a separate topic later in this chapter.

## Vector and Matrix Definition

Vectors and matrices are defined in the usual fashion—either implicitly by referencing an element of the array or explicitly with the DIM statement.

Once an array is defined, either implicitly or explicitly, it cannot be redefined with the DIM statement. However, an array can be redefined with one of the MAT statements as long as the number of dimensions in the array remains the same and the number of elements in the redimensioned array does not exceed the number of elements in the old array. Thus if array A is dimensioned A(5,9), then the following redimensions would be valid: A(9,5), A(3,15), and A(5,5), whereas A(5,10) would be invalid since the number of elements in the redimensioned array exceeds the number of elements in the old array.

MAT operations are defined on arithmetic arrays that must be defined either implicitly or explicitly before they can be used as an operand in a MAT statement. The reason that an array must be defined is that the computer uses its dimension during a MAT operation to which that array serves as an operand. Consider the following MAT statement where A, B, and C are defined matrices:

MAT A=B+C

It specifies that matrix C is added to matrix B on an element-by-element basis, and the result is stored as matrix A. The result is the same as if the following statements were used (where M is the row dimension of A, B, and C and N is the column dimension of A, B, and C):

```
FOR I= 1 TO M
    FOR J= 1 TO N
        A(I,J)=B(I,J)+C(I,J)
    NEXT J
NEXT I
```

Thus, even in one of the more simple cases, the reduction in the number of statements is 5 to 1.

## Input and Output of Vectors and Matrices

Three matrix input and output statements are described: MAT READ, MAT PRINT, and MAT INPUT. The MAT READ statement has the form:

> MAT READ arithmetic-array-variable$[(e_1[,e_2])]$
> $[,$arithmetic-array-variable$[(e_1[,e_2])]]$ ...

where "arithmetic-array-variable" is an arithmetic array and the "$e_i$s" are scalar arithmetic expressions evaluated at the point of reference. If the arithmetic array variable has been previously defined, then the dimension of the array is taken from the definition. If the array has not been defined or if the user desires to change its extents, as outlined previously, then array specifications must be included in the MAT READ statement as described below. The MAT READ statement causes arithmetic data items to be read from the data set established with DATA statements and assigned to the specified array by row. Thus, the execution of the following statements:

    DIM A(2,3)
    MAT READ A
    DATA -7,3,9,6,5,1

would cause the following matrix to be constructed in computer storage:

$$A = \begin{pmatrix} -7 & 3 & 9 \\ 6 & 5 & 1 \end{pmatrix}$$

The concept also applies to ordinary vectors (that is, one-dimensional arrays), column vectors (that is, a matrix with $n$ rows and one column), and row vectors (that is, a matrix with one row and $n$ columns). Similar to the previous example, the execution of the following statements:

    DIM B(7), C(4,1), D(1,5)
    MAT READ B,C,D
    DATA 1,1,2,3,5,8,13
    DATA 2,3,5,7
    DATA 1,4,9,16,25

would cause the following matrices to be constructed:

$$B = (1 \quad 1 \quad 2 \quad 3 \quad 5 \quad 8 \quad 13)$$

$$C = \begin{pmatrix} 2 \\ 3 \\ 5 \\ 7 \end{pmatrix} \qquad D = (1 \quad 4 \quad 9 \quad 16 \quad 25)$$

A new matrix can be defined or an existing matrix can also be redimensioned through the MAT READ statement, by utilizing the parenthesized expressions that are included in the above skeleton. A MAT READ statement of the form:

MAT READ $v(e_1, e_2)$

specifies that array $v$ should be dimensioned with row dimension $e_1$ and column dimension $e_2$, where $e_1$ and $e_2$ are evaluated at the point of reference, and the elements of $v$ are to be read in from the data set in row order. The concept also applies to one-dimensional arrays. The execution of the following statements:

DIM F(15), G(8,8)
READ U,V
MAT READ F(7), G(U,V)
DATA 4,3
DATA -7,3,9,6,5,1,4
DATA 1,1,2,3,5,8,1,3,2,1,3,4

causes the following vector and matrix to be constructed:

$$F = (-7 \quad 3 \quad 9 \quad 6 \quad 5 \quad 1 \quad 4$$

$$G = \begin{pmatrix} 1 & 1 & 2 \\ 3 & 5 & 8 \\ 1 & 3 & 2 \\ 1 & 3 & 4 \end{pmatrix}$$

The MAT PRINT statement has the following form:

MAT PRINT arithmetic-array-variable [{,|;}
     arithmetic-array-variable]...[,|;]

where "arithmetic-array-variable" is a previously defined arithmetic array. Array references, in the MAT PRINT statement, may be separated by either a comma or a semicolon, as specified below. The printing of an array is governed by the following conventions:

1. An array is printed in row order.
2. The printing of each row begins on a new line.

3. The first row of an array is separated from the preceding line by two blank lines.[2]
4. Other rows of the array are separated from the preceding row by one blank line.
5. The printing of an array is governed by its dimensions at the time the MAT PRINT statement is executed.

The separator (comma or semicolon) used between array references in the MAT PRINT statement governs how the elements of an array are printed. If an array reference is followed by a comma or a space, as with A, C, or D below:

```
MAT PRINT  A,B;C
MAT PRINT D
```

then the values are printed in zoned format. If an array reference is followed by a semicolon, as with F, H, or J below:

```
MAT PRINT E,F;G
MAT PRINT H;
MAT PRINT I,J;
```

then the values are printed in packed format (that is, they are closed up). Thus, a single array must be printed using the same format; however, distinct arrays in the same MAT PRINT statement can be printed using either format. The following program depicts the above concepts:

```
 10  DIM A(2,3), B(5,5), C(4), D(15)
 20  E(2)=17
 30  READ P
 40  MAT READ A,B(3,1),C,D(P),E(3)
 50  PRINT "MATRIX OUTPUT"
 60  MAT PRINT A;B,C,D;E
 70  DATA 5
 80  DATA -7,3,9,6,5,1
 90  DATA  1,1,2
100  DATA 1,3,2,1
110  DATA 3,4,5,5,8
```

---

[2]The manner in which arrays are printed differs among implementations of the BASIC language.

```
120  DATA 9,1,4
999  END
RUN
```

MATRIX OUTPUT

```
-7   3   9

 6   5   1

 1

 1

 2

 1           3           2           1

 3   4   5   5   8

 9           1           4
```

The MAT INPUT statement is similar to the MAT READ statement except that input is requested from the user's terminal. The form of the MAT INPUT statement is:

```
MAT INPUT arithmetic-array-variable[(e₁[,e₂])]
     [,arithmetic-array-variable[(e₁[,e₂])]]...
```

where the meaning of the metanotation is the same as for the MAT READ statement. In response to the MAT INPUT statement, the user is requested to enter data on a row-by-row basis. The user is prompted with two question marks for the first row of the matrix and by a single question mark for each subsequent row. Values are separated by commas and the last value in a row is followed by a carriage return. If an input line must be continued, then the carriage return for that row must be preceded by a comma to denote continuation. The following example depicts the use of the MAT INPUT statement:

```
10  DIM W(2,3)
20  MAT INPUT W
30  MAT PRINT W;
```

40 END
RUN

?? 6,3,9    [carriage return]
?  4,2,-1   [carriage return]

6   3   9

4   2  -1

### Elementary Operations

The general form of a MAT statement that causes an elementary arithmetic operation or the assignment operation to be performed is:

MAT arithmetic-array-variable = { arithmetic-array-variable |
{ arithmetic-array-variable{ + | - }arithmetic-array-variable }|
{(arithmetic-scalar-expression)*arithmetic-array-variable } }

where "arithmetic-array-variable" is an arithmetic array and "arithmetic-scalar-expression" is an expression that evaluates to a single scalar value at the point of reference. The various alternatives inherent in this format are described below. Matrices used as operands must be previously defined. A matrix variable that appears to the left of the assignment symbol (=) may be defined or redimensioned through the execution of the MAT statement.

The *array assignment* statement takes the form:

MAT A=B

where B must be a previously defined matrix. The statement copies the elements of array B into array A. The elements of B remain unchanged. If the dimension of B is $(m,n)$, then A is given the same dimensions and the result of the array assignment statement is $A(i,j)=B(i,j)$, for $i=1,2,...,m$ and $j=1,2,...,n$. If the dimension of B is $(n)$, then A is given that dimension and the result of the array assignment statement is $A(i)=B(i)$, for $i=1,2,...,n$. Essentially, array assignment is used to make a copy of an existing matrix.

The *matrix addition* statement takes the form:

MAT C = A+B

where A and B are matrices of the same size. The statement adds matrix A to matrix B, on an element-by-element basis and replaces matrix C with the result. If the dimension of A and B is $(m,n)$, then C is given the same dimension and the result of the matrix addition statement is $C(i,j)=A(i,j)+B(i,j)$, for i=1,2,...,$m$ and j=1,2,...,$n$. If the dimension of A and B is $(n)$, then C is given that dimension and the result of the matrix addition statement is $C(i)=A(i)+B(i)$, for i=1,2,...,$n$.

The *matrix subtraction* statement takes the form:

MAT C=A-B

where A and B are matrices of the same size. The statement subtracts the matrix B from matrix A, on an element-by-element basis; and replaces matrix C with the result. If the dimension of A and B is $(m,n)$, then C is given the same dimension and the result of the matrix subtraction statement is $C(i,j)=A(i,j)-B(i,j)$, for i=1,2,...,$m$ and j=1,2,...,$n$. If the dimension of A and B is $(n)$, then C is given that dimension and the result of the matrix subtraction statement is $C(i)=A(i)-B(i)$, for i=1,2,...,$n$.

The *scalar multiplication* statement multiplies a matrix by the value of an expression evaluated at the point of reference. The form of the scalar multiplication statement is:

MAT A = $(e)*$B

where B must be a previously defined matrix and $e$ is an expression that is evaluated prior to the multiplication. The statement multiplies matrix B by the value of scalar expression $e$, on an element-by-element basis, and replaces matrix A with the result. If the dimension of B is $(m,n)$, then A is given the same dimension and the result of the scalar multiplication statement is $A(i,j)=e*B(i,j)$, for i=1,2,...,$m$ and j=1,2,...,$n$. If the dimension of B is $(n)$, then A is given that dimension and the result of the scalar multiplication statement is $A(i)=e*B(i)$, for i=1,2,...,$n$.

MAT addition, subtraction, and scalar multiplication statements have a useful characteristic in common. These statements permit the same array variable to appear on both sides of the assignment symbol (=). Thus, a statement such as:

MAT A=A+B

or

MAT C=(3)*C

is permitted. In general, this facility is allowed since an element of an operand matrix is used in the computation of only one element of the result matrix. The following example depicts some of the preceding concepts:

```
 10 DIM B(2,3)
 20 MAT READ B
 30 MAT A=(2)*B
 40 PRINT "MATRIX B"
 50 MAT PRINT B;
 60 PRINT "MATRIX A=(2)*B"
 70 MAT PRINT A;
 80 MAT C=A+B
 90 PRINT "MATRIX C=A+B"
100 MAT PRINT C;
110 DATA 1,2,3,4,5,6
120 END
RUN
```

MATRIX B

1  2  3

4  5  6

MATRIX A=(2)*B

2  4  6

8  10  12

MATRIX C=A+B

3  6  9

12  15  18

## Special Matrices

A matrix is usually initialized in one of two ways:

1.  The elements are entered as DATA for use in a MAT READ statement.
2.  A FOR loop is written to perform the required initialization.

The use of either method becomes cumbersome when it is needed with any degree of regularity. Therefore, the BASIC language includes three statement options that facilitate matrix initialization. The form of the MAT statement options to generate special matrices is:

MAT arithmetic-array-variable={ZER|CON|IDN}$[(e_1[,e_2])]$

where "arithmetic-array-variable" is an arithmetic array and the "$e_i$s" are scalar arithmetic expressions evaluated at the point of reference. If the arithmetic array variable has been previously defined, then the dimension of the array is taken from the definition. If the array has not been defined or if the user desires to change its extents, then array specifications must be included with the statement. If $e_1$ is given, then a one-dimensional array is specified and $e_1$ gives its dimension. If both $e_1$ and $e_2$ are given, then a matrix is specified and $e_1$ and $e_2$ give its row and column extents, respectively.

The ZER option denotes an array of all zeros. Thus, the execution of the following statements:

```
DIM A(2,3),C(5,10)
MAT A=ZER
MAT B=ZER(6)
MAT C=ZER(4,3)
```

would cause the following matrices to be constructed in computer storage:

$$A = \begin{pmatrix} 0 & 0 & 0 \\ 0 & 0 & 0 \end{pmatrix} \qquad B = (0 \quad 0 \quad 0 \quad 0 \quad 0 \quad 0)$$

$$C = \begin{pmatrix} 0 & 0 & 0 \\ 0 & 0 & 0 \\ 0 & 0 & 0 \\ 0 & 0 & 0 \end{pmatrix}$$

The CON option denotes an array of all ones. Thus, the execution of the following statements:

```
DIM A(2,3),C(5,10)
```

MAT A=CON
MAT B=CON(6)
MAT C=CON(4,3)

would cause the following matrices to be constructed in computer storage:

$$A = \begin{pmatrix} 1 & 1 & 1 \\ 1 & 1 & 1 \end{pmatrix} \qquad B = (1 \quad 1 \quad 1 \quad 1 \quad 1 \quad 1)$$

$$C = \begin{pmatrix} 1 & 1 & 1 \\ 1 & 1 & 1 \\ 1 & 1 & 1 \\ 1 & 1 & 1 \end{pmatrix}$$

The IDN option denotes an identity matrix. An identity matrix contains ones in its main diagonal and zeros elsewhere; it must be defined or specified as a square matrix—that is, a matrix with the same number of rows as columns. Thus, the execution of the following statements:

DIM A(3,3),B(2,10)
MAT A=IDN
MAT B=IDN(4,4)
MAT C=IDN(2,2)

would cause the following matrices to be constructed in computer storage:

$$A = \begin{pmatrix} 1 & 0 & 0 \\ 0 & 1 & 0 \\ 0 & 0 & 1 \end{pmatrix} \qquad B = \begin{pmatrix} 1 & 0 & 0 & 0 \\ 0 & 1 & 0 & 0 \\ 0 & 0 & 1 & 0 \\ 0 & 0 & 0 & 1 \end{pmatrix} \qquad C = \begin{pmatrix} 1 & 0 \\ 0 & 1 \end{pmatrix}$$

**Matrix Multiplication, Transpose, and Inverse**

The *multiplication* of two matrices A and B is defined as:

$$C(i,j) = \sum_{k=1}^{n} A(i,k)*B(k,j)$$

for i=1,2,...,$m$ and j=1,2,...,$p$.

where C is the result matrix and the dimensions of the three matrices are A($m,n$), B($n,p$), and C($m,p$). Thus,

$$\begin{pmatrix} 1 & 2 \\ 3 & 4 \end{pmatrix} * \begin{pmatrix} 5 & 6 \\ 7 & 8 \end{pmatrix} = \begin{pmatrix} 19 & 22 \\ 43 & 50 \end{pmatrix}$$

The *matrix multiplication* statement in BASIC has the format:

MAT arithmetic-array-variable-1=arithmetic-array-variable-2*
arithmetic-array-variable-3

where "arithmetic-array-variable-$i$" is an arithmetic array, arithmetic array variable 2 and arithmetic array variable 3 must be previously defined, and the following conditions hold:

1. Arithmetic array variable 1 may not be the same variable as arithmetic array variable 2 or arithmetic array variable 3.[3]
2. The number of columns in arithmetic array variable 2 must equal the number of rows in arithmetic array variable 3.

Thus, the execution of the statements:

```
DIM A(2,3), B(3,2)
DATA 1,2,3,1,4,2
DATA 2,1,4,2,1,3
MAT READ A,B
MAT C=A*B
```

would cause the following matrix to be computed in computer storage:

$$C = \begin{pmatrix} 11 & 14 \\ 20 & 15 \end{pmatrix}$$

The *transpose* of a matrix is generated by interchanging its rows and columns. The transpose B of matrix A is defined as: B($j,i$)=A($i,j$) for $i=1,2,...,m$ and $j=1,2, ...,n$. The dimensions of A are ($m,n$); the dimensions of B are ($n,m$). (The trans-

[3] The same variable cannot be used on both sides of the assignment symbol (=) since each element of an operand is used several times during the computation.

pose of a matrix A is frequently denoted by $A^T$). The *matrix transpose* statement in BASIC has the format:

MAT arithmetic-array-variable-1=TRN(arithmetic-array-variable-2)

where "arithmetic-array-variable-$i$" is an arithmetic array and arithmetic array variable 1 and arithmetic array variable 2 must not be the same variable. Arithmetic array variable 2 must be previously defined. Thus, the execution of the following statements:

    DIM C(2,3)
    DATA 1,2,3,4,5,6
    MAT READ C
    MAT D=TRN(C)

would cause the following matrix to be computed in computer storage:

$$D = \begin{pmatrix} 1 & 4 \\ 2 & 5 \\ 3 & 6 \end{pmatrix}$$

A theorem in mathematics states that:

$$(AB)^T = B^T A^T$$

The validity of this theorem is demonstrated in the next example that depicts matrix multiplication and the transpose operation.

```
 10  DIM A(3,2),B(2,3),C(3,3),D(3,3),E(2,3),F(3,2),G(3,3)
 20  MAT READ A,B
 30  MAT C=A*B
 40  MAT D=TRN(C)
 50  PRINT "TRANSPOSE(A*B)"
 60  MAT PRINT D;
 70  MAT E=TRN(A)
 80  MAT F=TRN(B)
 90  MAT G=F*A
100  PRINT "TRANSPOSE(B)*TRANSPOSE(A)"
110  MAT PRINT G;
120  DATA 1,2,3,4,2,1
```

130  DATA 3,1,1,2,4,3
999  END
RUN

TRANSPOSE (A*B)

7   17   8

9   19   6

7   15   5

TRANSPOSE(B)*TRANSPOSE(A)

7   17   8

9   19   6

7   15   5

The *inverse* of a matrix A is a matrix B such that A*B=B*A=I, where I is the identity matrix. Only square nonsingular matrices have an inverse.[4] The *matrix inverse* statement in BASIC has the format:

---

MAT arithmetic-array-variable-1=INV(arithmetic-array-variable-2)

---

where "arithmetic-array-variable-*i*" is an arithmetic array and arithmetic array variable 1 and arithmetic array variable 2 must not be the same variable. Arithmetic array variable 2 must be previously defined, square, and nonsingular for its inverse to exist; if the matrix inverse does not exist, an error condition is generated.

As an example of the concept of an inverse, consider the inverse of matrix $\begin{pmatrix} 1 & 2 \\ 3 & 4 \end{pmatrix}$. A matrix is needed such that

$$\begin{pmatrix} a & b \\ c & d \end{pmatrix} * \begin{pmatrix} 1 & 2 \\ 3 & 4 \end{pmatrix} = \begin{pmatrix} 1 & 0 \\ 0 & 1 \end{pmatrix}$$

---

[4] A matrix is singular if the value of its determinant is zero.

Performing the matrix multiplication on the left, the following identity is obtained:

$$\begin{pmatrix} a+3b & 2a+4b \\ c+3d & 2c+4d \end{pmatrix} = \begin{pmatrix} 1 & 0 \\ 0 & 1 \end{pmatrix}$$

such that (since matrices are equal if their corresponding elements are equal):

$$a+3b=1 \qquad 2a+4b=0$$
$$c+3d=0 \qquad 2c+4d=1$$

solving for $a$, $b$, $c$, and $d$, the matrix $\begin{pmatrix} -2 & 1 \\ 1.5 & -.5 \end{pmatrix}$ is obtained, which is the inverse of the original matrix. The reader can verify that $\begin{pmatrix} -2 & 1 \\ 1.5 & -.5 \end{pmatrix} * \begin{pmatrix} 1 & 2 \\ 3 & 4 \end{pmatrix}$ $= \begin{pmatrix} 1 & 0 \\ 0 & 1 \end{pmatrix}$. The matrix inverse is frequently used in the solution of simultaneous linear equations. Consider the system of equations:

$$x_1 + x_2 + x_3 = 2$$

$$2x_1 + x_2 + 2x_3 = 3$$

$$x_1 + 3x_2 + x_3 = 4$$

If $A = \begin{pmatrix} 1 & 1 & 1 \\ 2 & 1 & 2 \\ 1 & 3 & 1 \end{pmatrix}$, $X = \begin{pmatrix} x_1 \\ x_2 \\ x_3 \end{pmatrix}$, and $B = \begin{pmatrix} 2 \\ 3 \\ 4 \end{pmatrix}$, then the system can be expressed as:

$$AX=B$$

Multiplying each side by the inverse of A (that is, $A^{-1}$) and simplifying,

$$A^{-1}AX=A^{-1}B$$
$$IX=A^{-1}B$$
$$X=A^{-1}B$$

the solution X is obtained. A BASIC program, using the matrix inverse, to solve the above problem is given as follows:

```
10 DIM A(3,3),B(3),X(3),N(3,3)
20 MAT READ A,B
30 MAT N=INV(A)
40 MAT X=N*B
50 MAT PRINT X
60 DATA 1,1,1,2,1,2,1,3,1
70 DATA 2,3,4
RUN

 2
 1
-1
```

where the result values of 2, 1, and -1 are the required values for $x_1$, $x_2$, and $x_3$, respectively.

## Character Matrices

Some implementations of BASIC include a limited capability for using one-dimensional character-string arrays. Actually, the MAT operations on character arrays are restricted to MAT READ, MAT PRINT, and MAT INPUT since character data is not in the domain of most matrix operations. Character arrays were introduced in Chapter 4 and must satisfy the same definitional requirements in MAT statements that exist for arithmetic arrays. The following example depicts the use of the MAT READ statement with character arrays:

```
10 READ N
20 MAT READ A$(N)
30 INPUT I
40 PRINT A$(I)
50 DATA 4
60 DATA "JONES,J.K.","SMITH, PETE","ADAMS, MIKE",
        "WEXLER, TOM"
99 END
RUN

?3
ADAMS, MIKE
```

The processing of character arrays plays a minor role in BASIC because of the predominance of applications involving arithmetic data. However, character data is frequently used for labeling purposes and the use of character arrays is often useful in that regard.

## 5.5 COMMENTS ON THE BASIC LANGUAGE

In a sense, the BASIC language has been used as an introduction to the remainder of the book. The BASIC language restricts variable names to a few simple forms and includes only two data types: arithmetic and character string. In addition, the kinds of statements are limited and extremely easy to use. Obviously, BASIC was designed to be this way and to users of the language, these attributes are a definite asset. As an introduction to programming languages, BASIC allows the reader to "get his feet wet" so that he can appreciate and understand some of the more subtle features found in the other languages. The presentation of BASIC is also more tutorial than the other parts of this book. This is so for three reasons:

1. The beginning of a book is the logical place to include tutorial information.
2. It would be inefficient to repeat tutorial information for each language covered.
3. Most readers like to see examples of how programming languages are used since it gives them some feel for the relative importance of the various statements in the language.

Thus, the remaining parts of the book are less oriented toward how a programming language is used and more oriented toward the essential characteristics of a given language.

In another sense, the BASIC language is misleading. One could easily infer that because the language is easy to learn and use, it is not a powerful language. Although BASIC is not considered to be a "general-purpose" programming language, some features in BASIC (such as the MAT operations) are very powerful and give the user a considerable amount of computational capability with a few statements.

## EXERCISES

1. Write user-defined functions for the following relational and logical operators:

(a)  greater than or equal to
(b)  equal to
(c)  not equal to
(d)  less than
(e)  less than or equal to
(f)  or
(g)  not

2.  Write a user-defined function that evaluates the step function:

$y=0$, if $x \leq 0$
$y=13.2$, if $0 < x < 131.4$
$y=50$, if $x \geq 131.4$

3.  Write a user-defined function that computes the modulus function; e.g., the value 5 (modulus 3) yields the value 2. The function header statement should take the form:

DEF FNM(A,N)

where A is the numeric value that should be transformed modulus N.

4.  Write user-defined functions that perform the following:

(a)  Convert degrees to radians
(b)  Convert radians to degrees

5.  Write subroutines to perform the following:

(a)  Compute the transpose of a matrix
(b)  Compute the matrix product
(c)  Generate the identity matrix
(d)  Generate a matrix of all ones

Do not use the MAT operations. However, use adjustable dimensions, such as:

M=...
N=...
GOSUB $n$

etc.

6. Write a BASIC program that determines whether M*N=N*M for two square matrices M and N. (Allow the program to compensate for small computational errors.)
7. Write a program similar to exercise 6 that verifies that TRN(A*B)= TRN(B)*TRN(A).
8. Write a BASIC subroutine to raise a matrix to the $n$th power, where $n$ is variable.
9. Given

       DIM A(5,1),B(1,5)
       DATA 1,2,3,4,5
       MAT READ A
       RESTORE
       MAT READ B
       MAT C=A*B
       MAT D=B*A

   What do C and D contain?
10. Generate the following matrix by using MAT statements alone:

$$F = \begin{pmatrix} -5 & -5 & -5 \\ 0 & -5 & -5 \\ -5 & 0 & -5 \\ -5 & -5 & 0 \\ -5 & -5 & -5 \end{pmatrix}$$

## SELECTED READINGS

1. Coan, J. S. *Basic BASIC.* New York: Hayden Book Company, 1970.
2. Kemeny, J. G., and T. E. Kurtz. *Basic Programming.* New York: John Wiley and Sons, Inc., 1971.
3. Nolan, R. L. *Introduction to Computing through the Basic Language.* New York: Holt, Rinehart and Winston, Inc., 1969.
4. *Proposed BASIC Standard,* IBM Corporation, 1970, Reference 3-9070CPS.

# PART 3

## THE
## FORTRAN
## LANGUAGE

# 6

# FORTRAN LANGUAGE CHARACTERISTICS

## 6.1 INTRODUCTION

The first programming language to be used with any degree of regularity is FORTRAN, which is an acronym for FORmula TRANslation. Under the leadership of John Backus, FORTRAN was developed by the IBM Corporation in the years 1954-1957 for their type 704 computer. The first version of FORTRAN was released for general use in 1957. In 1958, FORTRAN II, which incorporated extensions to the FORTRAN concept, was released and FORTRAN IV first became available in 1962. (FORTRAN III never formally existed.) FORTRAN IV, which is described in this part of the book, is an improved version of FORTRAN that includes many language enhancements originating from within IBM, from users, and from other computer manufacturers. Throughout its history, FORTRAN has been enthusiastically supported by practically all that have been involved with it. In fact, a variety of dialects of the language have been developed over the years. A FORTRAN standard was established by the (then called) American Standards Association (ASA) in 1966 and that specification has served as a guideline for subsequent implementations of the language. The level of the FORTRAN language described in this book is ASA FORTRAN. (The American Standards Association is now called the American National Standards Institute.) Ideas for the improvement of FORTRAN are continually being generated and versions of FORTRAN to meet special needs, such as the educational area, are frequently developed. Many of the improvements that would have been made to standard FORTRAN have been included in the PL/I language as "normal" language features.[1]

[1] Most implementations of FORTRAN contain extensions to the language but include ASA standard FORTRAN as a minimum subset. Therefore, programs written using only the language facilities in ASA standard FORTRAN can be run on most computers.

FORTRAN is designed as a mathematically oriented language for the development of scientific computer programs. The objectives of the language are three-fold:

1. To provide a programming language that the scientist or engineer can use himself instead of having to communicate his problem to a professional programmer.
2. To provide a programming language that subordinates many of the details ordinarily associated with programming to the compiler so that the lead time to construct programs and the errors involved are minimized.
3. To provide a programming language that contributes to the generation of efficient object code by a compiler.

Obviously, the need for a programming language like FORTRAN was very great and the objectives were well founded because the response to the FORTRAN language has been overwhelming. It is the most widely used of the higher-level programming languages, and has been applied to large and small programs for a wide range of applications.

FORTRAN was originally developed for scientific applications on a word-oriented computer. Thus, language facilities for processing character data and large data files are minimal. Another consideration is that when FORTRAN was originally developed, most installations did not use an operating system so that statements relating to the operating environment, other than PAUSE and STOP, are not included in the language. Time sharing was not even heard of at that time. Since then, FORTRAN has been made available in several time-sharing systems such that language conventions supporting that operational environment have been developed. These language conventions vary from one time-sharing system to another and are not covered here.

A FORTRAN version of the Indian problem, given in Chapter 3, is included in the next section so that the reader can obtain a flavor for the FORTRAN language and compare it, to a limited degree, with the BASIC language.

## 6.2 FORTRAN VERSION OF THE INDIAN PROBLEM

The FORTRAN version of the Indian problem provides some insight into the nature of the FORTRAN language:

|  |  |
|---|---|
| REAL RATE (4) | (1) |
| DATA RATE/.05,.06,.07,.08/ | (2) |

```
      DO 100 I=1,4                                          (3)
      PRINC=24.0                                            (4)
      DO 50 J=1627,1973                                     (5)
   50 PRINC=PRINC+PRINC*RATE(I)                             (6)
  100 WRITE (6,9000)PRINC                                   (7)
      STOP                                                  (8)
 9000 FORMAT(29H PRESENT VALUE OF MANHATTAN =,F17.2)        (9)
      END                                                   (10)
```

Output:

```
PRESENT VALUE OF MANHATTAN =       540627280.00
PRESENT VALUE OF MANHATTAN =     14499279000.00
PRESENT VALUE OF MANHATTAN =    377035310000.00
PRESENT VALUE OF MANHATTAN =   9511615900000.00
```

The REAL statement (statement 1) defines the type of variable RATE and specifies that it is a one-dimensional array containing four elements. The DATA statement (statement 2) initializes the elements of RATE to the values .05, .06, .07, and .08. The DO statement (statement 3) begins a loop that is to be executed as I ranges from 1 to 4. The subscript I is used to select one of the elements of RATE. Statement 4 initializes the principal (PRINC) to 24 dollars. The DO statement in statement 5 begins a series of iterations that compute the present value of PRINC from 1627 to 1973. The WRITE statement prints the computed value of PRINC using the format numbered 9000. The remainder of the program is self-explanatory.

The FORTRAN version is similar to the BASIC version, or vice versa, since the FORTRAN language was developed earlier. The biggest difference is the WRITE statement in FORTRAN that requires a FORMAT statement and the DATA statement that is used to initialize variables rather than build an internal data set, as in BASIC. Otherwise, program structure is essentially the same.

At a detailed level, however, there are marked differences between the two languages that include the form of variable identifiers, data types, storage organization, and subprograms.

## 6.3  CHARACTERS AND SYMBOLS

FORTRAN officially uses the alphabet given in Table 6.1, although most implementations of the language allow an extended character set. As with BASIC,

Table 6.1

Characters of the FORTRAN Alphabet

*Alphabetic Characters (26)*

A B C D E F G H I J K L M N O P Q R S T U V W X Y Z

*Digits (10)*

0 1 2 3 4 5 6 7 8 9

*Special Characters (11)*

| Name | Character |
|------|-----------|
| Blank | (no visual representation) |
| Equal sign | = |
| Plus sign | + |
| Minus sign | − |
| Asterisk | * |
| Solidus (slash) | / |
| Left parenthesis | ( |
| Right parenthesis | ) |
| Comma | , |
| Decimal point | . |
| Currency symbol (dollar sign) | $ |

the characters of the FORTRAN alphabet are represented as bit configurations in the computer so that any character can be used in a character literal (referred to as a Hollerith literal).

Some sequences of characters have special meaning to the FORTRAN compiler; they are used to form statements, which are used to form programs. Sequences of characters from which statements are formed generally fall into three categories: identifiers, constants, and symbols of the language. A *symbol of the language* is a sequence of one or more characters that have special meaning to the user of the language and to the compiler. Typical symbols are the plus sign (+) and the comma, used as a separator. As is usually the case, a symbol consisting of more than one character is termed a *composite symbol*. Typical composite symbols are ** for exponentiation and .AND. for logical conjunction. The symbols of the FORTRAN language are given in Table 6.2.

Blank characters (that is, spaces) are ignored in FORTRAN (except in Hollerith constants) in the statement portion of a line and may be used freely to improve readability. Statements can be labeled with a statement number for reference and some minor conventions on the use of blank characters with a statement number exist. These are covered later.

Table 6.2

Symbols of the FORTRAN Language

| Symbol | Function |
|--------|----------|
| + | Addition or prefix + |
| − | Subtraction or prefix − |
| * | Multiplication or repetition |
| / | Division or separator |
| ** | Exponentiation |
| .LT. | Less than |
| .LE. | Less than or equal to |
| .EQ. | Equal to |
| .NE. | Not equal to |
| .GE. | Greater than or equal to |
| .GT. | Greater than |
| .AND. | Logical conjunction (And) |
| .OR. | Logical disjunction (Or) |
| .NOT. | Logical negation (Not) |
| , | Separator |
| . | Decimal point |
| = | Assignment symbol |
| ( ) | Enclose lists or group expressions |

In general, the question of upper-case and lower-case letters does not apply to FORTRAN and only upper-case letters are defined with the language. However, some implementations of the language, especially in a time-sharing environment, permit upper-case and lower-case letters to be used interchangeably.

## 6.4 DATA TYPES AND CONSTANT VALUES

Six types of data are permitted in FORTRAN: integer, real, double precision, complex, logical, and Hollerith. Integer, real, double precision, and complex are arithmetic data types, associated with numeric values. The logical data type is associated with "true" or "false" values and the Hollerith[2] data type is associated with character data (occasionally referred to as descriptive information). Another means of processing character data is permitted. With the READ and WRITE statements, information can be transferred between an external medium

[2] In FORTRAN, character data are referred to as Hollerith data in honor of Herman Hollerith, who invented the "IBM card."

and main storage in character form using an "A" format specification. (Format specifications are covered later.) Once character data is placed in main storage, it can be processed using many of the statements defined for arithmetic values. Obviously, severe limitations on the processing of character data exist. This topic is covered as a special section in Chapter 8.

### Integer Data

An integer data item is an exact representation of an integer stored in fixed-point form. An integer data item can be positive, negative, or zero but no places to the right of the radix point are maintained; that is, in other words, the result of an integer expression is always an integer. When an integer data item is stored, the radix point is normally assumed to be immediately to the right of the low-order digit (rightmost digit) of the integer value.

An identifier that names an integer data item is termed an "integer variable." In FORTRAN, an identifier can be declared to be an integer variable or it can assume that attribute by default. This subject is discussed in the next section.

An *integer constant* is a whole number written without a decimal point and optionally preceded by a plus or minus sign. Thus −174, 15, and +3000 are valid integer constants while 25.0 is not because it contains a decimal point. Consider the following assignment statement:

IJOB=NT+15

It specifies that the integer value 15 should be added to integer variable NT and integer variable IJOB should be replaced with the result.

Formally, an integer constant is defined as:

[+|−] digit [digit]...

where "digit" is one of the characters 0 through 9 in the FORTRAN alphabet.

### Real Data

As mentioned in Part 1 of the book, the magnitude of an integer data item is limited by the size of the fixed-point word in main storage. Thus, if $n$ bits are used to store the numeric value of an integer, then the magnitude of the largest integer that can be stored there is $2^n - 1$. An alternative to the question of representation, of course, is to use floating-point notation.

In FORTRAN, a *real data item* is one that is stored in floating-point notation. It can assume a real value in the mathematical sense; that is, it can be positive or negative and represents a rational or irrational number. The magnitude and precision of a real data item are determined by the size of the exponent and the fraction, respectively, of the floating-point format used in storing the number.

A *basic real constant* is composed of the following constituents in the given order: a sign, an integer part, a decimal point, and a decimal fraction. The sign is optional and the decimal point is required. Either or both of the integer and decimal fraction parts must be present. Thus 3., –25.126, and +.000123 are valid basic real constants.

An *exponent* can be used to scale a numeric value. As in BASIC, an exponent is the letter E followed by a signed or unsigned integer. For example, E2, E–11, and E+4 are valid exponents.

Finally, a *real constant* is one of the following: a basic real constant, a basic real constant followed by an exponent, or an integer constant followed by an exponent. The following are valid real constants: –198.30, 123E–4, and 1.693E7. Consider the following assignment statement:

$$ZT301 = 1.32E{-}11*Y**(E{-}34.389)$$

It specifies that the variable Y is to be raised to the power denoted by the value of the expression E–24.289, that the result of the exponentiation is to be multiplied by the real constant 1.32E–11, and that the value of the variable ZT301 is to be replaced with the result of the multiplication. E–34.389 is an expression; 1.32E–11 is a real constant. A real constant is stored as a floating-point number.

Formally, a real constant is defined as

$$[+|-]\{\{\{\text{digit}[\text{digit}]...\,.\,[\text{digit}]...\,|\,[\text{digit}]...\,.\,\text{digit}[\text{digit}]...\}[E[+|-]$$
$$\text{digit}[\text{digit}]...\}\,\}|\,\text{digit}[\text{digit}]...E[+|-]\text{digit}[\text{digit}]...\}$$

where "digit" is one of the characters 0 through 9 in the FORTRAN alphabet.

## Double Precision Data

A *double precision data item* is a value with a precision greater than that of a real data item. A double precision data item is usually stored as an extended floating-point word or as two floating-point words. In most cases, the exponent field of a double precision floating-point value is the same size as that of a real floating-point value so that both data types have the same range. The size of the fraction field of a double precision floating-point value is always greater than the size of the fraction field of a real floating-point value (usually, it is twice as large) so that a double precision value has a greater precision than that of a real value.

A *double precision constant* is written as a basic real constant followed by a double precision exponent or as an integer constant followed by a double precision exponent. A *double precision exponent* is the same as a real exponent except that the letter E is replaced with the letter D. The following are valid double precision constants: −1.23D17, 3D−12, and .000000000073D0.

Formally, a double precision constant is defined as:

$$[+|-]\{\{\{ \text{digit[digit]}... \, . \, \text{[digit]}...| \text{[digit]}... \, . \, \text{digit[digit]}...\}D[+|-]$$
$$\text{digit[digit]}...\}| \text{digit[digit]}... D[+|-] \text{digit[digit]}...\}$$

where "digit" is one of the characters 0 through 9 in the FORTRAN alphabet.

## Complex Data

A *complex data item* is used to represent a complex number; it consists of a pair of real data items: the first represents the real part of the complex number and the second represents the imaginary part. Other than the fact that the components of a complex number are stored in floating-point format, complex data can be utilized effectively without knowing exactly how it is stored. Usually, it is stored as two contiguous floating-point words.

A *complex constant* is written as a pair of real constants, separated by a comma, and enclosed in parentheses. The following are valid complex constants:

| Complex Constant | Mathematical Meaning[3] |
| --- | --- |
| (4.0,3.5) | $4+3.5i$ |
| (2.0,0.0) | 2 |
| (0.0,.00123) | $.00123i$ |
| (1E6,−13.1) | $1000000−13.1i$ |
| (2.0,.45E−5) | $2+.0000045i$ |

## Logical Data

A *logical data item* can only assume the true values of true or false. The manner in which a logical data item is represented on a storage medium is implemen-

[3] The letter $i$ represents the value of $\sqrt{-1}$.

tation defined. Some examples of conventions that have been used to represent logical data are:

| Unit of Storage | True Value | False Value |
|---|---|---|
| Bit | 1 | 0 |
| Byte | At least one bit nonzero | All bits zero |
| Word | Nonzero | Zero |

In general, the storage of logical data is implementation defined and is not of concern to the programmer.

A *logical constant* can be one of the two composite symbols .TRUE. or .FALSE., representing "true" and "false," respectively. A logical constant can only be used in a logical expression. As an external data item for input or output, "true" and "false" are represented by the single letters T and F, respectively.

## Hollerith Data

*Hollerith data* is character data. Originally, Hollerith data was included to serve descriptive purposes, and Hollerith data was permitted in a FORMAT statement used for input and output. As the use of FORTRAN expanded into non-scientific applications, however, the need for a Hollerith constant became evident. There is no Hollerith variable in FORTRAN and character data is usually stored as a variable of type real or type integer.

A Hollerith constant takes the form:

$$nHxxx \ldots x$$

$\underbrace{\phantom{nHxxx \ldots x}}$

$\quad n$ characters

where $n$ is a nonzero positive integer and $x$ is any character in the FORTRAN alphabet, including blank characters. The $n$ characters comprise the Hollerith data item. The following are valid Hollerith constants:

| Hollerith Constant | Characters Comprising the Hollerith Data Item |
|---|---|
| 3HEQU | EQU |
| 5HDON'T | DON'T |
| 11HTEA FOR TWO | TEA FOR TWO |
| 5HA=B+C | A=B+C |
| 7H%*  /− | %*  /− |

In ASA FORTRAN, a Hollerith constant can only be used as an argument in a CALL statement or in a data initialization statement. This topic is covered later.

## 6.5 IDENTIFIERS

As in the BASIC language, an *identifier* in FORTRAN is a string of alphabetic or numeric characters, the first of which must be alphabetic. Identifiers are used to name scalar variables, array variables, or user-defined subprograms and are used as part of the FORTRAN language as keywords.

### Keywords

Keywords are used as statement identifiers, separating keywords, and as built-in functions. A *statement identifier* names a statement and specifies the operational function that it performs. Sample statement identifiers are CALL, INTEGER, and WRITE in the following statements:

    CALL INIT2(3HSIN,CAL**2,I)
    INTEGER ALPHA,B,COW
    WRITE (6,9000) DOG,IT,WONDER

A *separating keyword,* such as TO in the following ASSIGN statement:

    ASSIGN 250 TO LTOK

is used to distinguish between constituent parts of a statement and to make the language more readable. *Built-in function* names are defined to be part of the language. For some built-in functions, such as ABS in the following statement:

    I2 = ABS(I1)+300

the compiler recognizes the name and generates appropriate machine code. For others, such as SQRT in the following statement:

    HYP = SQRT(BASE**2+HGT**2)

the compiler generates control information such that the SQRT function is retrieved from the subroutine library when the program is loaded into main storage for execution.

## Variables

Identifiers that name variables may be up to six characters in length, and the same naming conventions apply to scalar and array variables. Each variable has a *type* which may be integer, real, double precision, complex, or logical. The type of a variable may be specified implicitly or explicitly.

Five statements govern type specifications; these are the INTEGER, REAL, DOUBLE PRECISION, COMPLEX, and LOGICAL statements. When a variable is "declared" in a LOGICAL statement, for example, it is of type logical and only logical data items can be stored in the main storage space assigned to that variable. Thus, in the following statements:

```
INTEGER BOW,ITJAM,Z
REAL FOXIT, JELLO, MONKEY, T
DOUBLE PRECISION A,NUB,XEROX
COMPLEX KAM,PULL
LOGICAL P,Q,BOX,WAIT
```

each variable is assigned the type specified by its statement identifier, regardless of the characters that comprise the name of the variable. A given variable may not have two types and may not appear in more than one type statement.

A variable that is not specified in a type statement is assigned a type implicitly. Variable names beginning with the letters I, J, K, L, M, or N are implicitly assigned type integer. All other implicitly defined variables are assigned type real. Thus, in the statements:

```
I=JERK+13
PETE=TOM+1.23E7
```

I and JERK are implicitly defined as type integer and PETE and TOM are implicitly defined as type real, provided that neither of these variables had been specified in a type statement. If any one of the variables had been specified in a type statement, then it would have been assigned a type governed by the statement identifier of the type statement in which it was included. Thus, a type statement overrides the implicit naming conventions.

Double precision, complex, and logical variables must always be defined explicitly.

## Comment on Arrays

An *array* is a collection of data items of the same type that is assigned a single array name. In ASA FORTRAN, an array can have up to three dimensions; however, the restriction seems to be obsolete since most implementations of FORTRAN allow at least seven dimensions. An element of an array is selected with a subscript and can be used in an expression in the same manner that a scalar variable or a constant can be used. The above naming and type conventions apply to array names as well as to scalar variable names.

The topic of arrays is presented as a separate section in Chapter 7.

## 6.6 OPERATORS AND EXPRESSIONS

### Introduction

In a scientifically oriented programming language such as FORTRAN, operators are naturally very important. The emphasis, obviously, is on what an operator means and on how it can be used. Most operators are infix operators of the form:

operand ⊕ operand

where ⊕ is an infix operator and "operand" is a constant, scalar variable, element of an array, function reference, or a value of a subexpression—each in the domain of the infix operator. Three prefix operators are defined: +(identity), −(negation), and .NOT.(complement). A prefix operator is written as:

⊕ operand

where ⊕ is the prefix operator and "operand" is a constant, scalar variable, element of an array, function reference, or value of a subexpression—each in the domain of the prefix operator.

As mentioned previously, operators have a hierarchy and one with a higher priority is executed before one with a lower priority. More generally, however, arithmetic operators, as a class, have a higher priority than comparison operators, which have a higher priority than the logical operators. This convention has an indirect meaning. Only arithmetic operators and arithmetic operands are permitted in an arithmetic expression. A comparison operator, arithmetic operands, and arithmetic operators are permitted in a comparison expression. The arithmetic operations are executed before the comparison operator. Lastly, logical operators, logical operands, comparison operators, arithmetic operands, and arithmetic operators are permitted in logical expressions. Operators are executed in the following order: arithmetic operators, comparison operators, and then logical operators. In other words, arithmetic expressions can be used in comparison expressions which can be used in logical expressions, but the process cannot be reversed.

### Arithmetic Expressions

An arithmetic expression is composed of arithmetic operators and arithmetic operands. (The precise nature of an arithmetic operand is considered later.) At the point in a program that an arithmetic expression is evaluated, the expression has a value that assumes one of the data types mentioned previously, that is, integer, real, double precision, or complex. Moreover, the operands in that expression are restricted to data items of the same type, within the specifications given below. Thus, if I is an integer variable and A and B are real variables, then the arithmetic expression A+B is legal in FORTRAN while the expression I+A is illegal.

The reader will recall that in Chapter 3, only the form of an expression in BASIC was given. As a variation to that approach, this section describes both the form of an arithmetic expression in FORTRAN and its interpretation. This method is consistent with the FORTRAN standard and is similar to the method used to define an arithmetic expression in ALGOL 60.[4]

The following arithmetic operators are used in FORTRAN:

| Prefix or Infix | Name | Symbol | Example | Meaning |
|---|---|---|---|---|
| Infix | Addition | + | A+B | A *plus* B |
| Infix | Subtraction | – | A–B | A *minus* B |
| Infix | Multiplication | * | A*B | A *times* B |
| Infix | Division | / | A/B | A *divided by* B |
| Infix | Exponentiation | ** | A**B | A *power* B (i.e., $A^B$) |
| Prefix | Identity | + | +A | 0+A |
| Prefix | Negation | – | –A | 0–A |

In general, the operators are combined with operands and parentheses to form expressions in the usual manner. Parentheses are used for grouping and expressions in parentheses are executed before operations of which they are an operand.

[4] P. Naur (ed.), "Revised Report on the Algorithmic Language ALGOL 60," *Communications of the ACM*, Vol. 6, No. 1 (January 1963).

The following rules govern the syntheses of arithmetic expressions:[5]

1. The elements of an arithmetic expression are: "primary," "factor," "term," "signed term," "simple arithmetic expression," and "arithmetic expression."
2. A *primary* is an arithmetic expression enclosed in parentheses, an arithmetic constant, a scalar variable, an element of an array, or a function reference.
3. A *factor* is a primary or an expression of the form:

   *factor* ** *primary*

   (This rule specifies that exponentiation has the highest priority since its operands are limited to primaries.)
4. A *term* is a factor or either of the following constructions:

   *term* { *|/ } *factor*

   (This rule states that the multiplicative operators—that is, * and /—have the next highest priority and the order of execution is left to right.)
5. An *arithmetic expression* is a term immediately preceded by a + or a –, that is,

   {+|–} *term*

   or an arithmetic expression followed by a + or a – followed by a term, that is,

   *arithmetic expression* {+|–} *term*

   (This rule states that the additive operators have the lowest priority and that prefix + and prefix – have the same priority as their infix counterparts; the order of execution of additive operators is left to right.)

Thus, in the expression

$$-A+B*C**(D-1)+E$$

---

[5] See the ASA FORTRAN standard, reference [7], p. 11, and the ALGOL report, op. cit. The rules given here are based on the FORTRAN standard and the ALGOL report; the interpretation is that of the author.

A,B,C,(D–1), and E are primaries. C**(D–1) is a factor. B*C**(D–1) is a term as are A and E. Then from left to right, –A is an arithmetic expression to which is added the value of the term B*C**(D–1); lastly, the term E is added to that result. The process of evaluation can be depicted somewhat as follows:

$$-A+B*C**\underbrace{(D-1)}_{1}+E$$

$$\begin{array}{c} -A+B*C**\underbrace{(D-1)}_{1}+E \\ \underbrace{\phantom{C**(D-1)}}_{2} \\ \underbrace{\phantom{B*C**(D-1)}}_{3} \\ \underbrace{\phantom{-A}}_{4} \\ \underbrace{\phantom{-A+B*C**(D-1)}}_{5} \\ \underbrace{\phantom{-A+B*C**(D-1)+E}}_{6} \end{array}$$

Therefore, the expression –3**2 in FORTRAN evaluates to –9. The hierarchy of FORTRAN arithmetic operations is summarized in the following list:

| Operator | Hierarchy |
|---|---|
| ** | highest |
| *,/ | ↓ |
| infix +, infix –, prefix +, prefix – | lowest |

where operators of the same priority are executed from left to right.

The use of operands with different data types (that is, *mixed modes*) is governed by the following operational conventions:

1. A primary of any data type may be raised to an integer power (that is, exponentiated) and the result is of the same data type as the data item being exponentiated.
2. A primary of either the real or double precision data type may be raised to either the real or double precision power. If both operands are real, the result is of the real data type. Otherwise, the result is double precision.
3. Only exponentiation that is covered by rules (1) and (2) is defined.
4. For arithmetic operators other than exponentiation, operands must have the same data type except that a real operand may be combined with a complex or double precision operand and the result is complex or double precision, respectively.

Practically, the following rules apply:

1. Two operators may not appear in succession, for example, A*–B. A prefix operator may only be used at the beginning of an expression (for example, –A*B) or following a left parenthesis (for example, A*(–B).
2. In FORTRAN A**B**C means (A**B)**C which may not be the intended order of evaluation. Remember, $(a^b)^c$ does not necessarily equal $a^{(b^c)}$. For example, $(2^3)^2 = 64$, whereas $2^{(3^2)} = 512$.
3. A negative quantity may not be raised to a real power. This restriction, in most implementations of FORTRAN, is caused by the fact that a power series expansion is used to approximate exponentiation with a real exponent.

Ordinarily, the above operational conventions cause no difficulty and arithmetic expressions are written directly from the corresponding mathematical notation. The biggest problem is mixing data types, especially where constants are used. This is precisely the reason why many extensions to ASA standard FORTRAN permit mixed-mode expressions.

### Comparison Expressions

A *comparison expression* is used to compare two arithmetic values for use in a logical expression. The result of a comparison expression is one of the truth values, "true" or "false." A comparison expression consists of a pair of arithmetic expressions separated by a comparison operator, as follows:[6]

arith-expression{ .LT.|.LE.|.EQ.|.NE.|.GT.|.GE.}arith-expression

where "arith-expression" is an arithmetic expression, as defined above, subject to the following restrictions:

1. If one "arithmetic expression" is of type real or double precision, the other must be of type real or double precision. If mixed real and double precision operands are used, then the real operand is converted to double precision.
2. If one operand is of type integer, then the other must be of type integer.

---

[6]Comparison operators are listed in Table 6.2.

3. No other operands are permitted in comparison operations.

These rules reflect the ASA standard, which is unnecessarily restrictive. Most implementations additionally allow complex operands to be compared for equality. The following are valid comparison expressions (where A, B, and C are real; I, J, and K are integer; and E, F, and G are double precision):

A+B .GT. 25.3
I .EQ. J+1
A .LT. G**2
A*(E+C) .GE. F
A+B*C .LE. (F+G)**2

In all cases, the arithmetic operands are evaluated before the comparison operation is executed.

### Logical Expressions

A logical expression is used for decision making, with the logical IF statement, and to assign a truth value to a logical variable. A *logical expression* is formed from logical operands, logical operators, and parentheses and returns a truth value to the point of reference. As usual, parentheses are used for grouping. Logical infix operators are .AND. (meaning logical conjunction) and .OR. (meaning logical disjunction). The logical prefix operator is .NOT., meaning logical complement.

The following rules govern the synthesis of logical expressions:

1. A *logical operand* (that is, a logical element) is a "logical primary," a "logical factor," a "logical term," and a "logical expression."
2. A *logical primary* is a logical expression enclosed in parentheses, a comparison expression, a logical constant, a logical scalar variable, an element of a logical array, or a logical function reference.
3. A *logical factor* is a logical primary or the prefix operator .NOT. followed by a logical primary, that is,

   .NOT. *logical-primary*

   (This rule states that .NOT. has the highest priority and its operand is limited to a logical primary.)

4. A *logical term* is a logical factor or an expression of the form:

    *logical-term* .AND. *logical-factor*

(This rule states that .AND. has the next highest priority and that successive .AND. operations are executed from left to right.)

5. A *logical expression* is a logical term or an expression of the form:

    *logical-expression* .OR. *logical-term*

(This rule states that .OR. has the lowest priority; successive .OR. operations are also executed from left to right.)

Thus, in the expression (where P, Q, and R are logical variables):

    .NOT. XLO .LT. YES .AND. (P .OR. Q) .OR. (A+B)\*\*2.EQ.C .AND. R

the following are logical primaries:

| | |
|---|---|
| XLO.LT.YES | *Comparison expression* |
| (P .OR. Q) | *Logical expression in parentheses* |
| (A+B)\*\*2.EQ.C | *Comparison expression* |
| R | *Logical scalar variable* |

.NOT. XLO.LT. YES is a logical factor. .NOT. XLO .LT. YES .AND. (P.OR.Q) and (A+B)\*\*2.EQ.C .AND. R are logical terms and the entire expression (that is, the two logical terms separated by .OR.) is a logical expression.

The process of evaluation is depicted conceptually as follows:

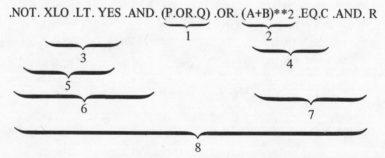

Clearly, the order of evaluation of logical operators is .NOT. followed by .AND. followed by .OR.

**Comments on Expressions**

Table 6.3 lists the hierarchy of FORTRAN operators. The most straightforward approach to the evaluation of expressions is to list the operators and their hierarchies and to simply state that higher priority operators are executed before those with a lower priority. The approach taken here avoids the use of a hierarchy table and a left-to-right rule for operators of the same priority and exists as a variation to the other method. The end result is obviously the same.

The curious reader has probably wondered if the order of evaluation is important when operators are commutative or associative. Clearly, the above rules specify that the order of evaluation for operators of the same priority is left to right. Actually, this is a slight departure from the FORTRAN standard and is based upon actual implementation experience and the ALGOL report. The left-to-right rule is necessary for integer operations and is always a "correct" method of evaluation for all expressions. The FORTRAN standard actually allows more flexibility as stated in the following quotation:[7]

> When two elements are combined by an operator, the order of evaluation of the elements is optional. If mathematical use of operators is associative, commutative, or both, full use of these facts may be made to revise orders of combination, provided only that integrity of parenthesized expressions is not violated. . . . The associative and commutative laws do not apply in the evaluation of integer terms containing division, hence the evaluation of such terms must effectively proceed from left to right.

## 6.7 STRUCTURE OF STATEMENTS

The structure of a statement in FORTRAN involves two considerations: statement format and actual statement structure. Statement format involves the conventions for entering a statement into the computer and for labeling a statement. Statement structure involves the manner in which statements are constructed.

**Statement Format**

A *line* in FORTRAN is a string of 72 characters usually taken as columns 1-72 of a punched card or the first 72 characters of a data record. The characters in a line are numbered consecutively as 1,2,...,72 and are referred to as such, reading

[7]See the ASA FORTRAN standard, reference [7], p. 12.

Table 6.3

Hierarchy of FORTRAN Operators

| Operator | Hierarchy |
|---|---|
| ** | Highest |
| *,/ | |
| prefix +, prefix –, infix +, infix – | |
| .GT.,.GE.,.EQ.,.NE.,.LE.,.LT. | |
| .NOT. | |
| .AND. | |
| .OR. | Lowest |

from left to right. A line can represent a FORTRAN statement, a continuation to a FORTRAN statement, or a comment.

The first line of a FORTRAN statement is referred to as an "initial line." An *initial line* is characterized by the fact that it is not a comment line (see below) and that column 6 is either zero or blank. Columns 1 through 5 of an initial line can contain the statement number of the statement (also covered below) or must be blank. The actual FORTRAN statement is contained in columns 7 through 72 and most statements are entered as a single line. A statement can be continued on up to 19 continuation lines. A *continuation line* is characterized by the fact that it is not a comment line and that column 6 contains a nonblank nonzero character. Frequently, column 6 is used to order continuation lines. However, the magnitude of the character in column 6 (if it is a numeral) is ignored by the language processor and the physical position of a continuation line in a program deck determines the logical order of continuation lines. A continuation line must follow an initial line or another continuation line.

A *comment line* has the character C in column 1 and is ignored by the compiler; it may be used by the programmer to place remarks in a program. A comment line must be followed by another comment line or an initial line. A program unit cannot end with a comment line.

The last line in a program must be an initial line with the characters END in columns 7 through 72. Columns 1 through 6 of the END line must be blank and columns 7 through 72 must contain only the characters E, N, D, in that order, or be blank.

Blank characters are ignored in the statement portion of a line—except in Hollerith literals.

A *FORTRAN statement* is placed in columns 7 through 72 of a line and consists of an initial line followed by up to 19 continuation lines. A statement can be given a *statement number* so that it can be referred to in other statements. A statement number consists of from one to five digits placed in columns one through five of the initial line of a statement. A statement number is only a label; thus, the value of the statement number is not significant and statement numbers need not be ordered. Some necessary conventions on the use of statement numbers exist: (1) A statement number must not be zero; (2) the same statement number may not be assigned to more than one statement; and (3) leading zeros in a statement number are not used in distinguishing between statement numbers.

Usually, statements in FORTRAN are assigned a statement number only when they are to be referred to in another statement. However, this is not a necessary condition.

### Statement Structure

A statement is a string of characters formed by concatenating the characters in columns 7 through 72 of the initial and continuation lines. A statement has the following structure:

statement-identifier | statement-body | statement-identifier statement-body

where "statement-identifier" is a keyword that identifies a particular type of statement and "statement-body" is a series of characters that comprise the body of the statement. From the statement format, it is obvious that a statement can be composed of a statement identifier, a statement body, or both. A statement without a statement identifier is the assignment statement. A statement may not be blank. The following are valid FORTRAN statements:

| | |
|---|---|
| READ(5,9010),A,BETA,IFIX | (1) |
| GOTO 150 | (2) |
| END | (3) |
| A=B+C | (4) |

In statement (1), READ is the statement identifier and the remainder of the statement is the statement body. In statement (2), GOTO is the statement identifier and 150, which is the statement body, refers to the statement number of another statement in that program. Statement (3) depicts an END statement that does not require a statement body. Statement (4) is the assignment statement; it does not use a statement identifier.

## 6.8  PROGRAM STRUCTURE

As with the BASIC language, a FORTRAN program is composed of a series of statements that are executed sequentially until a statement is executed that terminates execution of the program or a statement, such as GOTO or IF, is executed that alters the sequential flow of execution. Conceptually, the complete program is compiled into machine language and loaded into the computer before any of it is executed.

### Operating Environment

FORTRAN is conveniently described with respect to a batch-processing environment, as presented in section 1.6. A program is compiled and executed using a deck setup similar to the one depicted in Figure 1.13.

Whereas in BASIC, a program is composed of a series of statements the last of which is an END statement, in FORTRAN, a program is a set of "program units" that are compiled independently and combined along with library subprograms when the program is loaded into the computer for execution.

### Elements of Program Structure

A *program unit* is a main program or a subprogram; a *subprogram* can be the subroutine type or the function type. Although subprograms are presented in detail later, the following general structure is given:

| *Subroutine Structure* | *Function Structure* |
|---|---|
| SUBROUTINE... | FUNCTION... |
| [body of subroutine] | [body of function] |
| END | END |

Thus, a subprogram begins with either a SUBROUTINE or FUNCTION header statement and ends with an END statement, and as mentioned, it is compiled individually. A *main program* has no header statement but ends with an END statement. A FORTRAN program consists of a main program and zero or more subprograms. There must be only one main program and when the program is loaded for execution, the main program is executed. (A main program in FORTRAN corresponds to a complete program in BASIC.) Subprograms are invoked with either a function reference or a CALL statement, depending upon the type of subprogram being called, in an executing program unit.

The FORTRAN language has restrictions on the form of a program unit—remembering that it can be a main program or a subprogram. This structure is presented through a set of definitions. A *program part* is a set of the following FORTRAN statements: executable statements, FORMAT statements, and data initialization statements. A program part must contain at least one executable statement and the executable statements, which comprise the program part, may be optionally preceded by statement function definitions, data initialization statements, and FORMAT statements. (Each of these constituents is described later.) In fact, FORMAT statements may be interspersed in the program part. A *program body* is a set of specification statements (such as REAL or INTEGER) followed by a program part, followed by an END statement. More formally, then, the following definitions can be made:

1. A main program consists of a program body.
2. A subroutine consists of a SUBROUTINE statement followed by a program body.
3. A function consists of a FUNCTION statement followed by a program body.
4. An executable program consists of a main program and any number of subroutines, functions, or library subprograms.

Except for a BLOCK DATA subprogram, which is used to initialize COMMON storage, the above description is a complete description of program structure. The significance of these concepts in addition to other topics is presented in subsequent chapters.

### Example of Program Structure

This section gives an example of a FORTRAN program consisting of three program units—a main program, a subroutine, and a function. The program reads a list of real numbers, sorts them, and computes the average of the list. One built-in function is used; it is the FLOAT function that converts an argument from an integer data item to a real data item.

```
C     MAIN PROGRAM TO READ AND PRINT LIST OF VALUES
C
      REAL VALUES(100)
      READ (5,9000) N
```

```
      READ (5,9010)(VALUE(I),I=1,N)
9000 FORMAT (I3)
9010 FORMAT (10F8.3)
C
C     PRINT ORIGINAL LIST OF VALUES
C
      WRITE(6,9020)(VALUES(I),I=1,N)
9020 FORMAT(14 H ORIGINAL LIST/(10F10.3))
C
C     CALL SORT SUBROUTINE TO ORDER LIST OF VALUES
C
      CALL SORT (VALUES,N)
C
C     PRINT SORTED LIST OF VALUES
C
      WRITE(6,9030)(VALUES(I), I=1,N)
9030 FORMAT(11H SORTED LIST/(10F10.3))
C
C     COMPUTE AVERAGE USING FUNCTION SUBPROGRAM
C
      X=AVER(VALUES,N)
C
C     PRINT AVERAGE AND STOP
C
      WRITE(6,9040) X
9040 FORMAT(10H AVERAGE=, F12.3)
      STOP
      END
      SUBROUTINE SORT (A,N)
      REAL A(N)
      INTEGER F
      NN=N-1
10    F=0
      DO 50 I=1,NN,2
         IF (A(I).LE.A(I+1)) GOTO 50
         T=A(I)
         A(I)=A(I+1)
         A(I+1)=T
         F=1
```

```
50    CONTINUE
      DO 100 I=2,NN,2
         IF (A(I).LE.A(I+1)) GOTO 100
         T=A(I)
         A(I)=A(I+1)
         A(I+1)=T
         F=1
100   CONTINUE
      IF (F.EQ.0) RETURN
      GO TO 10
      END

      FUNCTION AVER(DUM,NUM)
      REAL DUM(NUM)
      SUM=0.0
      DO 10 I=1,NUM
10    SUM=SUM+DUM(I)
      AVER=SUM/FLOAT(NUM)
      RETURN
      END
```

Input:[8]

```
  28.12    6.20    -14.00    10.08    5.10

5
```

Output:

```
ORIGINAL LIST
   28.120    6.200    -14.000    10.080    5.100

SORTED LIST
   -14.000    5.100    6.200    10.080    28.120

AVERAGE = 7.10
```

[8]Input and output characters are not formatted precisely.

Many important features of FORTRAN have not been discussed. For example, in the READ statement:

READ(5,9000)N

which obviously causes data to be read from an input unit, the number 5 identifies a specific input unit and 9000 gives the statement number of the FORMAT statement used to control the input editing operation. Similarly, the statements:

DO *m* I=1,N
_____
_____
_____
*m* _____

comprise a program loop where I is the control variable and the body of the loop is the set of statements following the DO up to and including the statement numbered *m*. However, an overall view of FORTRAN is important here; the details are covered in Chapters 7 and 8.

The above program is depicted structurally in Figure 6.1 where the relationship between the program parts is shown.

## EXERCISES

1. Write the following FORTRAN real constants in ordinary decimal notation:

   (a) 2E5
   (b) .104E–6
   (c) .28164E+01
   (d) .4E0

2. Write the following real numbers as FORTRAN real constants using an exponent:

   (a) $5.15 \times 10^{17}$
   (b) 1.369
   (c) .00003629
   (d) 651382.

3. Explain what is meant by the statement, "The magnitude and precision of a

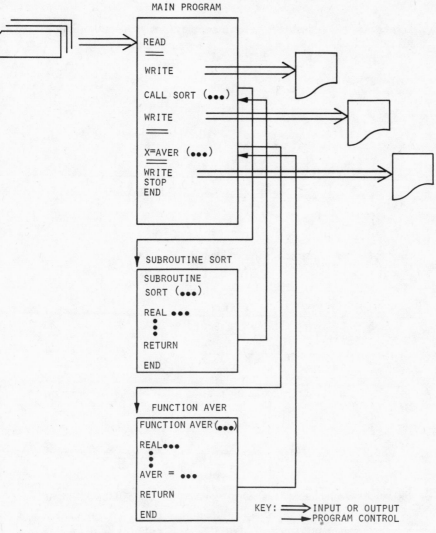

MAIN PROGRAM

READ

WRITE

CALL SORT (•••)

WRITE

X=AVER (•••)

WRITE
STOP
END

SUBROUTINE SORT

SUBROUTINE
SORT (•••)

REAL •••

RETURN

END

FUNCTION AVER

FUNCTION AVER(•••)

REAL•••

AVER = •••

RETURN

END

KEY: ⟹ INPUT OR OUTPUT
→ PROGRAM CONTROL

Fig. 6.1. Example of FORTRAN program structure.

real data item are determined by the size of the exponent and fraction, respectively, of the floating-point format used in storing the numbers."

4. Using the implicit naming conventions, identify integer, real, and illegal variable names:

| | | |
|---|---|---|
| (a) IDENT | (e) KOUNT | (i) 2IT |
| (b) QUOT | (f) PRODUCT | (j) WRITE |
| (c) XYZ | (g) IO | (k) DIMENSION |
| (d) E7 | (h) W123 | (l) IF |

5. If I=5, and J=2, evaluate the following expressions in the integer mode:

   (a) I/J+2
   (b) 2*I/J
   (c) I/J*2

6. Write FORTRAN expressions for the following mathematical expressions:

   (a) $\dfrac{x^3 + y^2}{3}$

   (b) $a + bx$
   (c) $a^2x - b^3y + abz$

7. Give the sequence in which the following FORTRAN expressions are evaluated:

   (a) (Q/R+S)**2-(WT-4.1)*(-P)
   (b) X**2+B*X .GT. 13.1 .AND. Q
   (c) A**B**I-3.0*W*Z
   (d) .NOT. 2.1*T**(J-1) .LT. X/Y .OR. A.GT.B

8. Write the following complex numbers as FORTRAN complex constants:

   (a) $3i$
   (b) $4 + 5i$
   (c) $11.1 + 0i$

9. Flowchart a procedure designed to read and classify FORTRAN input lines as to whether they are initial lines, continuation lines, comment lines, or the END statement. Concatenate initial and continuation lines to form a complete statement.
10. Distinguish between a program part, a program body, and a program unit.

# 7

# FORTRAN LANGUAGE FACILITIES

## 7.1  INTRODUCTION

This chapter follows the pattern established in Chapter 4 where the most frequently used statements in the BASIC language are presented. The language here, of course, is FORTRAN. Relatively simple topics are covered in their entirety. More complex topics are introduced in this chapter and continued in Chapter 8. Thus, Chapters 6 and 7 present a working knowledge of FORTRAN. Chapter 8 extends the capability of the user by covering more advanced topics.

This chapter, as well as Chapter 8, is less pedagogical than Chapters 4 and 5 for two reasons: (1) The need does not exist since the reader is now more experienced with the subject matter; and (2) FORTRAN is a more extensive language than BASIC and the chapter would become lengthy and tedious. Also, at this point, it is hoped that the reader is becoming more interested in programming languages, per se, than in what is usually done with them.

## 7.2  INPUT AND OUTPUT

Input and output is performed for several reasons: (1) To enter data into the computer for processing; (2) to output results in a form suitable for printing; and (3) to store large amounts of information on a temporary or permanent basis. In the latter case, information may be placed on a mass storage medium because it is too voluminous to occupy main storage; or information may be placed on a mass storage medium between distinct runs on the computer. A temporary file used during a sort operation is an example of the former case; a payroll master file is an example of the latter case.

### System Input and Output

Every job that is run on the computer has a system input device and a system output device. Usually, the *system input device* corresponds to the input job stream and allows the user to read the input data that accompanies the program deck. The *system output device* usually corresponds to the line printer and data written to the system output device is formatted for printing. In FORTRAN, each input and output device is assigned a number by the computer installation. The system input device number is frequently 5; the system output device number is frequently 6. These numbers are used here although they may vary at any given installation.

The actual devices are not important. For example, the system input device is sometimes a card reader, sometimes a magnetic tape, and sometimes a magnetic disk. Similarly, the system output device can be a line printer, a magnetic tape, or a magnetic disk. All one needs to know is that input cards are placed on the system input device and lines written to the system output device are printed with the aid of the operating system control programs using the installation's operational procedures.

All input and output devices that are recognized in ASA FORTRAN are sequential and data is read and written consecutively. When a magnetic disk is used, the input and output routines of the operating system use it as a sequential device. Some advanced versions of FORTRAN permit direct-access data files to be defined for use with direct-access devices. This technique is not, at this time, a standard feature in FORTRAN and is not covered here.

### Formatted and Unformatted Data Transmission

Formatted input and output is used for reading source data, for displaying printed information, and for storing information in an external form—such as BCD. As depicted in Figure 1.7, data is edited during both the input and output processes and is stored (in main storage) in a computational (or binary) form. Unformatted output and input is used to store information on a storage medium in an internal form (that is, a computational or binary form) and to retrieve that information without having to go through the editing process, which takes computer time.

Formatted input and output uses a FORMAT statement that describes the external appearance of the data. Input and output is performed by subroutines that are supplied by the FORTRAN compiler and/or the operating system. An input operation is used as an example. The READ statement is compiled into a call to an input subroutine; the list of data variables to be read and the format specification are supplied as arguments with the subroutine call. The input subroutine reads a data record, converts the data items to internal form using the format statement, and places the results in main storage in the locations assigned to the variables. Program control then returns to the statement following the READ statement. The process is reversed for formatted output.

Figure 7.1 depicts the process of doing formatted input and output. The following comments are useful for understanding Figure 7.1:

1. I format is used for integer data.
2. F format is used for real data without an exponent.
3. X format means "skip characters."
4. H format is used to include Hollerith (that is, literal) data.
5. The first character of the printed line is used for carriage control. (In the example, 1Hɓ, where ɓ means the blank character, places a blank character in column 1 of the output record and single spacing is used for that line.)
6. Except for X and H formats, a one-to-one correspondence exists between format items and variables.

Obviously, Figure 7.1 and the above discussion is simply an overview. The objec-

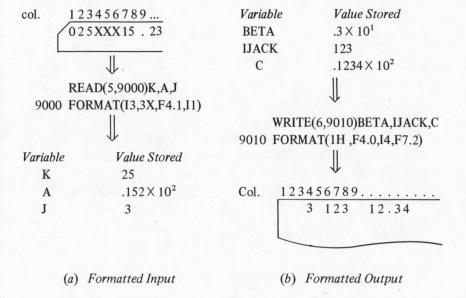

(a) Formatted Input       (b) Formatted Output

Fig. 7.1. Conceptual view of formatted input and output.

tive of the chapter is to present the information in more detail. Unformatted input and output is covered in Chapter 8.

## The READ and WRITE Statements

The READ statement causes data to be transferred from an external storage medium to main storage under format control. The form of the READ statement is:

> READ(unit,format)[list]

where "unit" is an integer variable or an integer constant specifying an input device number and "format" is the statement number of a FORMAT statement or is a "character" array name. (The use of a "character" array as a format is considered as an advanced topic in Chapter 8.) The "list" is optional. It specifies the names of variables, elements of an array, and arrays to which values are assigned. A list is defined as follows:

1. A *simple list* is a scalar variable, an element of an array, an array name, or two simple lists separated by a comma.
2. A *DO-implied list*[1] is a list, followed by a comma, followed by an implied DO specification of the form:

   $i = m_1, m_2 [,m_3]$

   where $i$ is an integer variable and $m_1$, $m_2$, and $m_3$ are integer values (that is, an integer constant or an integer variable). A DO-implied list means that the list is "effectively copied" where $i$ takes on the values $m_1$ to $m_2$ in increments of $m_3$. If $m_3$ is elided, then it is assumed to be one. A DO-implied list is enclosed in parentheses to denote the scope of the specification. Examples follow.
3. A *list* is a simple list, a simple list enclosed in parentheses, a DO-implied list, or two lists separated by a comma.

An example of a READ statement with a simple list is:

READ(5,8193)COW,AL2,JABBER,T

---

[1] The meaning of the terminology "DO-implied" will become obvious when the subject of looping is presented.

An example of a DO-implied list is:

READ(5,9000) (A(I),I=1,5)

where A is a one-dimensional array. This DO-implied list is equivalent to:

READ(5,9000) A(1),A(2),A(3),A(4),A(5)

The increment in the implied DO can be used to specify nonconsecutive array elements, such as:

READ(5,9005)(DOG(JJ),JJ=2,N,2)

which specifies the elements of array DOG with even-numbered subscripts. The above definition of a list also states that implied DOs can be nested, as shown in the following example:

READ(5,9010) ((A(I,J),J=1,2),I=1,3)

which is equivalent to:

READ(5,9010) A(1,1),A(1,2),A(2,1),A(2,2),A(3,1),A(3,2)

Note that the inner implied DO list is executed first. Lastly, the various forms of lists can be used in combination as stated in the definition; as an example, consider the statement:

READ(5,9020)N,(A(K2),K2=1,N,2),PETE(I+1,N1)

where the value read in for variable N is used in the next list element.

Lists are a good example of the importance of formal definitions. It would be ridiculous to attempt to list all of the forms that a list could take. However, a formal definition in a few short rules can define all possible forms.

The READ statement is rarely used without a list—but it can be. It can be used to read in a Hollerith literal for use in a subsequent WRITE statement (which, for now, takes the same general form as READ); this case is depicted in Figure 7.2.

The WRITE statement causes data to be transferred from main storage to an external storage medium under format control. The form of the WRITE statement is:

> WRITE(unit,format)[list]

where "unit," "format," and "list" are defined the same as for the READ statement. An example of the WRITE statement is:

> WRITE(6,7070)NIL,A(3),(WOW(I),I=1,3)
> 7070 FORMAT(1H ,I5,F10.4,3F12.6)

It should be remembered that the READ and WRITE statements in FORTRAN are used to transfer data between an external storage medium (such as the card reader, magnetic tape, disk, or the line printer) and main storage. The READ statement in FORTRAN should be distinguished from the READ statement in BASIC. Although they both perform an input function, the READ statement in BASIC reads from an internal data file constructed with DATA statements.

### The Record Concept

FORTRAN reads records and writes records. Each execution of a READ statement causes the next record to be read from the specified input unit. The amount of data that is taken from the record is determined by the input list. Excess data is ignored. If insufficient data exists to satisfy the input list, then an error condition is generated and execution of the program is terminated in most versions of FORTRAN. Each execution of a WRITE statement causes a record to be written to the specified device. The amount of data that is written is governed collectively by the output list and the FORMAT statement. When the output list is satisfied, the output record is complete, regardless of whether unused field descriptors exist in the format specification.

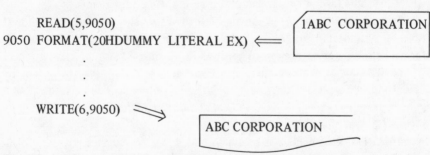

Fig. 7.2. A program segment showing how a Hollerith literal can be used to read in descriptive information.

## The FORMAT Statement and Field Descriptors

The FORMAT statement is used with formatted input and output statements to permit conversion and data editing under the user's direction. The FORMAT statement is the only statement that requires a statement number since it must be specified in an appropriate input or output statement. The form of the FORMAT statement is:

$$m \ \text{FORMAT}(q_1 t_1 z_1 t_2 z_2 \dots t_n z_n q_2)$$

where:

1. $m$ is the statement number.
2. $(q_1 t_1 z_1 t_2 z_2 \dots t_n z_n q_2)$ is the format specification.
3. Each $q$ is a series of slashes or is empty.
4. Each $t$ is a field descriptor or a series of field descriptors.
5. Each $z$ is a field separator (comma, slash, series of slashes, or parentheses).
6. $n$ may be zero—in other words, there may be no field descriptor.

A sample FORMAT statement is:

9000 FORMAT(I3,3F12.6/(I2,10I4))

where I3, F12.6, I2 and I4 are field descriptors that correspond on a one-to-one basis with a variable in an input or output list. The 3 before the F12.6 is a repetition factor; thus, 3F12.6 is equivalent to F12.6,F12.6,F12.6. The slash (/) means that the input or output routine should go to the next record. The parentheses around I2,10I4, that is (I2,10I4), is used when the input or output list is not complete but the format specification is exhausted. The input or output routine returns to the first open parenthesis in the FORMAT statement. (When an input or output routine returns to the first open parenthesis in a FORMAT statement, it automatically goes to the next input or output record.) If, for example, a user has a long input or output list and desires to read six values from each input record, he might use statements such as:

READ(5,9500)(A(I),I=1,1000)
9500 FORMAT(6F12.5)

The repetition factor can also be applied to a parenthesized list of field descriptors. Thus, 3(I4,F10.2) is equivalent to I4,F10.2,I4,F10.2,I4,F10.2. It is *important to recognize* that 3(I4,F10.2) is *not* equivalent to I4,I4,I4,F10.2,F10.2, F10.2.

A working set of field descriptors and separators is given in this section. Others are covered later.

The *I field descriptor* is used for conversion between an internal integer data item and an external integer in decimal form. The form of an I format specification is:

I*w*

where *w* is the size of the external field, including blanks and a sign. On output, the sign is printed only if the number is negative. A decimal point is not permitted in an input field. For example, on input, the external values ƀƀ12, ƀ621ƀ, and −ƀ210ƀ using format specifications I4, I5, and I6, respectively, cause the values 12, 6210, and −2100 to be stored. For output, the values −987 and 123 using format specifications I5 and I4, respectively, cause the following fields:

ƀ−987 and ƀ123

to be generated.

For all numeric input conversions, leading blanks are ignored and all trailing blanks are treated as zeros. An all-blank field is regarded as zero. For all output conversions, the output field is right justified. Leading blanks are supplied, as required.

The *F field descriptor* is used for conversion between an internal real data item and an external real number in decimal form without an exponent. The form of an F field descriptor is:

F*w.d*

where *w* is the width of the field, including blanks, the sign, and the decimal point and *d* is the number of places to the right of the decimal point. On *input,* use of the decimal point is optional. If the decimal point is not used on input, then the rightmost *d* digits in the field are interpreted as decimal places. If the decimal point is used with input data, then it overrides *d*. On *output,* the decimal point is always generated with *d* decimal places to the right of it. Thus, with F field descriptor F6.2, the following input values achieve the same result (where ƀ denotes the blank character):

ƀƀ−123     ƀ−1.23     −1.230     −1.23ƀ

and cause the value $-.123 \times 10^1$ to be placed in main storage. On output, for example, the values $.98134 \times 10^2$ and $-.63472 \times 10^1$ are converted using field descriptors F7.2 and F8.3, respectively, so that the values

¢¢98.13 and ¢¢–6.347

are generated.

As implied previously, a field separator is used between field descriptors. A *comma* is simply used to separate distinct field descriptors. For example, the following descriptors:

F20.12I4

could be interpreted as F20.12 and I4 or F20.1 and 2I4. This is a case where a comma is needed. In other cases, it is used mainly for readability. The *slash* (/) causes the input or output routine to go to the next record so that for output, $n$ slashes in succession generate $n-1$ blank lines. As an example of the use of the slash for input, suppose it were desired to read a value N with I4 format from a single card and then read N values from subsequent cards in format F12.6 with six values per card. The following statements would be used:

        REAL A(100)
        READ (5,9000) N,(A(I),I=1,N)
   9000 FORMAT (I4/(6F12.6))

The example depicts the use of a slash to go to the next card, a repetition factor, and a return to the first open parenthesis.

The *H field descriptor* is used for Hollerith data, as described previously with regard to READ and WRITE statements without a list. An H field descriptor has the following format:

$n$HXXX...X

      $n$ characters

where $n$ is an unsigned integer constant that denotes the number of Hollerith characters that comprise the Hollerith literal; the $n$ characters from the FORTRAN alphabet follow the H. The H field descriptor is most frequently used for printing comments and headings and does not require a corresponding variable in the input or output list, as demonstrated in the following example:

```
              K=10
              ...
              WRITE(6,9010)K
         9000 FORMAT(13H THE ANSWER =,I5)
```

that would generate the following output:

```
    THE ANSWER =      10
```

The *X field descriptor* is used to *skip characters* on the external medium during input or output. The format of the X field descriptor is:

   *n*X

where *n* is an unsigned integer constant that denotes the number of characters to be skipped. For input, *n* character positions of the input record are skipped, regardless of their contents. For example, if columns 1-8 of an input record contained an integer value to be read into KAT and columns 14-25 contained a real value to be read into RAT, then the following FORMAT and READ statements would be used:

```
              READ(5,9030)KAT,RAT
         9030 FORMAT(I8,5X,F12.5)
```

For output, the output record for formatted output is initially filled with blanks. Data fields are moved into the output record from left to right as conversions and editing are performed under format control. Use of the X field descriptor simply moves a pointer the indicated number of positions to the right, resulting in blank characters in the output record. Thus, if it were desired to output the values of JOHN and JIM separated by 12 blank characters, the following FORMAT and WRITE statements might be used:

```
              WRITE(6,9040)JOHN,JIM
         9040 FORMAT(I5,12X,I5)
```

**Carriage Control**

Frequently, the eventual disposition of output data written to an output device is the line printer. In fact, this is always the case with the system output device. Formatted data written to an output device exists as a set of records; each record is composed of characters. When information in this form is printed, the first character is used for carriage control and is not printed. The following standard for interpretation of the first character of each printed record is established:

| Character | Vertical Spacing Before Printing of That Line |
|-----------|-----------------------------------------------|
| Blank | One line |
| 0 | Two lines |
| 1 | To first line of next page |
| + | No advance (overprint of last line) |

It is always best for the user to *explicitly* take care of the first character of each record to be printed. For example, to have the values of JOHN and JIM printed, the user should use statements similar to the following:

```
      WRITE(6,9050)JOHN,JIM
9050 FORMAT(1H ,2I5)
```

that is, if the user desired single spacing. Users sometimes use an oversized field width for the first field descriptor in a format specification to obtain a blank in column one, as follows:

```
      JOE=10
      WRITE(6,9060)JOE
9060 FORMAT(I4)
```

which is essentially the same as

```
      JOE=10
      WRITE(6,9070)JOE
9070 FORMAT(1H ,I3)
```

If the nature of the output data is not known, however, surprises are frequently the result. For example, the statements:

```
      JIL=123
      WRITE(6,9080)JIL
9080 FORMAT(I3)
```

would cause a 1 to be placed in column one. The result: the carriage would be ejected and the 1 would not be printed.

If, on the other hand, the user desired to print on the top of a page (that is, eject the page), he would use statements such as:

> WRITE(6,9090)
> 9090 FORMAT(1H1,20X,15HTITLE OF REPORT)

The other carriage control characters are used in a similar fashion.

## Comments on Other Input and Output Facilities in FORTRAN

As promised, there is more to come on this complex subject, which is better in small doses. Field descriptors for logical, double precision, and character data have not been presented, in addition to data files, unformatted input and output, and relevant control statements. Other field descriptors for real data also exist. However, the preceding information should enable the user to utilize FORTRAN effectively. In general, input and output is a complicated topic and the facilities in FORTRAN are a good introduction to it.

## 7.3 ASSIGNMENT STATEMENTS

The "workhorse" of the FORTRAN language is the assignment statement; it is defined to have two forms: arithmetic assignment and logical assignment. Arithmetic assignment also permits type conversion under some circumstances.

### Arithmetic Assignment

The arithmetic assignment statement is used to assign the value of an arithmetic expression to an arithmetic variable. The form of the arithmetic assignment statement is:

> | arithmetic-variable = arithmetic-expression |

where "arithmetic-variable" is a scalar arithmetic variable or an element of an arithmetic array and "arithmetic-expression" is an arithmetic expression, defined previously, that is evaluated at the point of reference using the current values of the operands of which the expression is composed. The following sets of statements compute identical values for D:

| | |
|---|---|
| A=10. | A=10. |
| B=20. | B=20. |
| C=A+B | C=A+B |
| D=C+1. | A=30. |
| | B=40. |
| | D=C+1. |

During assignment, only the value of the variable to the left of the equal sign is changed and variable references that are part of the expression retain their original values.

FORTRAN allows a type conversion "across the equals sign," to a limited extent. For example, the following statement is valid (where A is a real variable):

A=10

and is interpreted to mean: (1) Take the integer constant 10, stored as an integer fixed-point value, and convert it to a floating-point value; and (2) replace the value of A with the result. Similarly, the statement (where I is an integer variable):

I=13.4

is interpreted to mean: (1) Take the real constant 13.4, stored as a floating-point value, and convert it to an integer fixed-point value; and (2) replace the value of I with the result. The reader should recall that mixed-mode expressions, such as (where A is real and I is integer):

10 + 13.4
I + A
I + 13.4
A + 10

are illegal in standard FORTRAN. Type conversion during assignment also applies when an intermediate result is computed, as in the following set of statements (where A is real and I and J are integer):

I=5
J=6
A=I+J

that are interpreted to mean: (1) Assign integer constant 5 to integer variable I;

(2) assign integer constant 6 to integer variable J; (3) add the value of integer variable I to the value of integer variable J; (4) convert the intermediate result from an integer fixed-point value to a floating-point value; and (5) replace the value of floating-point variable A with the floating-point result.

Table 7.1 lists the conversion rules for type conversion during arithmetic assignment. The only combinations that are illegal are those that involve either a variable or an expression that is of type COMPLEX.

Table 7.1

Type Conversion Rules for Arithmetic Assignment of the Form V=E

| Type of V | Type of E | Conversion Rule |
|---|---|---|
| Integer | Integer | Assign |
| Integer | Real | Convert to fixed-point and assign |
| Integer | Double precision | Convert to fixed-point and assign |
| Integer | Complex | Illegal |
| Real | Integer | Convert to floating-point and assign |
| Real | Real | Assign |
| Real | Double precision | Truncate double precision to real and assign |
| Real | Complex | Illegal |
| Double precision | Integer | Convert to floating-point double precision and assign |
| Double precision | Real | Extend to floating-point double precision and assign |
| Double precision | Double precision | Assign |
| Double precision | Complex | Illegal |
| Complex | Integer | Illegal |
| Complex | Real | Illegal |
| Complex | Double precision | Illegal |
| Complex | Complex | Assign |

## Logical Assignment

The logical assignment statement is used to assign the true or false value of a logical expression to a logical variable. Logical assignment takes the form:

```
logical-variable = logical-expression
```

where "logical-variable" is a scalar LOGICAL variable or an element of a LOGICAL array and "logical-expression" is a logical expression, defined previously, that is evaluated at the point of reference using the current values of the operands of which the expression is composed. The following are valid logical assignment statements:

| | |
|---|---|
| LOGICAL P,Q,R,T | (1) |
| REAL A,B,C | (2) |
| INTEGER I,J,K | (3) |
| P=.TRUE. | (4) |
| Q=A.GT.B | (5) |
| R=I.EQ.J.AND.Q | (6) |
| T=A+B.LE.C.AND.(I+J)**2+K.GT.15 .OR. P | (7) |

Statements (1), (2), and (3) are type specification statements; they are covered later although these examples are self-explanatory. Statement (4) depicts the assignment of a logical constant to the logical variable P. Statement (5) assigns the value of a comparison expression (which has the value true or false) to the logical variable Q. Statement (6) includes a logical operator (.AND.) and a comparison expression and assigns the value of the logical expression to the logical variable R. Statement (7) includes arithmetic expressions, comparison expressions, and logical operators that are evaluated according to the hierarchy of FORTRAN operators given previously. The result of the logical expression in statement (7) is a logical value that is assigned to logical variable T. In addition, statement (7) depicts an important point; the comparison expression A+B.LE.C includes real operands and the comparison expression (I+J)**2+K.GT.15 includes integer operands. This is valid because when the logical operator .AND. is applied, both comparison expressions are reduced to logical values.

### Comment on the Use of the Assignment Statement

The assignment statement is used for both data movement and computation where the computed result is stored for subsequent use in the program. Data movement takes the form $v_1 = v_2$, which is simply a special case of the assignment statement of the form $v = e$, where the $v$s are variables and $e$ is an expression. As in BASIC, the same variable can appear to the left and to the right of the equals sign. Thus, statements such as

    K=K+1
    A=(A**2)+3.*A+A

and even

    I=I

are valid, even though I=I does not appear to serve a useful purpose. (It will as described in the section on looping.)

Multiple replacement is not defined in FORTRAN.

## 7.4  PROGRAM CONTROL

Program control statements affect the order in which statements are executed in a program unit. The order is usually sequential depending on the sequence in which the statements are placed in the source deck. Program control statements allow the normal sequence to be altered.

### The GOTO Statement

The GOTO statement unconditionally directs program control to the statement numbered by the specified statement number. The form of the GOTO statement is:

```
GOTO statement-number
```

where "statement-number" is a valid statement number of an executable statement in the same program unit. Examples of the GOTO statement are:

| GOTO 150 | 575... | GOTO 1436 |
|----------|--------|-----------|
| . | . | 1436... |
| . | . | |
| . | . | |
| 150... | GOTO 575 | |

### The Computed GOTO Statement

The computed GOTO statement is a normal extension to the "unconditional" GOTO statement, presented directly above. The computed GOTO statement directs program control to one of a set of statement numbers, depending on the value of an integer variable. The form of the computed GOTO is:

GOTO (statement-number[,statement-number]...),integer-variable

where "statement-number" is a valid statement number of an executable statement in the same program unit and where "integer-variable" contains one of the values 1,2,... up to the number of statement numbers contained in the statement. Thus,

GOTO $(S_1, S_2, ..., S_n)$,I

directs program control to executable statement numbered $S_i$ where $i$ is the value of I. In the following statements:

I=5

...

GOTO (819,420,1280,3,100,9000),I

program control is directed to statement numbered 100 after the computed GOTO is executed.

When the computed GOTO statement is executed, the integer variable must not be negative, zero, or greater than the number of statement numbers in the statement.


## The Arithmetic IF Statement

The arithmetic IF statement directs program control to one of three statements depending on the value of an arithmetic expression evaluated at the time the IF statement is executed. The form of the arithmetic IF statement is:

IF(arithmetic-expression)$s_1, s_2, s_3$

where "arithmetic-expression" is evaluated at the point of referer ce and "$s_1, s_2,$ and $s_3$" are valid statement numbers of executable statements ·n the same program unit. Program control is directed to the statements numbered by $s_1$, $s_2$, and $s_3$ if the value of the arithmetic expression is less than zerc, equal to zero, or greater than zero, respectively. $s_1$, $s_2$, and $s_3$ need not be unique. Thus, if A=10, B=15, and C=20, then the statement:

IF(A+B–C)350,50,7324

directs program control to executable statement numbered 7324.

The arithmetic expression in the arithmetic IF statement may be either of the integer, real, or double precision data types; it must not be a complex arithmetic expression.

### The Logical IF Statement

The logical IF statement causes a single executable statement to be executed depending upon the truth value of a logical expression. The form of the logical IF statement is:

> IF(logical-expression)executable-statement

where "logical-expression" is a logical expression evaluated at the point of reference and "executable-statement" is any executable statement except a DO statement or another logical IF statement. If the value of the logical expression is true, then the executable statement accompanying the logical IF statement is executed. If the value of the logical expression is false, then the first executable statement following the IF is executed in sequence.

The executable statement accompanying the logical IF statement can be one that directs program control to another point in the program unit (such as a GOTO statement) and one that does not (such as an assignment statement). If program control is directed to another point in the program, then sequential execution continues from there. Otherwise, the statement is executed and sequential execution continues with the first executable statement following the IF statement.

Examples of the use of the logical IF statement follow:

IF(A.GT.B**2) CALL SAM(B)
IF(CLOCK .LT. 0.0) A=0.0
IF(I .EQ.J .AND. YOU .GE. YOW) IF(I) 160,20,5140

In many cases, the logical IF is more convenient than the arithmetic IF. If it were desired to test whether the value of variable A is greater than the value of variable B and branch to statement 7400 if it were true, the arithmetic IF requires a subtraction, a determination of the greater than case, and a statement number on the executable statement following the arithmetic IF. The logical IF requires only a comparison expression and a GOTO statement. Both cases are depicted as follows:

|              *Arithmetic IF*        |  *Logical IF*  |
| :---: | :---: |

      IF(A–B)100,100,7400    IF(A .GT. B) GOTO 7400

100 ...                        ...

The logical IF is frequently referred to as a *compound statement,* that is, a statement that contains at least one other statement as part of its statement body. The compound statement in programming languages like FORTRAN, COBOL, and PL/I should be distinguished from the compound statement in ALGOL. In ALGOL, a compound statement is a series of statements $S_i$ enclosed in "begin" and "end," that is,

    **begin** $S_1, S_2, ..., S_n$ **end**

A compound statement of this type is treated as a single statement.

### The Assigned GOTO Statement

One of the least-used statements in FORTRAN is the assigned GOTO statement. It provides a "subprogram" facility similar to that provided with the GOSUB statement in BASIC. The assigned GOTO operates as follows:

```
        ASSIGN 100 TO NTAB
        GOTO 5000
100 ...
      .
      .
      .
        ASSIGN 200 TO NTAB
        GOTO 5000
200 ...
      .
      .
        ASSIGN 750 TO NTAB
        GOTO 5000
750 ...
      .
      .
```

> 5000 ...
>
> .
>
> .
>
> GOTO NTAB,(100,200,750)
>
> .
>
> .
>
> .

The statements that comprise the "subprogram" begin with the statement numbered 5000 and end with the GOTO NTAB,(100,200,750). Two different statements are used: the ASSIGN statement and the assigned GOTO. The form of the ASSIGN statement is:

| ASSIGN statement-number TO integer-variable-name |
| --- |

where "statement-number" is the number of the statement to which the corresponding assigned GOTO should return control and "integer-variable-name" is an integer variable that is used with an ASSIGN/GOTO pair. When the integer variable is in use as an ASSIGN variable, it may not be used as a numeric integer variable. The form of the assigned GOTO statement is:

| GOTO integer-variable-name,(statement-number[,statement-number]...) |
| --- |

where "integer-variable-name" is an integer variable referenced in an ASSIGN statement, which has been executed, and "statement-number" is one of a set of statement numbers that specify statements to which the assigned GOTO *can* return.

The use of the assigned GOTO has diminished because modern versions of FORTRAN include a subroutine capability. The assigned GOTO was defined in the original IBM FORTRAN (that is, before FORTRAN II was released) that did not contain a subroutine capability. The ASSIGN/GOTO statements were used for subroutines in the same manner that GOSUB/RETURN statements are used for subroutines in BASIC today.

### Other Program Control Statements

Other program control statements include a DO statement, for controlled looping, CALL and RETURN statements for use with subprograms, and PAUSE and STOP statements for halting and terminating a program. The DO, CALL, and

RETURN statements are covered as separate topics. The PAUSE and STOP statements are briefly covered here.

The PAUSE statement has its origin in the days when programs were run without the use of an operating system. The basic idea was that the execution of a program could be halted while a tape was mounted, and so forth. The form of the PAUSE statement is:

```
PAUSE [n]
```

where "$n$" is a string of from one to five octal digits. In general, the manner in which the PAUSE statement is implemented is dependent on the operational environment. A summary of the FORTRAN standard definition of the PAUSE statement is:

1. The execution of the PAUSE statement causes the execution of the program to halt temporarily.
2. The octal string is displayed to the system operator.
3. The decision to continue with program execution is not under program control.
4. If execution of the program is resumed, the normal execution sequence is continued.

The execution of the STOP statement causes the execution of a program to be halted permanently. The form of the STOP statement is:

```
STOP [n]
```

where, again, "$n$" is a string of from one to five octal digits. In an operating system environment,[2] execution of the STOP statement causes an exit to the operating system and the octal string is usually displayed, in some fashion, on the system output device. In a basic programming environment, the program simply terminates and the octal string is displayed to the system operator.

## 7.5  TYPE DECLARATIONS

A type declaration is used to specify the type of a variable. FORTRAN II, to regress momentarily, did not include type declaration facilities and implicit typ-

---

[2]Chapter 1 gives an introductory discussion of basic programming support and operating systems.

ing was the only means of distinguishing between integer and real variables. (To answer an obvious question, logical and double precision facilities were not available in FORTRAN II. Statements involving complex data were flagged with an I in column one.[3])

The type statements in FORTRAN IV permit the user to declare INTEGER, REAL, DOUBLE PRECISION, LOGICAL, and COMPLEX variables and to override the implicit typing conventions. The form of a type declaration is:

---

type { identifier | array-declarator } [,{ identifier | array-declarator }] ...

---

where "type" is one of the keywords INTEGER, REAL, DOUBLE PRECISION, COMPLEX, or LOGICAL, "identifier" is a variable name, an array name, or a function name, and "array-declarator" has the form

identifier (subscript)

where the subscript is composed of 1, 2, or 3 expressions, each of which may be an integer constant or an integer variable. The expressions are separated from each other with a comma. The constituents declared in a type statement are assigned the type corresponding to the keyword used in the statement. Thus, the following statement:

INTEGER ADOG,I3,PIG

specifies that the names ADOG, I3, and PIG are to be assigned the integer data type. Similarly, the statements:

REAL I,BOY,ZEBRA
LOGICAL ALL,JIME
COMPLEX VIM,SOL,KILT
DOUBLE PRECISION FOX,NIT,WOWY,D

declare I, BOY, and ZEBRA as real names; ALL and JIME as logical names; VIM, SOL, and KILT as complex names; and FOX, NIT, WOWY, and D as double precision names. Usually the names are assigned to scalar or array variables; in some cases, however, the type of a function is declared since it is used as a primary in

---

[3]Boolean (that is, logical operations on bit string) statements were flagged with a B in column one and the IBM 704 FORTRAN programming system permitted assembler language statements to be used *in* FORTRAN programs. Assembler language statements were flagged with an S in column one.

an expression and its type may need to be known if it deviates from the implicit naming conventions.

The array declarator is used to define an array in addition to specifying its type. The subscript is used to give the bounds and extent of the named array. This topic is covered in the next section.

A type declaration must be placed at the beginning of a program unit and can be used to:

1. Confirm implicit typing
2. Override implicit typing
3. Declare arrays, variables, and functions to be of types double precision, complex, and logical

The scope of a type declaration is the program unit in which it is included. A program unit may contain any number of type statements with the same keyword. Thus, the statements:

```
REAL K25,X4TP,JONSON
LOGICAL M,P,Q
REAL ABC,LEGGY,I
```

are equivalent to:

```
REAL K25,X4TP,JONSON,ABC,LEGGY,I
LOGICAL M,P,Q
```

The type statement and the FORMAT statement covered previously with regard to input and output are examples of what are usually referred to as nonexecutable statements. Use of statements such as the assignment statement and the GOTO causes computation to be performed, hence, the name "executable statement." Nonexecutable statements provide information to the language processor concerning the manner in which executable statements are to be processed.

## 7.6 ARRAYS AND SUBSCRIPTS

Arrays must be declared in the FORTRAN language and can be any of the data types mentioned previously, that is, integer, real, double precision, complex, or logical. The FORTRAN standard allows three dimensions; however, most modern versions of FORTRAN allow at least seven dimensions. Arrays cannot have a variable number of dimensions or even variable-sized dimensions and storage for an array is allocated in the program unit in which it is declared. The only exception to the above convention exists in subprograms[4] in which an array is specified as a parameter. In that case, an array can have adjustable dimensions since no storage is allocated for the array in the subprogram and the location of the actual storage to be used is passed as an argument in the reference to the subprogram.

### Array Specifications

Array specifications are made with the DIMENSION statement, with one of the type statements, or with the COMMON statement introduced in Chapter 8. The DIMENSION statement is used to give the number of dimensions and the size of one or more arrays and has the form:

DIMENSION array-declarator[,array-declarator]...

where "array-declarator" has the form:

identifier(subscript)

"Identifier" is the name of the array and "subscript" is one, two, or three expressions, separated by commas, that must be integer constants or integer variables. The subscript in an array declarator gives the number of dimensions and the bounds and extent for each dimension. Thus, the statement:

DIMENSION A(7,13)

defines a two-dimensional array that has 7 rows and 13 columns. The lower bound for each dimension is one and the upper bound and extent for each dimension is the value specified in the array declarator. The data type of an array may be specified implicitly or explicitly with a type statement. The array A, defined above, is of type REAL because of the implicit type assignments.

Consider the following statements:

DIMENSION FOXES(2,3),IMY(100),A(7,13),JACOB(6,3,2),
   APPLE(10000)
REAL IMY
DOUBLE PRECISION JACOB

---

[4]FORTRAN subprograms are covered in the next chapter.

```
COMPLEX FOXES
LOGICAL APPLE
```

FOXES is a two-dimensional array with two rows and three columns; its data type is COMPLEX so that each element of FOXES has two components: a real component and an imaginary component. IMY is a real one-dimensional array that contains 100 elements. A is included in the DIMENSION statement but not in a type statement. It is implicitly given the data type REAL; as an array it is given 7 rows and 13 columns as mentioned above. JACOB is a three-dimensional DOUBLE PRECISION array with extents of six, three, and two, respectively. APPLE is a large LOGICAL array; it contains 10,000 logical elements.

The DIMENSION statement is another example of a nonexecutable statement; it supplies information to the language processor on the amount of storage that should be allocated to an array and the manner in which an element of an array should be referenced.

The preceding example has depicted a case in which the same identifier is used in two different nonexecutable statements (frequently referred to as *specification statements*). For example, the identifier FOXES is found in the statement body of the DIMENSION statement and the COMPLEX statement. As mentioned previously, FORTRAN allows a type specification and an array declaration to be made with a type statement. The form of a type statement with this capability was given in the preceding section. Using only type statements, the preceding example can be simplified as:

```
REAL A(7,13),IMY(100)
DOUBLE PRECISION JACOB(6,3,2)
COMPLEX FOXES(2,3)
LOGICAL APPLE(10000)
```

Since arrays can be declared in the type statements (and the COMMON statement), the DIMENSION statement is no longer needed in FORTRAN. In fact, it is placed in the "other statements" section of some FORTRAN manuals. However, the DIMENSION statement probably never will be removed from FORTRAN, because of the need to compile programs written for earlier versions of FORTRAN.

### Subscripts

A subscript is used to select an element of an array and must contain a subscript expression for each dimension of the array. Subscript expressions are separated by a comma when more than one is needed in an array reference. In standard FORTRAN, a subscript expression is limited to one of the following forms:

$$c * v$$
$$c * v + k$$
$$c * v - k$$
$$v + k$$
$$v - k$$
$$v$$
$$k$$

where $c$ and $k$ are integer constants and $v$ is a scalar integer variable. (Most modern versions of FORTRAN allow generalized subscripts consisting of conventional arithmetic expressions that are evaluated and truncated to an integer before selection is performed.) Thus given:

    INTEGER ABLE(10,3)
    REAL JOE(50)

and K=2 and I=4, then ABLE(2*K−1,2) selects the integer value located in the third row and second column of ABLE and JOE(10*I) selects the real value located as the fortieth element of JOE.

The elements of an array occupy contiguous storage locations and no array subscript expression may assume a value when evaluated during the execution of a program that is higher than the declared dimensionality for that array. Obviously, this is not a condition that can be detected during compilation, and in most versions of FORTRAN explicit tests of a subscript value are not made during the execution of a program. In general, the results of using an oversized subscript are unpredictable.

Except as specified otherwise, an element of an array can be used anywhere that a constant or a scalar variable of the same type can be used.

### Input and Output of Entire Arrays

The FORTRAN language includes a language facility for reading or writing entire arrays. Consider the following statements:

    REAL ALIST(5)
    READ(5,9000) ALIST

```
9000 FORMAT(7F10.2)
```

The READ statement specifies that the entire array ALIST is to be read in; the array specifications for ALIST are determined from the array declarator. Data items must be placed on the input medium by increasing order of array index in accordance with the FORMAT specification. (In the example, the field descriptor reads 7F10.2; however, input is terminated when the list is exhausted. In this case, only the first five fields of the input record are used.)

Input of entire arrays is referred to as *short list input;* output of entire arrays is referred to as *short list output.*

Short list input or output can be used in a conventional input/output list, such as:

```
      INTEGER I(5)
      REAL FOX(2),JOKER(100)
      WRITE(6,9000)DOG,I,JOKER(34),FOX
 9000 FORMAT(1H ,F5.2,5I3,F16.8,2F10.3)
```

When short list input or output involves two- or three-dimensional arrays, a preestablished convention determines the order in which array elements are transmitted. Arrays are stored in column order in FORTRAN and the short list input and output conventions use that order. Array elements are transmitted in column order such that the first subscript varies most rapidly and the last subscript the least rapidly. Thus, if the following statements were executed:

```
      INTEGER BOY(2,3)
      WRITE(6,9000)BOY
 9000 FORMAT...
```

the array elements are transmitted from main storage to output device 6 in the following order: BOY(1,1), BOY(2,1), BOY(1,2), BOY(2,2), BOY(1,3), and BOY(2,3).

This convention makes the printing of arrays a problem since the line printer effectively prints by row and not by column. To print the matrix:

```
      REAL CONV(9,17)
```

for example, a DO implied output list of the form:

```
      WRITE(6,9000)((CONV(I,J),J=1,17),I=1,9)
```

would be required.

## 7.7 LOOPING

Clearly, looping can be performed with the IF and GOTO statements as outlined in Chapter 4. As with BASIC, however, the FORTRAN language includes a statement that permits controlled looping and facilitates the programming of iterative procedures.

In general, looping is performed to repeat a procedure while a control variable successively assumes a set of values or to iterate until a given condition is met. Looping can also be used when it is necessary to count the number of times an event takes place since the control variable of an interrupted loop can be inspected to determine the number of times the loop has been executed.

### The DO Statement

The DO statement is used to establish a controlled loop, specify the control variable and indexing (or control) parameters, and give the range of the loop. The form of the DO statement is:[5]

$$\boxed{\text{DO } s\ i = n_1, n_2\, [, n_3]}$$

where:

- $s$ is the statement number of the last statement in the range of the DO loop.
- $i$ is a scalar integer variable.
- $n_1$ is the initial value given to the control variable.
- $n_2$ is the limit value of the control variable.
- $n_3$ is the value by which the control variable is incremented prior to the execution of the loop. If $n_3$ is omitted, then it is interpreted to be the value one.

And $n_1$, $n_2$, and $n_3$ must be integer constants or scalar integer variables. The range of the loop is the statements following the DO statement up to and including the one numbered by $s$. The following example depicts a simple DO loop that computes the sum, product, and sum of squares of a one-dimensional array X containing N elements:

[5]The form of statement structure is relaxed here because of the length of the entries involved.

```
        SUM = 0.0
        PROD = 1.0
        SUMSQ=0.0
        DO50I = 1,N
        SUM=SUM+X(I)
        PROD=PROD*  X(I)
     50 SUMSQ=SUMSQ+X(I)**2
```

A DO loop is executed in the following manner:

1. The control variable $i$ is assigned the initial value $n_1$.
2. The body of the loop is executed.
3. The control variable $i$ is incremented by $n_3$.
4. The control variable $i$ is tested against $n_2$; if $i$ is greater than $n_2$, then the loop is terminated and normal execution proceeds with the first executable statement following the range of the DO, that is, the first executable statement following the statement numbered $s$.

### Operational Restrictions on the Use of the DO Statement

FORTRAN was designed as a language that lends itself to the generation of efficient object programs.[6] As a result, partially, of this objective, several restrictions are placed on the use of the DO statement:

1. At the time the DO statement is executed, the control parameters $n_1, n_2, n_3$ must be greater than zero.
2. The value of the control variable may not be modified from within the loop. (This restriction results from the fact that the value of the control variable was expected to be placed in an index register.)
3. DO loops may be nested but must not overlap.
4. A DO loop must be entered through its DO statement.
5. The last statement in the range of a DO loop must not be one of the following statements:

---

[6]When FORTRAN was designed, it was generally felt that a compiler could *not* generate an object program that could execute as efficiently as a hand-coded assembler language program. Therefore, many features in the FORTRAN language, such as subscripts and looping, incorporate operational restrictions that prevent the user from inadvertently causing the compiler to generate an inefficient object program.

> GOTO (of any form),
> Arithmetic IF,
> RETURN,
> STOP,
> PAUSE,
> Another DO statement, or a
> Logical IF containing any of these forms.

Restriction 5 presents an operational problem that is resolved with the CONTINUE statement.

### The CONTINUE Statement

Suppose, in the preceding example, it were necessary to perform the calculations only for positive values of the one-dimensional array X. One would probably start writing the program as follows:

```
SUM=0.0
PROD=1.0
SUMSQ=0.0
DO 50 I=1,N
IF(X(I) .LT.0.0)...
```

and realize that the DO loop could not be completed because of restriction 5. The situation is resolved with the CONTINUE statement as follows:

```
       SUM=0.0
       PROD=1.0
       SUMSQ=0.0
       DO  50  I=1,N
       IF  (X(I) .LT. 0.0)  GOTO  50
       SUM=SUM+X(I)
       PROD=PROD*X(I)
       SUMSQ=SUMSQ + X(I)**2
   50  CONTINUE
```

More specifically, the CONTINUE statement has the form:

```
CONTINUE
```

The execution of the CONTINUE statement causes the normal execution sequence to be continued. It can be used to end a DO loop or as an "entry point" in a series of statements as follows:

```
      SUM=0.0
150   CONTINUE
      READ(5,9000) VAL
      IF (VAL .LT. 0.0) GOTO 5000
      SUM=SUM+VAL
      GOTO 150
```

The CONTINUE statement is sometimes used in the latter fashion to avoid rekeypunching statement numbers when it is expected that statements are to be rearranged in a program.

### Miscellaneous Comments on Looping

The terminal statement in the range of one or more nested DO loops can be the same statement as shown in the following program segment that multiplies two matrices A and B and produces the result C:

```
      REAL  A(3,2),  B(2,4),  C(3,4)
      DO   200  I=1,3
      DO   200  J=1,4
      SUM=0.0
      DO   190  K=1,2
190   SUM=SUM+A(I,K)*B(K,J)
200   C(I,J)=SUM
```

Use of the variable SUM in the example is for efficiency since it reduces the number of times the subscript of array C must be computed.

The control variable in a DO loop cannot run backward; however, that facility can be simulated with statements such as the following:

```
      DO  750  I=1,N
      IDUM = N-I+1
         .
         .
         .
750   ...
```

where the "pseudo-control variable" that can be used for indexing is IDUM.

Many readers prefer a more formal description of how a DO loop is executed—similar to the one given in Chapter 4. The execution of a DO loop of the general form:

$$\text{DO } s \ i = n_1, n_2, n_3$$

.

.

.

Body of loop

.

.

.

s    ...

is functionally equivalent to the following statements:

$e_1 = n_1$
$e_2 = n_2$
C    IF $n_3$ is omitted, $n_3 = +1$
$e_3 = n_3$
$i \ = e_1$
99999 .

.

.

Body of loop

.

.

.

$i = i + e_3$
IF($i$ .LE. $e_2$) GOTO 99999

.

.

.

Thus, if a user wrote:

N=1
DO 50 I = 2,N

.

```
        .
        .
        .
50   ...
```

the loop would be executed once. This phenomenon is actually a carryover from the original version of FORTRAN where the situation existed. Many implementations of FORTRAN, however, test the value of the control variable against the limit value before the loop is executed for the first time.

One of the uses for the DO loop, as mentioned, is to count the number of times a given set of statements is executed, such that the control variable is not used in the loop, per se. Together with this use of the DO loop is the fact that an index register is frequently used to control the execution of the DO loop. Assume the control variable is I. If I is explicitly used in the loop, then each time the index register is incremented (or decremented), the current value is stored in I. This is called *materializing the control variable.* On the other hand, if I is not used explicitly, then it is not materialized. If the control variable is being used as a counter but not used explicitly as a variable, then a branch out of that DO loop would not reflect the current value for the control variable.[7] Therefore a statement such as:

```
    DO  100I=1,N
    I=I
        .
        .
        .
100  ...
```

serves to materialize the control variable and achieve the desired purpose.


## 7.8  BUILT-IN FUNCTIONS

*Built-in functions* are considered to be a part of the FORTRAN language in the sense that these functions comprise a minimum subset supplied by all implementations that satisfy the FORTRAN standard. Two kinds of built-in functions exist: intrinsic functions and external functions.

---

[7] Some FORTRAN compilers generate object code to materialize the control variable if program control passes out of the DO loop; others do not. Control can pass out of a DO loop in several ways, such as the GOTO, IF, and RETURN statements, or through the invocation of a subprogram.

## Intrinsic Functions

An *intrinsic function* is generated as part of the program unit in which it is referenced—hence the adjective intrinsic. Most intrinsic functions are implemented as open subprograms because the overhead instructions necessary to link to a closed subprogram are usually not justified. An intrinsic function is referenced by using its name as a primary in an expression followed by its arguments, separated by commas and enclosed in parentheses. Arguments may be expressions of the data type defined for the specific function. Sample functions are the real absolute value (ABS), the integer absolute value (IABS), and the real truncation function (AINT). In FORTRAN, the name assigned to an intrinsic function is governed by the data type of the argument(s) and the result of the function. Table 7.2 lists the intrinsic functions that are defined in standard FORTRAN.

## External Functions

An *external function* is usually referred to as a "library function" and exists independently of the program unit in which it is referenced. When the program units that comprise a program are loaded into the computer for execution, the required external functions are fetched from the system library and linked to the program units that use them. Mathematical functions, such as the trigonometric sine or square root, are normally implemented as external functions. Table 7.3 lists the external functions that are defined in standard FORTRAN. The set of external functions in a given system library is usually augmented by specific functions that pertain to the workload of the computer installation.

## 7.9 COMMENTS

It is obvious now why an easy-to-use language like BASIC was developed. FORTRAN is a comprehensive programming language for scientifically oriented applications; the designers of the language had to be aware of: (1) compilation times; (2) execution times; and (3) insuring that the language was powerful enough to cover a wide spectrum of applications. The result, of course, was the various data types, input and output conventions, operational restrictions, and so on. Actually, FORTRAN is easy to use, but more complicated than BASIC. From an overall point of view (that is, installation's, system's, and user's), FORTRAN is a more versatile programming language than BASIC and that versatility is manifest in the complications that are presented in this chapter.

There is more to come. The next chapter covers the general subject of subprograms and some advanced topics in FORTRAN.

**EXERCISES**

1.  Give sample input card formats for each of the following program segments:

```
      REAL A(20)
      READ(5,9000)(A(I),I=1,5)
 9000 FORMAT(10F8.2)

      REAL B(20)
      READ(5,9010)N,(B(I),I=1,N)
 9010 FORMAT(I5/(5F10.4))

      INTEGER JACK(50)
      READ(5,9020)M,(JACK(I),I=1,M)
 9020 FORMAT(I5,(15I4))
```

2.  Given the program segment:

```
      REAL A(100)
      INTEGER L(100)
      DO  10 I=1,100
      L(I)=I
   10 A(I) = I**2
      WRITE(6,9030) (L(I),A(I),I=1,100)
 9030 FORMAT(1H1,2X,1HL,8X,1HA/(1H ,I4,3X,F9.2))
```

describe what is printed.

3.  Modify the program segment of exercise 2 so that the listing is double spaced.
4.  Given:

```
      REAL A,B,C
      INTEGER I,J,K
      DOUBLE PRECISION Q,R,S
      COMPLEX D,E,F
      LOGICAL U,V,W
```

## Table 7.2

### Intrinsic Functions in Standard FORTRAN

| Function | Definition | Number of Arguments | Symbolic Name | Data Type of: Argument(s) | Function | Example |
|---|---|---|---|---|---|---|
| Absolute value | $|x|$ | 1 | ABS | R | R | ABS(−1.2)↔1.2 |
| | | | IABS | I | I | |
| | | | DABS | D | D | |
| Truncation to integer | Sign $(x)$* largest integer $\leq |x|$ | 1 | AINT | R | R | AINT(1.2)↔1.0 |
| | | | INT | R | I | |
| | | | IDINT | D | I | |
| Modulus (remainder function) | $x_1(\text{mod. } x_2)$ | 2 | AMOD | R | R | AMOD(5.0,2.0)↔1.0 |
| | | | MOD | I | I | |
| Largest value | $\text{Max}(x_1, x_2, \dots)$ | $\geq 2$ | AMAX0 | I | R | AMAX1(1.0,2.0)↔2.0 |
| | | | AMAX1 | R | R | |
| | | | MAX0 | I | I | |
| | | | MAX1 | R | I | |
| | | | DMAX1 | D | D | |
| Smallest value | $\text{Min}(x_1, x_2, \dots)$ | $\geq 2$ | AMIN0 | I | R | AMIN1(1.0,2.0)↔1.0 |
| | | | AMIN1 | R | R | |
| | | | MIN0 | I | I | |
| | | | MIN1 | R | I | |
| | | | DMIN1 | D | D | |

| | | | | | | |
|---|---|---|---|---|---|---|
| Float | Conversion from integer to real | 1 | FLOAT | I | R | FLOAT(5)↔5.0 |
| FIX | Conversion from real to integer | 1 | IFIX | R | I | IFIX(5.0)↔5 |
| Transfer of sign | Sign $(x_2)*(x_1)$ | 2 | SIGN<br>ISIGN<br>DSIGN | R<br>I<br>D | R<br>I<br>D | SIGN(3.1,–6.4)↔–3.1 |
| Positive difference | $x_1 - \mathrm{Min}(x_1,x_2)$ | 2 | DIM<br>IDIM | R<br>I | R<br>I | DIM(2.1,–1.0)↔3.1 |
| Significant part of double precision value | | 1 | SNGL | D | R | SNGL(.123456789)↔.1234 |
| Real part of complex value | | 1 | REAL | C | R | REAL((3.0,2.0))↔3.0 |
| Imaginary part of complex value | | 1 | AIMAG | C | R | AIMAG((3.0,2.0))↔2.0 |
| Convert single precision to double precision | | 1 | DBLE | R | D | DBLE(.1234)↔.12340000 |
| Construct complex value from two real values | $x_1 + x_2 i$ | 2 | CMPLX | R | C | CMPLX(3.0,2.0)↔(3.0,2.0) |
| Conjugate of complex value | | 1 | CONJG | C | C | CONJG((3.0,2.0))↔(3.0,–2.0) |

R–Real    I–Integer    D–Double precision    C–Complex

Table 7.3

External Functions in Standard Fortran

| Function | Definition | No. of Arguments | Symbolic Name | Data Type of: Argument(s) | Function |
|---|---|---|---|---|---|
| Exponential | $e^x$ | 1 | EXP | R | R |
| | | | DEXP | D | D |
| | | | CEXP | C | C |
| Natural logarithm | $\log_e(x)$ | 1 | ALOG | R | R |
| | | | DLOG | D | D |
| | | | CLOG | C | C |
| Common logarithm | $\log_{10}(x)$ | 1 | ALOG10 | R | R |
| | | | DLOG10 | D | D |
| Trigonometric sine | $\sin(x)$ | 1 | SIN | R | R |
| | | | DSIN | D | D |
| | | | CSIN | C | C |
| Trigonometric cosine | $\cos(x)$ | 1 | COS | R | R |
| | | | DCOS | D | D |
| | | | CCOS | C | C |
| Hyperbolic tangent | $\tanh(x)$ | 1 | TANH | R | R |
| Square root | $\sqrt{x}$ | 1 | SQRT | R | R |
| | | | DSQRT | D | D |
| | | | CSQRT | C | C |
| Arctangent | $\tan^{-1}(x)$ | 1 | ATAN | R | R |
| | | | DATAN | D | D |
| Arctangent | $\tan^{-1}(x_1,x_2)$ | 2 | ATAN2 | R | R |
| | | | DATAN2 | D | D |
| Double precision modulus (remainder function) | $x_1(\mathrm{mod}\ x_2)$ | 2 | DMOD | D | D |
| Modulus of complex value | | 1 | CABS | C | R |

R—Real    I—Integer    D—Double precision    C—Complex

which of the following statements are correct or incorrect and give the reason(s)?

> B=A**61.23
> C=B+S/2.3
> I=Q*R
> A=D+(3.0,2.1)
> U=I>J .OR. (A+B)/16.1
> K=V.AND.W
> E=A**Q
> F=D*E-(-16.123,4E-3)

5. Compare the ASSIGN/GOTO statements in FORTRAN with the GOSUB/ RETURN statements in BASIC.
6. Determine why the "executable statement" in a logical IF statement cannot be another logical IF statement.
7. Construct the following matrix in main storage by using short-list input only:

$$A = \begin{pmatrix} -7 & 3 & 9 \\ 6 & 4 & 1 \\ 4 & 3 & 2 \\ 8 & 1 & 9 \end{pmatrix}$$

Give the array declaration, input statement, and format statement, and data cards.
8. Write a short program segment that inspects each element of a M X N array. If the value of the element is negative, set it to zero.
9. Write a program segment to find the saddle point of a matrix. (See Chapter 5.)
10. Develop a flow chart of the "formal description" of a FORTRAN DO loop that was given in the chapter.

# 8

# ADDITIONAL TOPICS IN FORTRAN

## 8.1 INTRODUCTION

As presented thus far, FORTRAN is a powerful programming language for the solution of scientifically oriented problems. The "computational" features of FORTRAN have been presented without many of the operational conveniences available to users of the language. This chapter covers topics that facilitate the construction and execution of programs written in FORTRAN, and enable the language to be used for a broader class of applications. The topics covered are: subprograms, storage management, data initialization, additional input and output facilities, and the processing of character data.

## 8.2 SUBPROGRAMS

It would be impractical to include all functions that a user might want to use as a part of a programming language. Similarly, it would be equally unwise to require that each user of a computer develop each program unit he needs from "scratch" and thereby eliminate the possible advantage of utilizing work that was done previously. The subprogram facilities in FORTRAN provide a means for a user to define his own functions and subprograms. As a result, the following benefits are achieved:

1. Users can work cooperatively on a large program by structuring that program into subprograms.
2. Functions and subroutines can be shared between users and installations.

214

3. A user can develop a subprogram that is referenced several times in his program, thereby providing for efficiency of coding and storage utilization.

Subprograms have been used for programmer efficiency, for standardization, and simply for convenience.

Three types of subprogram facilities are available in FORTRAN: one-statement defined functions, defined function subprograms, and defined subroutine subprograms. A fourth type of subprogram, called a block data subprogram, is presented under section 8.3, "Storage Management."

A review of some terminology is necessary. A function subprogram returns an explicit result so that it can be used as a primitive in an expression. This is equivalent to saying that the name of a function, when used, has a value that can be used in the same manner that a variable or a constant can be used. A subroutine subprogram does not return an explicit result and is invoked with the CALL statement. However, a subroutine subprogram may return an implicit result through the use of parameters and arguments.

One of the key points behind the use of subprograms is that values must be passed to the subprogram so that it has the appropriate data to work on. In other words, a subprogram is a procedure representing an algorithm; the result of the procedure depends on the values to which the algorithm is applied. When a subprogram is defined, key values are represented by dummy variables called *parameters*. For example, in the function header statement:

FUNCTION SUBRA(A,B2,I)

the variables A, B2, and I are parameters. When the function SUBRA is used, it must be referenced with a primitive of the form:

SUBRA($e_1,e_2,e_3$)

where $e_1$, $e_2$, and $e_3$ are expressions that have the same respective data types as the parameters A, B2, and I. The expressions $e_1$, $e_2$, and $e_3$, in this case, are called *arguments*. In general, parameters must be scalar variables;[1] however, each parameter has a data type as an ordinary variable does. The main difference between a parameter and an ordinary variable is that no storage for a parameter is allocated, because it is a "dummy variable."

An argument may be an expression that is evaluated at the point of reference

---

[1] A parameter is a scalar variable in the sense that it is a nonsubscripted "dummy" identifier. It can, for example, represent the name of an array.

and whose value is passed to the subprogram. Not all arguments are expressions in the usual sense. For example, the name of an array can be passed to a subprogram and when it is, the address of the array in the calling program is passed to the subprogram. Similarly, when a scalar variable or an element of an array is passed to a subprogram, the address of the particular data item is passed to the subprogram. This is the means by which a subprogram can return an implicit result to a calling program. When an argument is an expression containing computational operations, the expression is computed at the point of reference and stored in a temporary location. The address of the temporary location, which is not accessible to the calling program, is passed to the subprogram.

### Statement Functions

A *statement function* is a one-line defined function that is internal to the program unit in which it is defined. A statement function is defined with an expression of the form:

> function-identifier(parameter[,parameter]...)=expression

where "function-identifier" is the function name, "parameter" is a scalar variable name, and "expression" is a valid FORTRAN expression. The function name is an identifier that is assigned a type either explicitly or implicitly. The parameters are scalar variables that serve as dummy variables; they also have a type. The expression may be composed of non-Hollerith constants, scalar variables, elements of an array, function references, operators, and parentheses. Variables in the expression that are not parameters assume the values assigned to them in the program unit at the time the statement function is referenced.

The statement function definition must be placed before the first executable statement in a program unit. Consider the following statement function definition:

$$ROOT(A,B,C)= (-B+SQRT(B**2-4.0*A*C))/(2.0*A)$$

The name of the function is ROOT and, unless declared otherwise, it is implicitly assigned the type real. A, B, and C are parameters that are effectively replaced with the value of corresponding arguments when the function is referenced.

A statement function reference has the form:

> function-identifier(expression[,expression]...)

where "function-identifier" is the name of the function and "expression" is an argument that must agree in order, number, and type with the corresponding parameter in the statement function definition. Each expression is evaluated at the point of reference and passed to the statement function. The function is evaluated using the arguments and the result is returned to the point in the program at which the statement function is referenced.

A statement function is known only to the program unit in which it is declared and is compiled as a closed internal function. Thus, the statement Y=ROOT(1.0, −5.0,6.0)+1.0 would assign the value 4.0 to the variable Y.

A frequent use of statement functions occurs when converting programs from FORTRAN II to FORTRAN IV. In FORTRAN II, built-in function names terminate with the letter F, such as SINF, whereas in FORTRAN IV, they do not. Therefore, this kind of conversion can be made very easily with a statement function such as:

SINF(X)=SIN(X)

As another case, the real logarithm function is written as LOGF in FORTRAN II and as ALOG in FORTRAN IV. (FORTRAN IV does implicit typing here.) A statement function to convert logarithm function references would require an additional type statement as follows:

REAL LOGF
LOGF(X)=ALOG(X)

A statement function requires at least one parameter.

## Function Subprograms

A *FUNCTION subprogram* is a program unit that is compiled independently of the program unit that references it. More specifically, a FUNCTION program is composed of a FUNCTION statement, followed by a program body, which terminates with an END statement; it has the "general" form:

FUNCTION name (parameter [,parameter]...)

.
. } Body of the function
.

END

The function name must appear to the left of an equal sign in an assignment statement in the body of the function so that the function reference is assigned a value.

The form of the function statement is:

---

[type] FUNCTION function-identifier(parameter [,parameter]...)

---

where "type" can be one of the following: INTEGER, REAL, DOUBLE PRECISION, COMPLEX, or LOGICAL; "function-identifier" is a FORTRAN identifier; and "parameter" is a scalar variable name, an array name, or a function name. If "type" is omitted, the type of the function reference is assigned implicitly using the naming conventions established for identifiers. The FORTRAN standard states that the name of a defined function may not appear in a nonexecutable statement in its program body. Thus, for example, the user cannot write

    FUNCTION CROOT (A,B,C)
    COMPLEX CROOT

but must write

    COMPLEX FUNCTION CROOT (A,B,C)

(However, this seems to be a restriction that has been relaxed in many versions of FORTRAN.) Similarly, each parameter that corresponds to a variable or array is assigned a type either implicitly or explicitly.

The name of a defined function must be assigned a value during each execution of the subprogram. Once the function name has been assigned a value, it may be used or reassigned in the function. The value of the function is the value most recently assigned to the function name when the RETURN statement is executed. The RETURN statement that has the form:

---

RETURN

---

causes program control to be transferred back to the calling program unit. Each function subprogram must include at least one RETURN statement.

A FUNCTION subprogram always returns a *scalar value* to the point of invocation in the calling program unit.

A reference to a FUNCTION subprogram in a calling program is similar to the reference of a statement function and takes the form:

> function-identifier(expression[,expression]...)

where "function-identifier" is the name of the function and "expression" is a valid argument that can be one of the following: an array name, an element of an array, a variable name, an expression, or the name of an external subprogram.

The arguments used with a function reference must agree in order, number, and type with the corresponding parameters in the function definition. If a parameter of a defined function is an array name, then the corresponding argument in the function reference must be an actual array name or an element of an array in the calling program unit. If the argument is the name of an external subprogram, then the corresponding parameter must be used as an external subprogram.

As an example, consider the step function

$$y = 0, \text{ if } x \leq 0$$
$$y = 13.4, \text{ if } 0 < x \leq 25$$
$$y = 97.8, \text{ if } x > 25$$

which cannot be programmed as a statement function. A FUNCTION subprogram, such as:

```
        FUNCTION STPFCN(X)
        IF(X)10,10,20
10      STPFCN=0.0
        RETURN
20      IF(X .GT. 25) GOTO 30
        STPFCN=13.4
        RETURN
30      STPFCN=97.8
        RETURN
        END
```

is needed. Thus, if real variable A contains 16.389, then the expression:

```
DOG = 2.0* STPFCN (A/2.0+5.0) −6.8
```

would assign the value 20.0 to the real variable DOG.

Although FUNCTION subprograms are used when a statement function cannot be used, this type of function (that is, the FUNCTION subprogram) achieves its greatest utility because of the fact that it is an external subprogram and can be referenced by any program unit in an executable program.

### Subroutine Subprograms

A *subroutine* is an external subprogram that does not return an explicit result and is invoked with the CALL statement. A subroutine is used when no result need be returned, the result is not a scalar value and must be returned implicitly, or when more than one scalar result is computed. A SUBROUTINE subprogram definition has the general form:

SUBROUTINE name [(parameter[,parameter]...)]

$\left.\begin{array}{c} . \\ . \\ . \end{array}\right\}$ Body of the subroutine

END

where the "body of the subroutine" must contain at least one RETURN statement, defined above, that returns program control to the calling program unit. More specifically, the form of the SUBROUTINE statement is:

SUBROUTINE subroutine-identifier[(parameter[,parameter]...)]

where "subroutine-identifier" is a standard FORTRAN identifier, which is not assigned a data type because there is no need to, and "parameter" is a scalar variable name, an array name, or a function name. All parameters corresponding to variables or arrays are assigned data types implicitly or explicitly. Unlike statement functions and FUNCTION subprograms, the subroutine need not utilize parameters.

A subroutine is invoked in a program unit with the CALL statement that has the form:

CALL subroutine-identifier[(expression [,expression]...)]

where "subroutine-identifier" is the name of the subroutine to be called and "expression" is a valid argument that can be one of the following: a Hollerith constant, a variable name, an array name, an element of an array, an expression, or the name of an external subprogram. As with function subroutines, the arguments used with a subroutine reference must agree in order, number, and type with the corresponding parameters in the subroutine definition.

As an example, consider a subroutine that prints a page title and page number each time it is called:

```
      SUBROUTINE PGNUM(I)
      WRITE(6,9000)I
 9000 FORMAT(1H1,30X,10HABC  REPORT,45X,4HPAGE,I5)
      RETURN
      END
```

A typical call to subroutine PGNUM would take the form:

```
      CALL PGNUM(N)
```

where N is a running count of the current page number.

Additional examples of subroutine structure, including the case where an implicit result is returned to the calling program, are given in the following sections.

### Passing Array Arguments to Subprograms

An array can be passed to a subprogram as an argument provided that the corresponding parameter is also an array. Recall here that storage is not assigned to parameters, but rather, the storage locations obtained from the calling program are used. Parameters declared as arrays can have either fixed dimensions or variable dimensions. (Variable dimensions are only permitted in subprograms.) The following function subprogram computes the sum of the elements of a vector with a dimension of 10:

```
      FUNCTION VSUM(A)
      REAL A(10)
      VSUM=0.0
      DO 100 I=1,10
  100 VSUM=VSUM+A(I)
      RETURN
      END
```

It would be referenced in a calling program unit as follows:

```
          REAL PLIST(10)
            .
            .
            .
          AVER=VSUM(PLIST)/10.0
```

The following subroutine subprogram computes the transpose of a matrix; it demonstrates variable dimensions and returns an implicit result.

```
          SUBROUTINE TRANSP(A,M,N,B)
          REAL A(M,N), B(N,M)
          DO 50 I=1,M
          DO 50 J=1,N
   50     B(J,I)=A(I,J)
          RETURN
          END
```

It would be called with a program segment such as:

```
          REAL PMAT(30,17), RMAT(17,30)
            .
            .
            .
          CALL TRANSP(PMAT,30,17,RMAT)
```

Suppose that a user desired to use the following subprogram to sum a row or column of a matrix:

```
          FUNCTION WSUM(BMAT,N)
          REAL BMAT(N)
          WSUM=0.0
    .     DO 3000 K=1,N
 3000     WSUM=WSUM+BMAT(K)
          RETURN
          END
```

Given the array declarations:

```
          REAL CAT(77), DOG(20,30)
```

the function reference WSUM(CAT,77) computes the sum of the elements of vector CAT and the function reference WSUM(DOG(1,I),20) computes the sum of the elements of column I of DOG. However, it is impossible to sum the elements of a row of a matrix with the function WSUM. Why? Because WSUM is defined on one-dimensional arrays and the address of any argument passed to WSUM is interpreted as a one-dimensional array. WSUM can only be used to sum columns of a matrix because matrices are stored in column order. A function subprogram to sum either rows or columns would take the following form:

```
      FUNCTION ANYSUM  (A,M,N,RC,L)
      REAL  A(M,N)
      LOGICAL RC
C     RC=.TRUE.DENOTES ROWS. RC=.FALSE. DENOTES COLS.
      ANYSUM=0.0
      IF(RC) GOTO 5000
C     L DENOTES COL TO BE SUMMED.
      DO  100 I=1,M
  100 ANYSUM=ANYSUM+A(I,L)
      RETURN
C     L DENOTES, IN THIS CASE, THE ROW TO BE SUMMED.
 5000 DO  5100 J=1,N
 5100 ANYSUM=ANYSUM +A(L,J)
      RETURN
      END
```

### Subprogram Names in Argument Lists and the EXTERNAL Statement

As a pedagogical problem, consider a subroutine that applies an external function to each element of an array and replaces a given array, that is, an implicit result, with the computed values. Suppose also that the name of the external function is to be passed to the subroutine. A user would probably write a CALL statement such as:

CALL ANYFCN(A,M,N,B,SIN)

where A and B are the arrays, M and N are the dimensions, and SIN is the name of the external function. Since FORTRAN uses no reserved names, however, SIN is treated as a scalar variable. The EXTERNAL statement permits SIN, in this case, to be declared as an external subprogram. The form of the EXTERNAL statement is:

---

EXTERNAL subprogram-identifier [,subprogram-identifier]...

---

where "subprogram-identifier" is an external subprogram name.

A definition of the ANYFCN subroutine is given as follows:

```
      SUBROUTINE ANYFCN(OLDARY,ROWS,COLS,NEWARY,FCN)
      REAL OLDARY(ROWS,COLS),NEWARY(ROWS,COLS)
      INTEGER ROWS,COLS
      DO 50 I=1,ROWS
      DO 50 J=1,COLS
50    NEWARY(I,J)= FCN(OLDARY(I,J))
      RETURN
      END
```

Note that in the subroutine, FCN is implicitly declared as a function because it is used with a parenthesized expression but is not specified as an array. The following program segment uses the ANYFCN subroutine to compute the SIN and COS of each element of an array:

```
      REAL FOX(10,3), LION(10,3), WOLF(15,10), TIGER(15,10)
      EXTERNAL SIN,COS
      .
      .
      .
      CALL ANYFCN(FOX,10,3,LION,SIN)
      .
      .
      .
      CALL ANYFCN(WOLF,15,10,TIGER,COS)
```

In general, an external subprogram name can be passed through several generations of subprogram references as long as it is declared in an EXTERNAL statement in the original calling program.

The above discussion gives some indication of why statement functions and function subprograms require at least one parameter and a subroutine subprogram does not. The parenthesized expression(s) following the function name are used to distinguish it from a scalar variable name.

## 8.3  STORAGE MANAGEMENT

Storage is managed statically in FORTRAN. This means that all the storage to be assigned by the operating system to a program (that is, all program units and external functions) is assigned when the program is loaded into the computer. Storage is allocated to variables and arrays in the program unit in which they are declared (either explicitly or implicitly)—except in subprograms where the variable or array is passed as an argument. This section covers language facilities that allow different variables and arrays to share the same storage in the program unit and others that permit different program units to share the same physical storage.

### Common Storage

Physical storage that is shared between two or more program units is referred to as *common storage*. The concept works as follows:

1.  A common area of main storage is established that can be accessed by any program unit of which a program is comprised.
2.  A COMMON statement is used to declare the variables that are assigned to the common area.
3.  If variables are placed in the common area appropriately, two or more distinct program units can access the same data.

The concept provides the following capabilities:

1.  Large tables of data can be shared among several program units instead of including the same table in each program unit. Thus, main storage is utilized more efficiently.
2.  Large amounts of data can be passed from a calling program to a subprogram without using extensive argument and parameter lists. Thus, the linking process is made more efficient and the program operates more efficiently.
3.  In many cases, the practice of using common storage is simply more convenient for the programmer.

Common storage is specified with the COMMON statement that has the following format:

> COMMON [/common-storage-identifier/]common-storage-list
> [[/common-storage-identifier/]common storage-list]...

where "common-storage-identifier" is a name assigned to a block of common storage and "common-storage-list" is an ordered list of variable names, array names, or array declarators (see section 7.6 on array declarations). *Blank common* refers to the case where the common storage identifier is elided. *Labeled common* refers to the case where a block of common storage is assigned a name. When two or more program units specify blank common, they reference the same area of main storage. When two or more program units specify labeled common with the same name, they reference the same area of main storage. Blank common and any number of labeled common blocks may be declared in the same program unit.

Variables and arrays are placed in common storage in the order specified in the COMMON statement. Although the variable and array names need not be the same in program units referencing the same common block, the entries must agree in order, type, and number.

The following example gives a variation to the transpose subroutine (given above) using common storage:

*Calling Program Unit*

```
COMMON A(50,50),B(50,50),M,N
      .
      .
      .
CALL TP
      .
      .
      .
```

*TP SUBROUTINE*

```
      SUBROUTINE TP
      COMMON OLDARY(50,50),NEWARY(50,50),R,C
      REAL NEWARY
      INTEGER R,C
      DO 50 I=1,R
      DO 50 J=1,C
50    NEWARY(J,I)=OLDARY(I,J)
      RETURN
      END
```

When the subroutine is invoked with a statement of the form

    CALL TP

the transpose of matrix A is placed in the storage occupied by matrix B. Matrix A has dimensions (M,N) and matrix B has dimensions (N,M).

Since array declarators in a COMMON statement refer to actual main storage space, variable (or *adjustable,* as they are sometimes called) dimensions are not permitted.

The declaration of labeled common with the COMMON statement is interpreted as follows:

1. The "common storage list" entries appearing after a "common storage identifier" and before the next identifier are placed in the first labeled common block.
2. Two slashes in succession denote blank common.

Thus, in the statement:

    COMMON A,B,C/BIG/X,Y,Z/SMALL/T,V//D/BIG/W

variables A, B, C, and D are in blank common; variables X, Y, Z, and W are in the common block labeled BIG; and variables T and V are in the common block labeled SMALL. As indicated, common block entries are strung together by order of their appearance in the same COMMON statement or successive COMMON statements.

The following program demonstrates the use of labeled common by applying a function to an array in blank common and by placing the result in labeled common.

*Calling Program Unit*

    COMMON VL(10)/FCNVL/VLXXX(10) //LEN
    EXTERNAL SIN,COS
        .
        .
        .
    CALL  COMFCN(SIN)
        .
        .
        .

*COMFCN Subroutine*

```
      SUBROUTINE COMFCN (FCN)
      COMMON DATA(10),N
      COMMON /FCNVL/RESLT(10)
      DO 25 J=1,N
25    RESLT(J)=FCN(DATA(J))
      RETURN
      END
```

The use of labeled common is important for a variety of reasons. Two of the most significant reasons are that: (1) The exclusive use of blank common causes the common block to become too long and cumbersome to manage accurately; and (2) labeled common can be used with "overlay" techniques to allocate a block of common storage with the highest program unit that uses it.[2]

### Storage Equivalence

It is sometimes desirable to have two or more variables or arrays share the same main storage locations. This is frequently done to conserve storage when large arrays are involved that are utilized consecutively. In other cases, storage is shared for operational purposes so that variables and arrays can be accessed in a certain manner in one part of a program and in another manner in a second part of the program. When two or more program units are involved, a common block can be used to share the same storage area. However, when it is desired to share variables and arrays within the same program unit, common storage cannot be used.

In a given program unit, the user can specify that he desires storage to be shared among variables or arrays with the EQUIVALENCE statement, which has the form:

> EQUIVALENCE(equivalence-list)[,(equivalence-list)]...

where "equivalence-list" is two or more variable names or array references; the equivalence list takes the form:

element,element[,element]

---

[2]When main storage is insufficient to hold a complete program, the program is structured into a hierarchical collection of program segments (called overlay segments) that successively reside in the main storage space allocated to the program.

For example, the statements:

    REAL  A(5),  B(6)
    EQUIVALENCE(A(1),  B(2))

establish the following equivalence between elements of the two arrays:

         A(1)    A(2)    A(3)    A(4)    A(5)
          ↕       ↕       ↕       ↕       ↕
 B(1)    B(2)    B(3)    B(4)    B(5)    B(6)

Array subscripts must be integer constants and the number of array subscripts must equal the number of dimensions declared for the array or must be one. In the latter case, the FORTRAN language definition allows an $n$-dimensional array to be referenced as a one-dimensional array for equivalence purposes since the array is stored in contiguous locations.

The EQUIVALENCE statement can be used with variables assigned to common storage as follows:

    COMMON  A,B,C(5)
    REAL  D(7)
    EQUIVALENCE  (A,D(1))

so that the following storage equivalence is established:

   A       B      C(1)    C(2)    C(3)    C(4)    C(5)
   ↕       ↕       ↕       ↕       ↕       ↕       ↕
  D(1)    D(2)    D(3)    D(4)    D(5)    D(6)    D(7)

and the storage locations are assigned from common storage.

The result of the EQUIVALENCE statement on the assignment of variables in common storage may be to lengthen the common block as depicted in the following example:

    REAL  A(8)
    COMMON  C(2),  B,D(3)
    EQUIVALENCE  (C(1),A(1))

so that common storage is organized as follows:

*Common Block*

| A(1) | A(2) | A(3) | A(4) | A(5) | A(6) | A(7) | A(8) |
|------|------|------|------|------|------|------|------|
| ↕ | ↕ | ↕ | ↕ | ↕ | ↕ | | |
| C(1) | C(2) | B | D(1) | D(1) | D(3) | * | * |

and the asterisk (*) denotes a position at which the common block is lengthened.

An obvious restriction on the use of COMMON and EQUIVALENCE statements is that when two variables or references to an array share main storage as specified in an EQUIVALENCE statement, the variables or array name may not both appear in a COMMON statement.

## 8.4 DATA INITIALIZATION

A variable is a quantity that can change in one of the following ways:

1. During the execution of a program
2. For a given run of a program
3. For a given version of a program

Frequently, a quantity, such as an input/output unit number, is referred to by a variable name instead of by a constant value. Then, if the physical input/output unit changes, only one card need be changed as compared to the case where the user has to go through the entire program and make a change in each statement where the unit is referenced. Even when the value of a variable changes during the execution of a program, it is frequently necessary to initialize the variable to a given value.

A variable can be initialized in one of three ways:

1. With the assignment statement
2. With an input statement that assigns a value to the variable to be initialized
3. With the DATA statement

When a single variable, or a few variables, needs to be initialized, the use of the assignment statement is often the most convenient method. When many variables need to be initialized, as is frequently the case, using the assignment statement for initialization would result in a lengthy and inefficient program. Instead, an input statement could be used, but this solution creates an operational problem and takes computer and IO time. The DATA statement is designed as an effective means of performing data initialization.

### The DATA Statement

When the DATA statement is used for initialization, variables to be initialized are assigned a value when the program is loaded. In other words, the initial values are incorporated into the object program. The DATA statement takes the form:

```
DATA  variable-list  /data-list/  [,variable-list/data-list/]...
```

where "variable-list" is a list that can include one or more variable names, array names, and array elements—separated by commas—and "data-list" is a list of optionally signed constants, each of which may be preceded with a repetition factor of the form $n*$, where $n$ is an integer. A one-to-one correspondence must exist between "variable-list" items and "data-list" items. Thus, with the statements:

```
       REAL  TOWL(3), CHARLY(5), WIZZY
       INTEGER  SIX, LIST(10),NAME(6)
       LOGICAL  Q,P(11)
       DATA  SIX, TOWL,WIZZY/6,3.1,3.2,3.3,-123.45/,
    1        Q,CHARLY,ABLE/.TRUE., 5*1.0,-.63E4/,
    2        LIST/8*0,63,0/,P(4)/.FALSE./
    3        NAME/13HJOHN H. JONES/
```

the following initialization is performed when the program unit is loaded (where ← denotes assignment):

```
       TOWL(1)←3.1, TOWL(2)←3.2, TOWL(3)←3.3
       CHARLY(1) through CHARLY(5) are assigned 1.0
       WIZZY← -123.45
       SIX←6
       LIST(1) through LIST(8) are assigned 0, LIST(9)←63, LIST(10)←0
       NAME(1) through NAME(6) are assigned characters "JOHN H. JONES"
            padded on the right with spaces (this is presented later)
       Q←.TRUE.
       P(4)←.FALSE.
       ABLE← -6300.
```

The concept is straightforward except for the restriction that variables in "blank COMMON" may not be initialized with the DATA statement and variables in "labeled COMMON" can only be initialized with a "BLOCK DATA subprogram," which is covered in the next section.

It is important to recognize that variables are initialized only once. If the value of an initialized variable is modified during the execution of a program, it "stays" modified—regardless of the execution time behavior of that program. This convention has at least one advantage. It can be used to detect the first time that a program unit is entered as in the following case:

```
      SUBROUTINE  BIGONE
      LOGICAL  FLAG
      DATA FLAG/.TRUE./
      IF (FLAG) GOTO 5000
100   .
      .
      .
5000  FLAG=.FALSE.
         (Initialization of subroutine)
      GOTO  100
      .
      .
      .
```

In the example, the statements beginning at the statement numbered 5000 are executed when the subroutine is entered the first time; the variable flag is then set to .FALSE.. On subsequent executions of the subroutine, the program then flows through the logical IF test.

### The BLOCK DATA Subprogram

The BLOCK DATA subprogram is used to initialize labeled common and has the general form:

```
BLOCK DATA
   .  }
   .  }  Specification statements
   .  }
END
```

As shown, the BLOCK DATA subprogram begins with the BLOCK DATA statement, ends with the END statement, and can only include specification statements, that is, the type statements, DIMENSION, COMMON, EQUIVALENCE, and DATA. The BLOCK DATA subprogram is processed (that is, compiled) as a separate program unit, and as a result, the complete common block must be declared if any variable or array in it is initialized. The following example depicts the use of a BLOCK DATA subprogram for the initialization of labeled common block ABC:

```
BLOCK DATA
REAL A(10),FOX(3)
INTEGER JL(5), COW
COMMON/ABC/A,FOX,JL,COW
DATA A,FOX /10*1.0,1.23,0.0,-139.4/,JL,COW/5*0,193/
END
```

The following initialization is performed when the program is loaded:

A(1) through A(10) are assigned 1.0
FOX(1)←1.23, FOX(2)←0.0, FOX(3)← -139.4
JL(1) through JL(5) are assigned 0
COW←193

A single BLOCK DATA subprogram can be used to initialize one or more labeled common blocks.

## 8.5  ADDITIONAL INPUT AND OUTPUT

### Auxiliary Input/Output Statements

A *data file* is a collection of data records on an external storage medium. Auxiliary input and output statements are intended primarily for use with data files.

The ENDFILE statement has the form:

```
ENDFILE unit
```

where "unit" is an integer variable or an integer constant specifying an output device number. The execution of the ENDFILE statement causes an end-of-data indicator to be written at the current position on the respective media. The end-of-data indicator is frequently referred to as a tape mark or an end-of-file mark.

The REWIND statement has the form:

```
REWIND unit
```

where "unit" is an integer variable or an integer constant specifying an input or output device number. The execution of the REWIND statement causes the specified data file to be positioned at its beginning or just prior to its first data record. If the specified unit is positioned at its initial point, the statement has no effect.

The BACKSPACE statement has the form:

```
BACKSPACE unit
```

where "unit" is an integer variable or an integer constant specifying an input or output device number. The execution of the BACKSPACE statement causes the specified unit to be positioned so that the preceding record becomes the next record. If the specified unit is positioned at its initial point, the statement has no effect.

### Unformatted Files

When formatted input and output is used, information is stored on the external storage medium in an external (or BCD) form. In the computer, information is stored in an internal (or binary) form. A conversion between the two forms is made during input and output. The conversion process, which operates under format control as mentioned previously, takes computer time and the external form of storage is less efficient than the internal form. However, the external form is necessary because it corresponds to the input record, the printed line, and the punched card used in the man-machine interface. When information is placed on an external storage medium for storage purposes only, it is frequently unnecessary to go through the conversion process.

Two forms of the READ and WRITE statements are designed for use with unformatted files. The forms are:

```
READ (unit) list
WRITE (unit) list
```

where "unit" is an integer variable or an integer constant specifying an input/

output device number, and "list" is a set of scalar variables, array names, elements of an array, and other specifications as defined in Chapter 7. The execution of each WRITE statement causes a logical record to be written on the specified external storage medium. The length of the logical record is the sum of the length attributes of the data values contained in it. The READ statement causes a logical record to be read from the specified external storage medium; values from the logical record are assigned to variables in the order denoted by the input list. On input, the data items from the logical record should agree in order, type, and number with the elements of the input list. If the logical record is too long, the excess data items, in general, are ignored and those values are not stored. If the logical record is too short, an error condition is raised.

Data files can contain either formatted data or unformatted data, but not both, depending on the needs of a particular application. Unformatted files are "FORTRAN oriented" and usually cannot be conveniently transferred between different models of computers or used with other programming languages. On the other hand, formatted files are less dependent on the characteristics of a given computer system or the implementation of a particular programming language.

### Additional Field Descriptors

The field descriptors, given in Chapter 7, for use in format statements are restrictive in the sense that exponential notation for floating-point data values was not included and field descriptors for several of the other data types were not mentioned at all.

The *E field descriptor* is designed for use with real data represented in exponential notation on the external medium. The form of an E field descriptor is:

Ew.d

where $w$ is the width of the field and $d$ is the number of decimal places. For *input,* the use of an actual decimal point overrides $d$, as with the F field descriptor. The exponent takes the form: $E \pm ee$, where the sign may be omitted if the exponent is positive and leading zeros in the exponent need not be written. If the exponent is signed, then the letter E may be omitted. The width indicator $w$ must include the exponent. The exponent should be right justified in the field since blank characters are interpreted as zeros. Using an input E field descriptor of E12.5, all of the following fields cause the same real value of $.314159 \times 10^1$ to be stored:

```
    3.14159E0
  314.159E-2
   314159E0
   .314159+1
```

For output, the E field descriptor produces a decimal number of the form:

$$\underbrace{\underbrace{\pm 0.d_1 d_2 ... d_n}_{d} \text{E} \pm ee}_{w}$$

where plus signs are replaced with blank characters during output editing. Thus the statements:

```
    A=987.123
    WRITE(6,9000)A
9000 FORMAT(1H ,E15.7)
```

would cause the following value to be printed:

```
ƀƀ0.9871230E 03
```

where the ƀ denotes a blank character. As with input, the magnitude of $w$ must include space for the exponent.

The *D field descriptor* is used for the editing and conversion of double precision data. The D field descriptor takes the form:

```
Dw.d
```

and operates in precisely the same fashion as the E field descriptor, except that the exponent is expressed with a D instead of an E.

A *complex data item,* which is composed of two real components, is edited using two consecutive real field descriptors. For example, the statements:

```
    COMPLEX  ARC
    ARC=  (4.0,3.0)
    WRITE(6,9001)ARC
9001 FORMAT(1H ,2F4.1)
```

would cause the following values to be printed:

ƀƀ4.0ƀƀ3.0

Complex input operates in an analogous fashion.

A *general (G) field descriptor* is defined for the conversion and editing of real data where the magnitude of the data is not known beforehand. The form of the G field descriptor is:

Gw.d

For input, the G field descriptor is equivalent to an F field descriptor. For output, the G field descriptor is equivalent to the following:

| Magnitude of Real Data Item | Equivalent Conversion Performed |
|---|---|
| $0.1 \leq v < 1$ | $F(w-4).d,4X$ |
| $1 \leq v < 10$ | $F(w-4).(d-1),4X$ |
| $10 \leq v < 100$ | $F(w-4).(d-2),4X$ |
| . | . |
| . | . |
| . | . |
| $10^{d-2} \leq v < 10^{d-1}$ | $F(w-4).1,4X$ |
| $10^{d-1} \leq v < 10^{d}$ | $F(w-4).0,4X$ |
| Otherwise | $Ew.d$ |

The G field descriptor is used to obtain the readability of the F field descriptor while eliminating the chance of obtaining a "too large" or "too small" error indication during output.

The *L field descriptor* is used for logical data and takes the form:

Lw

where $w$ is the width of the field. The input field consists of optional blanks, followed by T or F followed by optional characters, for true and false, respectively. For output, the field consists of either a T or an F, for true and false, respectively, followed by $w-1$ blank characters.

One field descriptor, defined in standard FORTRAN, has yet to be described. It is the A field descriptor used for alphanumeric input and output. It is described in section 8.6 on the "Processing of Character Data."

### Scale and Repetition Factors

Thus far, several field descriptors have been presented and the concept of a repetition factor has been mentioned. In addition, the F, E, G, and D field descriptors allow a scale factor to be used. A complete list of the forms of the format field descriptors is needed prior to a discussion of scale factors. Although many versions of FORTRAN allow additional format codes, those defined in standard FORTRAN are given as follows:

$srFw.d$
$srEw.d$
$srGw.d$
$srDw.d$
$rIw$
$rLw$
$rAw$
$nHc_1c_2...c_n$
$nX$

where $r$, $w$, $d$, and $n$ are integer constants and the $c_i$ are characters from the FORTRAN alphabet; $r$ is the repetition factor that can be used with F, E, G, D, I, L, and A field descriptors; $w$, $d$, and $n$ specify width, decimal places, and number of characters, respectively. The scale factor $s$ takes a different form.

A scale factor descriptor takes the form:

$nP$

where the scale factor $n$ is an unsigned or a minus integer constant. With F field descriptors, the scale factor has the following effect for input and output:

External value = internal value $*10^n$

For example, the statements:

```
    A=0.123
    WRITE(6,9002)A
9002 FORMAT(1H ,2PF5.1)
```

would cause A to be printed as:

$\emptyset$12.3

With the E and D field descriptors, the scale factor is ignored for input and scales the fraction without changing the magnitude for output. More specifically, the output fraction is multiplied by $10^n$ and the exponent is adjusted accordingly. For example, the statements:

```
        A= 12.345
        B= A
        WRITE(6,9003)A,B
   9003 FORMAT(1H ,E12.5,1PE12.5)
```

would produce the result:

ϸ0.12345E 02ϸϸ1.2345E 01

With the G field descriptor, input is handled as follows: (1) If the input field does not contain an exponent, it is processed in the same fashion as format F input; and (2) if the input field contains an exponent, then the scale factor has no effect. For format G output, the scale factor has no effect unless the data item is outside the range of format F output and format E conversion is used. If format E output conversion is required, the scale factor causes the same result as with format E output conversion.

The scale factor is said to be established once it is used with an appropriate field descriptor. Once a scale factor is established, it applies to the interpretation of subsequent F, E, D, and G field descriptors until another scale factor is encountered. The effect of a scale factor can be effectively nullified with a scale factor of the form:

        0P   (i.e., "zero P")

Therefore, if a scale factor is to affect only one field, the 0P scale factor should accompany the next F, E, D, or G field descriptor to be interpreted.


## 8.6  PROCESSING OF CHARACTER DATA

One of the characteristics that is used to classify FORTRAN as a scientific programming language is that facilities for the processing of character data are nonexistent. In fact, the only facility presented thus far is the H field descriptor for use with Hollerith constants and in FORMAT statements. The FORTRAN language also includes an A field descriptor that permits the input and output of character data that can be assigned to scalar or array variables. In FORTRAN, no operations, per se, are defined on character data.

### Storage of Character Data

The FORTRAN language is based on the concept of a computer word that can hold a numeric data item or a string of characters. Most implementations of FORTRAN permit four or six characters per word, although versions of FORTRAN exist that allow as few as two and as many as 10 characters per word. The actual number is "usually" dependent on the design of the computer involved.

A string of characters can be stored in two principal ways: (1) One character per word; and (2) with as many characters per word as possible. Thus, the character string "BINARY NUMBER" would be stored in one of the following forms (using a computer that allows four characters per word):

| location $n$ | BINA |
|---|---|
| $n$+1 | RY♭N |
| $n$+2 | UMBE |
| $n$+3 | R♭♭♭ |

| location $n$ | B♭♭♭ |
|---|---|
| $n$+1 | I♭♭♭ |
| $n$+2 | N♭♭♭ |
| $n$+3 | A♭♭♭ |
| $n$+4 | R♭♭♭ |
| $n$+5 | Y♭♭♭ |
| $n$+6 | ♭♭♭♭ |
| $n$+7 | N♭♭♭ |
| $n$+8 | U♭♭♭ |
| $n$+9 | M♭♭♭ |
| $n$+10 | B♭♭♭ |
| $n$+11 | E♭♭♭ |
| $n$+12 | R♭♭♭ |

where "♭" stands for the blank character. There obviously are variations in between (for example, three characters per word) and the actual form used is based on a particular application.

Character data are processed in FORTRAN using the input/output, replacement (that is, the assignment statement), and comparison facilities of the language. The only restriction on the use of variables is that they should be of the same type; otherwise, a type conversion is made during assignment that would change the representation and the meaning of a character item.

## The A Format Field Descriptor

The A field descriptor has the form:

A$w$

where $w$ is the width of an external character field. The A field descriptor operates as follows ($g$ is the number of characters that can be stored in a single computer word):

1. For input, if $w \geq g$, the rightmost $g$ characters are taken from the external input field; if $w < g$, the $w$ characters are left justified in the computer word followed (in the word) by $g-w$ trailing blank characters.
2. For output, if $w > g$, the external output field consists of $w-g$ blank characters followed by the $g$ characters from the computer word; if $w \leq g$, the external output field consists of the leftmost $w$ characters from the computer word.

For example, the following statements and associated input record:

```
      INTEGER PFX, LIST(5), SFX
      READ(5,9000)PFX,LIST,SFX
 9000 FORMAT(A5,5A4,A1)
```

col.  1    5 ¦6                        25¦26

| PL21X¦PRATT INSTITUTE USA ¦+ |

would cause the following data to be stored:

| PFX | L21X | | LIST(1) | PRAT | | SFX | +ɓɓɓ |
| | | | LIST(2) | TɓIN | | | |
| | | | LIST(3) | STIT | | | |
| | | | LIST(4) | UTEɓ | | | |
| | | | LIST(5) | USAɓ | | | |

For output, the following statements:

INTEGER A,B(2),C
WRITE(6,9001) A,B,C
9001 FORMAT(A2,2A4,A6)

and the associated storage structure:

A `XYZW`    B(1) `1234`    C `+ - / *`
            B(2) `5678`

would cause the following line to be printed:

XY12345678ƀƀ+-/*

### Formats Read in at Object Time

The A field descriptor can be used to "read in" a format during the execution of a program. This facility allows a degree of flexibility in that the precise format of the input records can be entered along with the data. The following example reads in a format, data, and a title and displays the result:

INTEGER ABLE(20),TITLE(20)
READ (5,9000)ABLE
9000 FORMAT(20A4)
READ(5,ABLE)A,B
READ(5,9000)TITLE
WRITE(6,9000)TITLE
WRITE(6,9001)A,B
9001 FORMAT(1H ,F3.1,2X,E10.3)

Using the following input records:

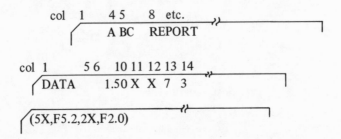

with the above program segment would produce the following result:

    ᑦᑦABC  REPORT
    1.5ᑦᑦᑦ0.730E  02

A format specification "read in" during program execution must always be enclosed in parentheses.

**Hollerith Constants**

Although many versions of FORTRAN allow statements such as:

    INTEGER  A(3)
    A='TEA  FOR  TWO'

or

    INTEGER  A(3)
    A= 11HTEA  FOR  TWO

standard FORTRAN restricts the use of Hollerith constants to FORMAT statements and as arguments in subprogram references. The following subroutine is programmed to use a Hollerith constant or a character array:

        SUBROUTINE PTNTIT(APPLE)
        INTEGER  APPLE(3)
        WRITE(6,9000)APPLE
    9000 FORMAT(1H ,3A4)
        RETURN
        END

If the subroutine PRNTIT were called in a program segment, such as:

    CALL PRNTIT(11HTEA  FOR  TWO)

the following line would be printed:

    TEA  FOR  TWO

One of the limitations on the processing of character data in FORTRAN is that the methods are dependent upon a particular implementation of the language. Unfortunately, this fact runs contrary to a basic objective in the design of programming languages, that is, to enable programs to be computer independent and interchangeable among different installations. In spite of this fact, an experienced and careful programmer can still produce a program that can be run on computers with a "standard" implementation of FORTRAN.

## 8.7 COMMENTS ON THE FORTRAN LANGUAGE

The FORTRAN standard has served its purpose well and has provided a high degree of interchangeability of FORTRAN programs among users and installations. However, it is the author's opinion that the standard is slightly out of date in the sense that most computer manufacturers have extended the language to some extent. The reader would do well to consult various reference manuals and bibliographical material.

After seven years, McCracken's guide to FORTRAN programming [5] is still worthy of the highest recommendation for both readability and clarity. The remainder of the reference list presents FORTRAN from different points of view. Couger and Shannon [2] present a programmed self-instructional approach for those that prefer programmed material. Haag [3] presents a complete introduction to standard FORTRAN. The major benefit from Haag's book is that he carefully describes what can be done and what cannot be done, along with a multiplicity of operational rules. This book is a suitable substitution for the ASA FORTRAN standard which is given as reference [7]. Campbell and Singletary [1] cover FORTRAN IV and WATFIV, which is an academically oriented version of FORTRAN developed at the University of Waterloo. Two other books are worthy of note. Murrill and Smith [6] cover FORTRAN from the point of view of the engineer or scientist, and Lee [4] presents an introduction to a modern up-to-date version of FORTRAN based on the IBM System/360 and System/370 computers.

## EXERCISES

1. Write FORTRAN subroutine subprograms that do the following:

    (a) Matrix transpose
    (b) Rotate a vector N places to the left
    (c) Multiply two matrices producing a third matrix
    (d) Read a matrix

(e)  Print a matrix
(f)  Generate an identity matrix

Use adjustable dimensions and pass the names of the arrays as arguments.
2.  Write FORTRAN function subprograms that do the following:

(a)  Sum the elements of a vector
(b)  Compute the product of elements of a vector

Again, use adjustable dimensions and pass the names of the arrays as arguments.
3.  Distinguish between labeled and blank common. Give an example of each.
4.  Using the DATA statement, construct the following matrices:

$$A = \begin{pmatrix} 1 & 1 & 1 \\ 2 & 2 & 2 \\ 3 & 3 & 3 \end{pmatrix} \qquad B = \begin{pmatrix} 1 & 2 & 3 \\ 1 & 2 & 3 \\ 1 & 2 & 3 \end{pmatrix}$$

5.  Describe the layout of main storage for the following cases:

(a)  REAL  A(5),B(4)
     EQUIVALENCE  (A(1),B(1))

(b)  REAL  A(10)
     COMMON  C(3),B,D,E(4)
     EQUIVALENCE  (C(2),A(1))

(c)  REAL  A(10)
     COMMON  B(5),C,D,E(6)
     EQUIVALENCE  (C,A(1))

6.  Develop a BLOCK DATA subprogram to initialize the following labeled common block:

COMMON/HOWDY/B,R,V,X,JOHN,Q
REAL  X(3),B
LOGICAL  Q,R
COMPLEX  V(2)
INTEGER  JOHN(2,3)

to the following values:

```
B=-123.4
X(1)=6E-2,X(2)=0, X(3)=-93.124E-6
Q=.TRUE., R=.FALSE.
V(1)=(6.1,-3.2), V(2)=(0,-.1E-4)
JOHN(1,1)=JOHN(2,1)=0
JOHN(1,2)=JOHN(2,2)=1
JOHN(1,3)=JOHN(2,3)=-4
```

7. Write a program segment to write the rows of the following matrix:

   REAL  BIGONE  (150,50)

   onto an unformatted file such that each row is a record. Then, rewind the storage volume and read the values back into main storage.

8. Describe the output from the following statements:

   ```
   LOGICAL P
   REAL A(3)
   DATA A/-.163E-1, 45.1, .89E2/,B/9.0/,P/.TRUE./
   WRITE (6,9000) A,B,P
   9000FORMAT(1H ,E11.4,2X, F6.2,1X,E9.2,2X,G7.2,3X, L3)
   ```

9. Write a program to read a card, delete blank characters, and print the result. (Hint: Use A format codes.)

10. Write a FORTRAN subroutine that plots a function, stored as a vector of functional values, against its indices. Use an adjustable dimension and pass the name of the array as an argument. (Hint: Construct a character matrix the size of the graph and fill each element with a blank character. Fill in elements that correspond to points with an asterisk. Print using an A1 format code.)

## SELECTED READINGS

1. Campbell, G. M., and W. E. Singletary. *A First Course in Programming: FORTRAN IV with WATFIV*. Philadelphia: Auerbach Publishers, Inc., 1971.
2. Couger, J. D., and L. E. Shannon. *FORTRAN IV: A Programmed Instruction Approach*. Homewood, Ill.: Richard D. Irwin, Inc., and The Dorsey Press, 1972.
3. Haag, J. N. *Comprehensive Standard FORTRAN Programming*. New York: Hayden Book Company, Inc., 1969.

4. Lee, R. M. *A Short Course in Basic FORTRAN IV Programming: Based on the IBM System/360 and System/370.* New York: McGraw-Hill Book Co., 1972.
5. McCracken, D. D. *A Guide to FORTRAN IV Programming.* New York: John Wiley and Sons, Inc., 1965.
6. Murrill, P. W., and C. L. Smith. *FORTRAN IV Programming for Engineers and Scientists.* Scranton, Pa.: International Textbook Company, 1968.
7. *American Standard FORTRAN.* American Standards Association, Inc., 1966.

# PART 4

# THE COBOL LANGUAGE

# 9

# COBOL
# LANGUAGE
# CHARACTERISTICS

## 9.1 INTRODUCTION

COBOL, which is an acronym for COmmon Business Oriented Language, is a programming language designed for the development of data processing programs. The development of COBOL was supported by the Department of Defense and a variety of computer manufacturers, user organizations, and users. The design and development of COBOL was begun in 1959 and was initially a hodgepodge of ideas—perhaps typical of efforts to design by committee. However, persistence, patience, and guidance by the CODASYL committee,[1] and a dozen years, have turned COBOL into a heavily used and widely supported programming language. Bemer[2] gives a very interesting history of the COBOL language.

As a programming language, COBOL is machine independent, relatively easy to learn and use, and readable in the sense that a reasonably good understanding of a COBOL program can be obtained by reading a listing of that program.

COBOL is an extensive language with special features for sorting, report writing, table handling, program segmentation, and library management—in addition to a full complement of descriptive, computational, and input/output facilities. Since the viewpoint here is pedagogical, not all of the special features are covered and the reader is directed to the bibliography. Otherwise, the complete COBOL language is covered including table handling and both sequential and random access input/output processing.

COBOL is a more verbose and a more readable language than either BASIC or FORTRAN. Using this fact as a starting point, a more casual introduction to

[1] CODASYL is an acronym for COmmittee on DAta SYstems Languages.
[2] R. W. Bemer, "A View of the History of COBOL," *Honeywell Computer Journal,* Vol. 5, No. 3, 1971, pp. 130-135.

COBOL is given. In addition, COBOL is a more "structured" language so that many of the programming details take care of themselves. The second and third chapters on COBOL use a more formal approach because of the large number of statements in the language.

The operational conventions for using COBOL are not covered and the reader is directed to the reference manual for a particular computer system.

The COBOL language standard is supported by the American National Standards Institute (ANSI), which requests the following acknowledgment to be reproduced in its entirety:

> Any organization interested in reproducing the COBOL report and specifications in whole or in part, using ideas taken from this report as the basis for an instruction manual or for any other purposes, is free to do so. However, all such organizations are requested to reproduce this section as part of the introduction to the document. Those using a short passage, as in a book review, are requested to mention "COBOL" in acknowledgment of the source, but need not quote this entire section.
>
> COBOL is an industry language and is not the property of any company or group of companies, or of any organization or group of organizations.
>
> No warranty, expressed or implied, is made by any contributor or by the COBOL Committee as to the accuracy and functioning of the programming system and language. Moreover, no responsibility is assumed by any contributor, or by the committee, in connection therewith.
>
> Procedures have been established for the maintenance of COBOL. Inquiries concerning the procedures for proposing changes should be directed to the Executive Committee of the Conference on Data Systems Languages.
>
> The authors and copyright holders of the copyrighted materials used herein: FLOWMATIC (Trademark of the Sperry Rand Corporation), Programming for the UNIVAC I and II, Data Automation Systems copyrighted 1958, 1959, by Sperry Rand Corporation; IBM Commercial Translator Form No. F28-8013, copyrighted 1959 by IBM; FACT, DSI 27A5260-2760, copyrighted 1960 by Minneapolis-Honeywell, have specifically authorized the use of this material in whole or in part, in the COBOL specifications. Such authorization extends to the reproduction and use of COBOL specifications in programming manuals or similar publications.

## COBOL and Data Processing

One of the characteristics of data processing is that most applications are file oriented in the sense that a program operates on one or more files and either modifies them or produces new ones. Files are composed of records and in data processing records usually adhere to a well-defined format. For example, a payroll program that produces paychecks requires a carefully designed format so that characters are placed in appropriate places on a previously specified form. Thus, data description is of prime importance. Actual computation also differs from that performed with the BASIC and FORTRAN languages. In data processing, numeric computation performs a minor role and input/output, data movement, editing, and conversion play a major role. Looping is also different in data processing. In numeric computations, a program frequently iterates until a solution is obtained. In data processing, a set of computations is usually developed for each record in a file and the program loops back to read the next record and perform the required computations.

In summary, a data-processing application is usually input and output oriented, in contrast to a scientific application which is usually CPU oriented. As a result, input and output is performed differently. Input data is read directly into main storage. Data conversion, if required, is performed before and after computation. During output, computed results are written to an external medium directly from main storage. Data processing was characterized in Section 1.3 and the input and output process was depicted in Figure 1.8.

The average data-processing program "tends" to run longer on the computer than the average scientific program—although there are obvious and notable exceptions—and relatively more data-processing programs go into a production status than in scientific computing. As a result, almost all COBOL programs are compiled into machine code before execution. Interpreters are infrequently used with COBOL.

## 9.2 OVERVIEW OF THE COBOL LANGUAGE

This section gives an overview of the COBOL language by presenting a relatively straightforward COBOL program and then discussing it. COBOL language elements are presented in subsequent sections.

### COBOL Reference Format

A source program in the COBOL language is prepared as 80-character data records, in BCD form, and punched on cards, placed on magnetic tape, and so on. A program is a set of consecutive data records, for example, a deck of cards. COBOL statements are prepared using a *reference format,* given as follows:

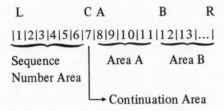

where:

> L   denotes the leftmost character position of a line.
> C   denotes the seventh character position relative to L.
> A   denotes the eighth character position relative to L.
> B   denotes the twelfth character position relative to L.
> R   denotes the rightmost character position in a line.

Four areas are defined: the sequence number, continuation, area A, and area B. The areas are used as follows:

1.  A six-digit sequence number occupies the sequence number area. The manner in which the sequence number is used is implementation-dependent.
2.  Division, section, and paragraph names begin in area A.
3.  COBOL sentences, that is, a set of COBOL statements, are written in area B.
4.  Any statement that requires more than one line is continued by starting subsequent lines in area B. In this case, the rightmost character of the preceding line is interpreted as though it were followed by a space. A line is usually "broken" between words or literals. In this case, nothing special need be done. However, a word or literal may be continued on another line by placing a hyphen in the continuation area (column 7); in this case, the first nonblank character in area B of the current line is the successor of the last nonblank character of the preceding line without any intervening space. A nonnumeric literal is continued by making the first nonblank character of area B of the continuation line a quotation mark; the nonnumeric literal is continued with the first character after that quotation mark.

The following examples demonstrate these concepts:

```
L     C A    B
                                                    ⁀
 001050 ENVIRONMENT DIVISION.
   •
   •
   •
 001100 FILE-CONTROL.
 001110      SELECT IN-FILE ASSIGN TO READER.
 001120      SELECT OUT-FILE ASSIGN TO PRINTER.
   •
   •
   •
 001500 PROCEDURE DIVISION.
   •
   •
   •
 001640 GET-DATA-PAR.
 001650      READ IN-FILE AT END GO TO CLOSE-UP.
   •
   •
   •
 001870      IF MALE ADD A TO B, MOVE GOOD TO BAD,...,
 001880      ADD TOP TO BOTTOM.
   •
   •
   •
 003410 CLOSE-UP.
 003420      CLOSE IN-FILE,  ...  ... DISPLAY 'END O
 003430-     'F JOB' UPON KEYBOARD.
   •
   •
   •
```

The following notes further explain the use of the COBOL reference format:

1. Line 001050 demonstrates a division name that must start in area A.
2. Line 001100 is a paragraph name that also must start in area A.
3. Lines 001110 and 001120 are COBOL statements that must be written in area B.
4. Line 001500 is another division name.
5. Line 001640 is a paragraph name. It must start in area A and can extend into area B, as required.

6.  Line 001650 is a COBOL statement; it is *not* continued. (In fact, it is a sentence because it ends with a period.)
7.  Line 001870 is a COBOL sentence; the last statement of this line is continued as line 001880. The continuation line begins in area B and *the hyphen in the C area is not used* because the statement is broken between words.
8.  Line 003410 is another paragraph name; it is referred to in line 001650.
9.  Line 003420 contains the beginning of a COBOL sentence, composed of COBOL statements. It is continued in line 003430 and a hyphen is used in the continuation area of the continuation line (that is, column 7) because the statement is broken in a nonnumeric literal. (Note that line 003430 begins with a quotation mark, which is required when a nonnumeric literal is continued.)

Most COBOL examples that follow in this part of the book depict only the A and B areas; however, in actual practice, the programmer is usually required to use sequence numbers.

### Sample COBOL Program

Figure 9.1 gives the flow diagram of a sample payroll program. The program is designed to process payroll information on a weekly basis and produces a listing that contains the following information for each input "pay card": social security number, payroll code (that is, either weekly or hourly), name, and total pay. The listing also contains a title and column headings.

Input to the program is a "pay card" that contains the following information in the specified columns:

    col. 1-9: Social Security Number (9 columns)
    col. 15-44: Employee's Name (30 columns)
    col. 47: Payroll code (1 column: W denotes weekly, H denotes hourly)
    col. 50-55: Payrate (6 columns: if weekly, this field contains weekly salary;
                    if hourly, this field contains hourly rate)
    col. 58-61: Hours worked (4 columns)

The program operates as follows:

1.  If the employee is "weekly," he receives his weekly salary regardless of hours worked. However, if hours worked exceed 40, then the employee

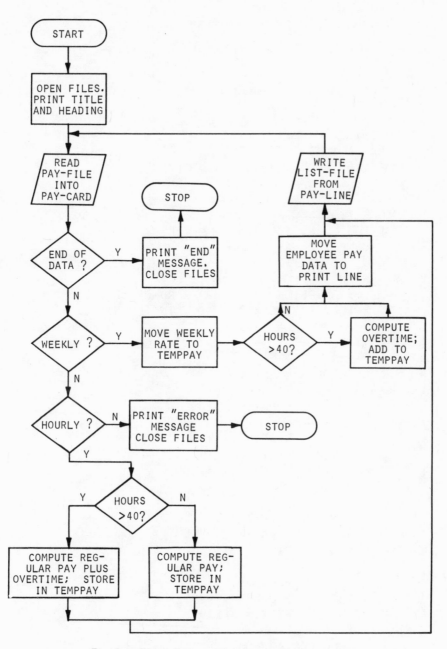

Fig. 9.1. Flow diagram of sample payroll program.

Program 9.1

| A | B |
|---|---|

```
IDENTIFICATION DIVISION.
PROGRAM-ID.  PAYROLL.
AUTHOR. JOE ANALYST.
INSTALLATION. ABC CORP.
REMARKS. INTRODUCTORY COBOL EXAMPLE.

ENVIRONMENT DIVISION.
CONFIGURATION SECTION.
SOURCE-COMPUTER. ABC-123.
OBJECT-COMPUTER. ABC-123.
INPUT-OUTPUT SECTION.
FILE-CONTROL.
     SELECT PAY-FILE ASSIGN TO CARD-READER.
     SELECT LIST-FILE ASSIGN TO LINE-PRINTER.

DATA DIVISION.
FILE SECTION.
FD  PAY-FILE
    LABEL RECORDS ARE OMITTED
    DATA RECORD IS PAY-CARD.
01  PAY-CARD.
    02  S-S-NO    PICTURE 9(9).
    02  FILLER    PICTURE X(5).
    02  NAME      PICTURE X(30).
    02  FILLER    PICTURE X(2).
    02  PAY-CODE PICTURE A(1).
        88 WEEKLY  VALUE IS "W".
        88 HOURLY  VALUE IS "H".
    02  FILLER    PICTURE X(2).
    02  RATE      PICTURE 9999V99.
    02  FILLER    PICTURE X(2).
    02  HOURS     PICTURE 999V9.
    02  FILLER    PICTURE X(19).
FD  LIST-FILE
    LABEL RECORDS ARE OMITTED
    DATA RECORD IS PAY-LINE.
01  PAY-LINE.
    02  FILLER    PICTURE X(6).
    02  SOCSECNO PICTURE 9(9).
    02  FILLER    PICTURE X(6).
    02  PAY-CODE PICTURE A(1).
```

```
A   B
    02  FILLER     PICTURE X(6).
    02  EMPL-NAME PICTURE X(30).
    02  FILLER     PICTURE X(2).
    02  TOTALPAY  PICTURE $$,$$$.99.
    02  FILLER     PICTURE X(63).
WORKING-STORAGE SECTION.
77  TEMPPAY        PICTURE 9999V99.
01  TITLE.
    02  FILLER PICTURE X(30) VALUE IS SPACES.
    02  FILLER PICTURE X(15)
        VALUE IS "PAYCHECK REPORT".
    02  FILLER PICTURE X(87) VALUE IS SPACES.
01  HEADING.
    02  FILLER PICTURE X(5) VALUE IS SPACES.
    02  FILLER PICTURE X(11)
        VALUE IS "S.S. NUMBER".
    02  FILLER PICTURE X(2) VALUE IS SPACES.
    02  FILLER PICTURE X(8)
        VALUE IS "PAY CODE".
    02  FILLER PICTURE X(10) VALUE IS SPACES.
    02  FILLER PICTURE X(4) VALUE IS "NAME".
    02  FILLER PICTURE X(20) VALUE IS SPACES.
    02  FILLER PICTURE X(9)
        VALUE IS "GROSS PAY".
    02  FILLER PICTURE X(63) VALUE IS SPACES.
01  ERR-MESS.
    02  FILLER PICTURE X(5) VALUE IS SPACES.
    02  FILLER PICTURE X(5) VALUE IS "*****".
    02  FILLER PICTURE X(32)
        VALUE IS "DATA ERROR - CHECK AND RERUN JOB".
    02  FILLER PICTURE X(5) VALUE IS "*****".
    02  FILLER PICTURE X(85) VALUE IS SPACES.
01  END-MESS.
    02  FILLER PICTURE X(30) VALUE IS SPACES.
    02  FILLER PICTURE X(18)
        VALUE IS "END OF PAY LISTING".
    02  FILLER PICTURE X(74) VALUE IS SPACES.

PROCEDURE DIVISION.
INITIALIZE.
    OPEN INPUT PAY-FILE.
    OPEN OUTPUT LIST-FILE.
```

```
A    B
PRINT-TITLE-AND-HEADING.
    WRITE PAY-LINE FROM TITLE
        AFTER ADVANCING 0 LINES.
    WRITE PAY-LINE FROM HEADING
        AFTER ADVANCING 2 LINES.
    MOVE SPACES TO PAY-LINE.
    WRITE PAY-LINE.
READ-PAY.
    READ PAY-FILE AT END GO TO END-OF-JOB.
    IF WEEKLY GO TO COMPUTE-WEEKLY-PAY.
    IF HOURLY GO TO COMPUTE-HOURLY-PAY.
    WRITE PAY-LINE FROM ERR-MESS.
        AFTER ADVANCING 2 LINES.
    CLOSE PAY-FILE, LIST-FILE.
    STOP RUN.
COMPUTE-WEEKLY-PAY.
    MOVE RATE TO TEMPPAY.
    IF HOURS GREATER THAN 40.0
        COMPUTE TEMPPAY = TEMPPAY + (RATE / 40) *
        (HOURS - 40) * 1.5.
    GO TO PRINT-PAY.
COMPUTE-HOURLY-PAY.
        IF HOURS GREATER THAN 40.0
            COMPUTE TEMPPAY = RATE * 40 +
            (HOURS - 40) * RATE * 1.5
            ELSE COMPUTE TEMPPAY = RATE * HOURS.
PRINT-PAY.
        MOVE SPACES TO PAY-LINE.
        MOVE S-S-NO TO SOCSECNO.
        MOVE PAY-CODE IN PAY-CARD TO PAY-CODE IN
            PAY-LINE.
        MOVE NAME TO EMPL-NAME.
        MOVE TEMPPAY TO TOTALPAY.
        WRITE PAY-LINE. GO TO READ-PAY.
END-OF-JOB.
        WRITE PAY-LINE FROM END-MESS AFTER ADVANCING
            2 LINES.
        CLOSE PAY-FILE, LIST-FILE.
        STOP RUN.
```

receives an overtime premium computed as follows:

$$(\text{hours} - 40) \times \left(\frac{\text{weekly salary}}{40}\right) \times 1.5$$

2. If the employee is hourly, then his pay is computed as: hours times rate plus time and one-half for hours over 40.

A COBOL program to compute a pay listing, as outlined, is given as Program 9.1. The complete program is composed of four divisions: identification, environment, data, and procedure. The blank line between the divisions is included for readability and is not required. Blank lines are ignored by the COBOL compiler. The divisions must be presented to the COBOL compiler in the given order. Each division is discussed in the following paragraphs.

**The Identification Division**

The purpose of the Identification Division is to identify the source program and the outputs of the compilation process. The only required lines in this division are the division header and the program identification, which assigns a name to the program. The identification division for the payroll program (Program 9.1) is repeated as follows:

```
A    B

IDENTIFICATION DIVISION.
PROGRAM-ID. PAYROLL.
AUTHOR. JOE ANALYST.
INSTALLATION. ABC CORP.
REMARKS. INTRODUCTORY COBOL EXAMPLE.
```

The "program name" line is written:

PROGRAM-ID. *program name.*

where "program name" is a user-defined COBOL name. The rules for forming a "name" are covered later.

The identification division is computer independent and causes no object code to be generated. The user may use this division to include in the program listing the date the program was written, programmer name, compilation date, installation, and any other information which is desired.

### The Environment Division

The Environment Division is the part of a source program that specifies the equipment being used. It includes information on the computers to be used for compiling the source program and for running the object program. This division allows memory size, input/output units, hardware switches, and so forth, to be specified. User names may be assigned to particular hardware units and to data files on specific input/output devices. The environment division tends to be machine or operating system dependent and is usually modified when a COBOL program is converted to run on another computer system.

The Environment Division for the payroll program is given as follows:

```
A    B
┌─────────────────────────────────────────────────────────────
│ENVIRONMENT DIVISION.
│CONFIGURATION SECTION.
│SOURCE-COMPUTER. ABC-123.
│OBJECT-COMPUTER. ABC-123.
│INPUT-OUTPUT SECTION.
│        SELECT PAY-FILE ASSIGN TO CARD-READER.
│        SELECT LIST-FILE ASSIGN TO LINE-PRINTER.
│
```

The configuration section specifies that the source and object computer is the ABC-123. In general, these entries take the form:

```
SOURCE-COMPUTER.    computer-name.
OBJECT-COMPUTER.    computer-name.
```

where "computer-name" is a set of characters recognized by the compiler. The source and object computers need not be the same and can also specify different hardware configurations.

The input-output section is used to assign symbolic file names to input/output devices to be used in the program. The form of the SELECT statement is:

```
SELECT file-name ASSIGN TO device-name.
```

where "file name" is the name assigned to a file by the programmer and "device name" is a name for a particular class of devices recognized by the compiler. In this example, the statements:

SELECT PAY-FILE ASSIGN TO CARD-READER.
SELECT LIST-FILE ASSIGN TO LINE-PRINTER.

specify that PAY-FILE is to be assigned to a card reader and LIST-FILE is to be assigned to a line printer. PAY-FILE and LIST-FILE are symbolic names of data files that *must be* described in the data division. The SELECT statement must begin in area B of the reference format.

Names of hardware units, such as CARD-READER, vary between different compilers, computer systems, and operating systems.

**The Data Division**

The Data Division describes the information on which the program operates. *All data files, data records, and temporary storage must be described.* This division is usually independent of a particular implementation of COBOL.

The data division consists of two sections: file and working storage. The *File Section* gives the attributes of input/output files and of the data records that comprise these fields. The *Working Storage Section* defines the main storage used during the execution of a program. (The reader should review Program 9.1 at this point to determine the relative position of the file and working storage sections and their general appearance.)

The *File Section* of the Data Division of the pay listing program is given as follows:

```
A    B

FILE SECTION.
FD   PAY-FILE
     LABEL RECORDS ARE OMITTED
     DATA RECORD IS PAY-CARD.
01   PAY-CARD.
     02  S-S-NO      PICTURE 9(9).
     02  FILLER      PICTURE X(5).
     02  NAME        PICTURE X(30).
     02  FILLER      PICTURE X(2).
     02  PAY-CODE    PICTURE A(1).
         88 WEEKLY VALUE IS "W".
         88 HOURLY VALUE IS "H".
```

A    B

```
         02  FILLER      PICTURE X(2).
         02  RATE        PICTURE 9999V99.
         02  FILLER      PICTURE X(2).
         02  HOURS       PICTURE 999V9.
         02  FILLER      PICTURE X(19).
FD   LIST-FILE
     LABEL RECORDS ARE OMITTED
     DATA RECORD IS PAY-LINE.
01   PAY-LINE.
         02  FILLER      PICTURE X(6).
         02  SOCSECNO    PICTURE 9(9).
         02  FILLER      PICTURE X(6).
         02  PAY-CODE    PICTURE A(1).
         02  FILLER      PICTURE X(6).
         02  EMPL-NAME   PICTURE X(30).
         02  FILLER      PICTURE X(2).
         02  TOTALPAY    PICTURE $$,$$$.99.
         02  FILLER      PICTURE X(63).
```

Two files are described: PAY-FILE and LIST-FILE. The letters FD denote "file description," followed by the file name and its attributes. The record descriptions of all records that belong to a file follow the FD statement. A record description is a structure[3] that must begin with a 01 level entry that contains the record name. In this case, the first FD statement describes the file named PAY-FILE and specifies that its data record is PAY-CARD. The record description of PAY-CARD follows the FD statement for PAY-FILE. The length of record PAY-CARD is implicitly given by the data items of which it is composed. The second FD statement describes the file named LIST-FILE and specifies that its data record is PAY-LINE. The record description of PAY-LINE follows the FD statement for LIST-FILE.

Most COBOL entries use reserved words. For example in the FD statement:

    FD   LIST-FILE
           LABEL RECORDS ARE OMITTED
           DATA RECORD IS PAY-LINE.

the only words supplied by the programmer are LIST-FILE and PAY-LINE; the remainder of the words in the statement are COBOL reserved words.

[3] See Chapter 2.

Data items within a record (02 level entries in this case) are either assigned a name or given the word FILLER in place of a name. The word FILLER can be assigned to a field when that field is not used in a program. Consider the input record named PAY-CARD. It has a length of 80 characters and each character position in the record is accounted for by a variable name or by a filler. The implication is that the record is read into an area of storage and when a variable is referenced, the correct field in the record is accessed. In other words, the record description serves as a template. The same concept holds true for output.

Each data item or field in a record is described with a PICTURE clause. As picture characters, 9 denotes a numeric character, A denotes an alphabetic character, X denotes any character in the COBOL alphabet, and V denotes an implied decimal point. Repetition of the same picture character is specified as follows:

$$\underbrace{CCC...C}_{n} \leftrightarrow C(n)$$

so that PICTURE X(4) is equivalent to PICTURE XXXX and PICTURE 9(5)V9(4) is equivalent to PICTURE 99999V9999.

The 88-level items in PAY-CARD denote condition names. The following specification:

    02    PAY-CODE PICTURE A(1).
          88  WEEKLY  VALUE IS "W".
          88  HOURLY  VALUE IS "H".

is interpreted as follows: The name of the condition that PAY-CODE="W" is WEEKLY and the name of the condition that PAY-CODE="H" is HOURLY. ("W" and "H" are nonnumeric literals.) Thus, in the procedure division of the program, the programmer can write:

    IF WEEKLY...

instead of

    IF PAY-CODE = "W" ...

The output record PAY-LINE contains the data item:

    02    TOTALPAY PICTURE $$,$$$.99.

that denotes data editing. When a value is moved to TOTALPAY, it is edited such that leading zeros are suppressed and the rightmost leading zero is replaced with a dollar sign. The comma is an insertion character; a comma is inserted into the edited result if digits appear to the right and to the left of it. The use of picture editing is consistent with the technique of computing, editing or converting, and then storing, mentioned earlier; so that editing or conversion is not performed during the actual output operation.

The output record PAY-LINE contains 132 characters—the precise length of a print line.

The *Working Storage* section of the data division describes storage used during execution of a program but not assigned to a particular file. Both data records and independent storage[4] can be defined. Consider the working storage section of the pay list program:

A    B

```
WORKING-STORAGE SECTION.
77  TEMPPAY        PICTURE 9999V99.
01  TITLE.
    02  FILLER    PICTURE X(30) VALUE IS SPACES.
    02  FILLER    PICTURE X(15)
        VALUE IS "PAYCHECK REPORT".
    02  FILLER PICTURE X(87) VALUE IS SPACES.
01  HEADING.
    02  FILLER PICTURE X(5) VALUE IS SPACES.
    02  FILLER PICTURE X(11)
        VALUE IS "S.S. NUMBER".
    02  FILLER PICTURE X(2) VALUE IS SPACES.
    02  FILLER PICTURE X(8)
        VALUE IS "PAY CODE".
    02  FILLER PICTURE X(10) VALUE IS SPACES.
    02  FILLER PICTURE X(4) VALUE IS "NAME".
    02  FILLER PICTURE X(20) VALUE IS SPACES.
    02  FILLER PICTURE X(9)
        VALUE IS "GROSS PAY".
    02  FILLER PICTURE X(63) VALUE IS SPACES.
01  ERR-MESS.
    02  FILLER PICTURE X(5) VALUE IS SPACES.
    02  FILLER PICTURE X(5) VALUE IS "*****".
    02  FILLER PICTURE X(32)
        VALUE IS "DATA ERROR - CHECK AND RERUN JOB".
```

[4]Independent storage is not a part of a record description.

```
A   B
|   02   FILLER PICTURE X(5) VALUE IS "*****".
|   02   FILLER PICTURE X(85) VALUE IS SPACES.
|01  END-MESS.
|   02   FILLER PICTURE X(30) VALUE IS SPACES.
|   02   FILLER PICTURE X(18)
|        VALUE IS "END OF PAY LISTING".
|   02   FILLER PICTURE X(74) VALUE IS SPACES.
```

The data item TEMPPAY is assigned six digits of independent storage because it has a level number of 77. The implied decimal point is after the fourth digit from the left. The record descriptions of TITLE, HEADING, ERR-MESS, and END-MESS describe records that will be moved to PAY-LINE before the "write" operation. None of the fields in either record is assigned a name, other than FILLER, because none of them is going to be referred to in the program. However, the fields of these records are assigned a value with the VALUE clause. The VALUE clause can only be used in the working storage section and may not be used in the file section, except in an 88-level item—that is, the specification of a condition name. Each of the records, that is, TITLE, HEADING, ERR-MESS, and END-MESS, is precisely 132 characters in length—the same length as PAY-LINE.

If the fields in one of the records under discussion (HEADING, for example) were not assigned a value with the VALUE clause, it would have to be given a name and then be assigned a value during the execution of the program. The clause:

VALUE IS SPACES

uses a figurative constant, which is SPACES (or SPACE—they are equivalent). A *figurative constant* is a frequently used value that is assigned a data name. Other frequently used figurative constants are ZERO and QUOTE. Figurative constants are discussed again later.

Independent storage (77-level items) may not be used in the file section.


**The Procedure Division**

The Procedure Division specifies the steps that the computer is to follow. The procedure division is composed of statements, sentences, paragraphs, and sections; it corresponds to the "program" in other programming languages except that declarative information is omitted. By itself, the procedure division is an incom-

plete specification of a program because information in other divisions of the
COBOL program is needed.

Of all the divisions of a COBOL program, the procedure division is more like
meaningful English. Verbs are used to denote actions and sentences, paragraphs,
and sections correspond to complex procedures.

The procedure division begins with the statement:

PROCEDURE DIVISION.

and is composed of sections and paragraphs. The paragraphs of the payroll program are described separately. The first paragraph is given as follows:

A    B

```
INITIALIZE.
     OPEN INPUT PAY-FILE.
     OPEN OUTPUT LIST-FILE.
```

where INITIALIZE is the paragraph name. The paragraph contains two OPEN
statements. The OPEN statement prepares the specified file for either input or
output. Functionally, this statement serves to "connect" the input/output device, assigned to the specified file in the environment division, to the program.
Each COBOL statement begins with a verb, such as OPEN, that denotes the function the statement is to perform. The verb is followed by words that augment
the verb and specify operands on which the computer is to operate.

The next paragraph of the procedure division is:

A    B

```
PRINT-TITLE-AND-HEADING.
     WRITE PAY-LINE FROM TITLE
          AFTER ADVANCING 0 LINES.
     WRITE PAY-LINE FROM HEADING
          AFTER ADVANCING 2 LINES.
     MOVE SPACES TO PAY-LINE.
     WRITE PAY-LINE.
```

where PRINT-TITLE-AND-HEADING is the paragraph name. The paragraph consists of four statements: WRITE, WRITE, MOVE, and WRITE—in that order. The
paragraph simply prepares the title for the report. When doing input and output
in COBOL, a good rule to remember is that the program *reads files* and *writes*

*records.* Therefore, a write statement is associated with a particular data file through the DATA RECORDS ARE . . . clause in the FD statement and the user must write a data record declared with the appropriate file. The first statement (that is, the WRITE statement) is equivalent to the following:

>   MOVE TITLE TO PAY-LINE.
>   WRITE PAY-LINE AFTER ADVANCING 0 LINES.

The ADVANCING 0 LINES clause tells the printer to go to the top of the next page. Similarly, the ADVANCING 2 LINES clause tells the printer to skip two lines before printing. The last statement, that is,

>   WRITE PAY-LINE

contains no ADVANCING clause and a default specification of one line is advanced before printing.

The succeeding paragraph named READ-PAY reads an input record and branches to the procedure defined for each type of input card. Incorrect input is recognized and error processing is performed.

A    B

```
READ-PAY.
     READ PAY-FILE AT END GO TO END-OF-JOB.
     IF WEEKLY GO TO COMPUTE-WEEKLY-PAY.
     IF HOURLY GO TO COMPUTE-HOURLY-PAY.
     WRITE PAY-LINE FROM ERR-MESS
           AFTER ADVANCING 2 LINES.
     CLOSE PAY-FILE, LIST-FILE.
     STOP RUN.
```

The READ statement reads the next input record into a storage area for that file. Each input file has a storage area. The data record defined with PAY-FILE is a template that allows information to be accessed by name. The first IF statement uses the condition name WEEKLY; it is the same as if the programmer had written:

>   IF PAY-CODE = "W" GO TO COMPUTE-WEEKLY-PAY.

If the condition is true, the statement(s) following the IF clause is (are) executed. Otherwise, the computer goes to the next sentence. The operand to the GO TO statement, in this case COMPUTE-WEEKLY-PAY, is a paragraph or section name. There are no statement labels in COBOL, per se. However, the programmer can achieve the same purpose by using a paragraph name. At this point, a paragraph or section name is nothing more than a statement label. Later statements are described that utilize the concept of a paragraph or section.

The second IF statement in the READ-PAY paragraph tests for the HOURLY condition and executes in a similar manner to the first IF statement. If the input record is neither weekly nor hourly, an error condition exists and an error message is printed. The CLOSE statement terminates processing of the specified files and logically disconnects the input/output devices from the program. The STOP RUN statement terminates processing of the program.

The COMPUTE-WEEKLY-PAY paragraph is the first case of actual computation being performed.

A    B

```
COMPUTE-WEEKLY-PAY.
    MOVE RATE TO TEMPPAY.
    IF HOURS GREATER THAN 40.0
        COMPUTE TEMPPAY = TEMPPAY + (RATE / 40) *
        (HOURS - 40) * 1.5.
    GO TO PRINT-PAY.
```

The MOVE statement moves the weekly rate to the temporary pay location. Numeric values are aligned by decimal point. The IF statement causes the COMPUTE statement to be executed if hours are greater than 40. The COMPUTE statement is analogous to the assignment statement in FORTRAN or the LET statement in BASIC. Several restrictions exist on the writing of expressions. Operators (such as =, +, −, *, /) must be preceded and followed by at least one space. The left parenthesis must not be followed by a space and the right parenthesis must not be preceded by a space. At this point, it is fairly obvious that hyphens can be used in names, but the reader has probably wondered about the minus operation. Placing a space before and after the minus sign, that is,

A − B

is used to distinguish the expression A *minus* B from the name A-B, since a name may not contain imbedded spaces.

In COBOL, the following hierarchy is established among operators:

| Operator | Hierarchy |
|----------|-----------|
| ** | Highest |
| * or / | ↓ |
| + or − | Lowest |

and parentheses are used for grouping as in FORTRAN and BASIC. The GO TO PRINT-LINE transfers program control to the named paragraph.

The COMPUTE-HOURLY-PAY paragraph demonstrates a compound IF statement, that takes the form:

$$\text{IF condition} \begin{Bmatrix} \text{statement-1} \\ \underline{\text{NEXT SENTENCE}} \end{Bmatrix} \begin{Bmatrix} \underline{\text{OTHERWISE}} \\ \underline{\text{ELSE}} \end{Bmatrix}$$

$$\begin{Bmatrix} \text{statement-2} \\ \underline{\text{NEXT SENTENCE}} \end{Bmatrix} .$$

and is depicted in Figure 9.2. In this format, "statement-1" and "statement-2" can each be one or more COBOL statements. The COMPUTE-HOURLY-PAY paragraph is given as follows:

```
A   B

COMPUTE-HOURLY-PAY.
    IF HOURS GREATER THAN 40.0
        COMPUTE TEMPPAY = RATE * 40 + (HOURS - 40) *
        RATE * 1.5
    ELSE COMPUTE TEMPPAY = RATE * HOURS.
```

If HOURS is greater than 40, the statement

COMPUTE TEMPPAY = RATE * 40 + (HOURS − 40) * RATE * 1.5

is executed and program control passes directly to the next sentence. If HOURS is not greater than 40, then the statement following the word ELSE is executed and program control is passed to the next sentence.

The PRINT-PAY paragraph is:

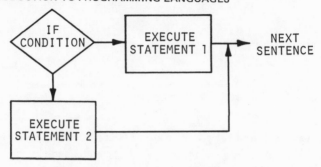

Fig. 9.2. The compound IF statement.

A    B

```
PRINT-PAY.
    MOVE SPACES TO PAY-LINE.
    MOVE S-S-NO TO SOCSECNO.
    MOVE PAY-CODE IN PAY-CARD TO PAY-CODE IN PAY-LINE.
    MOVE NAME TO EMPL-NAME.
    MOVE TEMPPAY TO TOTALPAY.
    WRITE PAY-LINE.  GO TO READ-PAY.
```

An area in storage is associated with the output record PAY-LINE. The first statement moves spaces to PAY-LINE to remove residual characters from previous write statements. The statement:

MOVE S-S-NO TO SOCSECNO

moves the numeric field S-S-NO to the numeric field SOCSECNO. The contents of S-S-NO are left unchanged. The fields are aligned by decimal point, which is assumed, in this case, to be to the right of the rightmost digit in the field. The statement:

MOVE PAY-CODE IN PAY-CARD TO PAY-CODE IN PAY-LINE

involves a movement of alphabetic information from left to right in the fields. The clause PAY-CODE IN PAY-CARD constitutes a qualified name that is required because the data item PAY-CODE is used in two structures. Thus, the qualification IN PAY-CARD denotes the structure in which PAY-CODE is found. The statement:

MOVE NAME TO EMPL-NAME

involves alphanumeric information that is also moved from left to right. The following general rules apply to data movement of character data. Consider the statement:

MOVE A TO B

*Rules:*
1. If the length of A is greater than the length of B, then A is truncated on the right during the replacement operation.
2. If the length of A is less than the length of B, then B is padded on the right with spaces.

Numeric fields are aligned by decimal point and padded on the left or right with zeros. The final MOVE statement:

MOVE TEMPPAY TO TOTALPAY

causes editing to be performed. Alignment is made by decimal point and zero suppression is performed on the left as denoted in the PICTURE clause for TOTALPAY. The WRITE statement transfers PAY-LINE to the associated file. After the WRITE statement is executed, the information in PAY-LINE is no longer accessible. The GO TO statement demonstrates that more than one statement and more than one sentence can be written on one line.

The final paragraph:

```
A    B

END-OF-JOB.
     WRITE PAY-LINE FROM END-MESS AFTER ADVANCING
          2 LINES.
     CLOSE PAY-FILE, LIST-FILE.
     STOP RUN.
```

is entered when an "end of data" condition is reached in the READ statement of paragraph READ-PAY. This paragraph writes a message, closes files, and terminates execution of the program.

In data processing, the "end of data" condition is frequently used to terminate processing of a file. An algorithm is defined for the processing of a single data record and is repeated for each record in the file.

## Comments on the Overview

The overview presents only a few of the statements in the COBOL language and practically ignores language details. This is left for later. However, the general structure of a program is given so that the reader can gain a conceptual view of the purpose of the different divisions of a COBOL program. From the viewpoint of programming languages, the data and procedure divisions have the most to offer and demonstrate the relationship between data and procedure. Some procedure is explicitly given in the procedure division in the form of statements. Other procedures are implied in the data division as a result of editing and conversion specified in the description of a particular data item.

## 9.3 LANGUAGE FUNDAMENTALS

This section describes the "basic facts" necessary for using COBOL. The material applies to all four divisions of a COBOL program. A key concept in COBOL is that of a word. The language is designed so that a programmer can express his program as a series of words familiar to the COBOL compiler. (This fact is obvious from the example of the preceding section.) Words are grouped to form statements; statements are grouped to form sentences; and so on. The term "word" is defined more explicitly after the COBOL character set is presented.

## Character Set

The complete COBOL character set consists of the following 51 characters:

| Character | Meaning or Name |
|---|---|
| 0.1,...,9 | Digit |
| A,B,...,Z | Letter |
|  | Space character (blank) |
| + | Plus sign |
| – | Minus sign or hyphen |
| * | Asterisk |
| / | Slash (stroke, virgule, solidus) |
| = | Equal sign |
| $ | Currency sign (dollar sign) |
| , | Comma |
| . | Period or decimal point |

| | |
|---|---|
| ; | Semicolon |
| " | Quotation mark |
| ( | Left parenthesis |
| ) | Right parenthesis |
| > | Greater than symbol |
| < | Less than symbol |

However, most implementations of COBOL permit other characters in alphanumeric data items.

Two sets of COBOL characters can be referred to by name to facilitate programming. *Numeric characters* consist of the digits 0 through 9. *Alphabetic characters* consist of the letters A through Z. Later, a class test is defined that allows the programmer to test if all characters in a data item are numeric or alphabetic.

The characters in the COBOL alphabet are also placed in categories on the basis of the function they serve in the language. Some characters serve more than one purpose. The characters used in *words* are: the letters A through Z, the digits 0 through 9, and the hyphen (-). The characters used for *punctuation* are:

| *Character* | *Meaning* |
|---|---|
| | Space |
| , | Comma |
| ; | Semicolon |
| . | Period |
| " | Quotation mark |
| ( | Left parenthesis |
| ) | Right parenthesis |

Rules for using the punctuation characters are given in a later paragraph. The characters used for *editing* are:

| *Character* | *Meaning* |
|---|---|
| B | Space |
| 0 | Zero |
| + | Plus |
| – | Minus |
| CR | Credit |
| DB | Debit |
| Z | Zero suppression |
| * | Check protection |

| | |
|---|---|
| $ | Dollar sign (currency sign) |
| , | Comma |
| . | Decimal point |

The function performed by each of these editing characters is presented under "Picture Editing." COBOL allows four characters to be used as *arithmetic operators* in the COMPUTE statement and in conditional expressions. Arithmetic operator symbols are:

| Character or Symbol | Meaning |
|---|---|
| + | Addition |
| - | Subtraction |
| * | Multiplication |
| / | Division |
| ** | Exponentiation |

*Comparison* (or relational) *operators* are permitted in conditional expressions (or "conditions," as they are called in COBOL); the following characters are used:

| Character | Meaning |
|---|---|
| > | Greater than |
| < | Less than |
| = | Equal to |

Arithmetic and comparison operators are discussed further under "Procedure Division."

### Words, Names, Nouns, and Constants

In COBOL, a *word* is a construct that can be "read," similar to a word in a natural language. More formally, a word is a series of not more than 30 characters chosen from the character set for words. A word may not begin or end with a hyphen. It is important to consider how a word is recognized, since many statements are composed of several words. A word is terminated by a space or by the following punctuation characters: a period, a right parenthesis, a comma, or a semicolon. It should be noted that this is an important rule. For example, it makes the expression A+B illegal, a fact which was also known because operators must be preceded and followed by a space. Also, when using a subscripted variable of the form:

data-name (subscript)

the rule implicitly states that the "data-name" must be followed by a space, and this is indeed one of the COBOL rules on the use of subscripts.

In the study of programming languages, it seems as though everything is classified in one way or another, and sometimes in more than one way. A convenient classification for words is to distinguish between reserved words and names. A *reserved word* is part of the COBOL language and may not be used by the programmer as the name of something. A *name* is a word defined by the programmer.

Reserved words are further classified as to whether they are keywords, optional words, or connectives. A *keyword* is required in the statement or clause of which it is a part. In most cases, the omission of a keyword or the substitution of another word for a keyword changes the meaning of a clause or a statement, or causes that construction to be interpreted as being syntactically incorrect. A keyword can be a verb, such as READ, ADD, or MOVE; a required word, such as TO in the MOVE statement; or a word that is assigned a functional meaning, such as NUMERIC, SPACE, or POSITIVE. An *optional word* can be included in a clause or statement at the programmer's option and is used to improve readability and understanding. For example, in the statement:

READ MFILE RECORD INTO DATA-AREA.

READ and INTO are keywords, MFILE and DATA-AREA are names, and RECORD is an optional word that can be omitted but not replaced by another COBOL word. A *connective* is used to qualify a data name, to link two or more consecutive operands, and to form compound comparison expressions. A *qualifier connective* uses the words OF and IN to establish a unique reference to a data item. A *series connective* uses the comma (,) to link two or more operands in a single statement, such as:

ADD A, B GIVING C.

(At this point, the reader is probably wondering if the author is still with it to classify a comma as a reserved word. However, the COBOL standard makes this classification and it is probably included for completeness.) A *logical connective* is one of the words AND, OR, AND NOT, and OR NOT that is used to form complex conditions. This subject is covered later.

A *name* is a word that contains at least one alphabetic character—not necessarily the first character in the word. There are several types of names in COBOL:

1. A *data name* identifies a data item. It is declared in the data division and used in the procedure division.
2. A *file name* identifies a data file. It is declared in the environment and data divisions and used in the procedure division.
3. A *record name* identifies a data record. It is declared in the data division and used in the procedure division.
4. A *procedure name* is either a paragraph or section name. In the environment and data divisions, section names are predefined as part of the COBOL language. In the procedure division, paragraph and section names are defined contextually by their presence in the program and are used as operands in some statements.
5. A *condition name* is a data name assigned to a particular value or a set of values of a data item. A condition name is defined as an 88-level item in the data division and is used as a condition in the IF statement.
6. A *special name* is a name assigned to a specific hardware component in the environment division.

"Extended COBOL" also allows user-defined names to be assigned to a program unit, library, report, a sort file, or a saved area (for random access input/output processing). The reader is directed to the COBOL standard (reference [9]) or a COBOL reference manual (for example, reference [4]) for additional information on extended COBOL.

A user-defined name is an instance of a set of operands frequently referred to as "nouns." More specifically, a *noun* is used as an operand in a COBOL statement and is *usually* a COBOL word, as defined previously. A noun can be a user-defined name, a constant, or a special register. Names are classified in the preceding paragraph. There are three types of constants in COBOL: numeric literals, nonnumeric literals, and figurative constants. A *numeric literal* is a fixed-point value composed from the numeric characters 0 through 9, the plus sign, the minus sign, and the decimal point in accordance with the following rules:

1. It must contain from 1 to 18 numeric characters.
2. It may be signed or unsigned. If a sign is used, it must be the first character in the numeric literal. An unsigned numeric literal is positive.
3. It must not contain more than one decimal point. If the decimal point is omitted, the numeric literal is an integer.
4. The value of a numeric literal is a number to the base ten using the positional number system.

Many implementations of COBOL allow floating-point numeric literals to be used. A floating-point literal is written with an exponent, that is,

[±]mantissa E[±]exponent

in precisely the same manner as in the FORTRAN language. The reader is directed to Chapter 6 for a complete discussion of floating-point notation.

A *nonnumeric literal* is a series of 1 to 120 characters from the COBOL alphabet, excluding the quotation mark; it is bounded by quotation marks. For example, the following are nonnumeric literals:

"TEA FOR TWO"
"123.4$"
"ADD A TO B."

All nonnumeric literals are classed as alphanumeric data items.

A *figurative constant* is a value to which a data name has been assigned. Figurative constants are reserved words, as defined previously. A figurative constant is used as an ordinary data name, that is, without quotation marks, and the singular and plural forms are equivalent. The following figurative constants are defined in COBOL:

| | |
|---|---|
| ZERO<br>ZEROES<br>ZEROS | Represents the character 0, or one or more occurrences of the character 0, depending on context. |
| SPACE<br>SPACES | Represents one or more spaces (blank characters) depending on context. |
| HIGH-VALUE<br>HIGH-VALUES | Represents one or more occurrences of the character that has the highest value in the computer's collating sequence. |
| LOW-VALUE<br>LOW-VALUES | Represents one or more occurrences of the character that has the lowest value in the computer's collating sequence. |
| QUOTE<br>QUOTES | Represents one or more occurrences of the quotation mark character. The word QUOTE cannot be used in place of the quotation mark as a delimiter. |
| ALL literal | Represents one or more occurrences of the string of characters representing the nonnumeric "literal." The |

literal may be a figurative constant, in which case the word ALL is superfluous.

In all cases, the class of a figurative constant must agree with the requirements of the statement in which it is used.

A *special register* is a storage area recognized and generated by the COBOL compiler for use in several of the COBOL statements. The only special register included in the COBOL "nucleus" of basic statements is TALLY, defined as an unsigned integer of five digits in computational form. The register TALLY may be used anywhere that a data name of integral value can be used. Extensions to COBOL allow additional special registers, such as LINE-COUNTER, PAGE-COUNTER, CURRENT-DATE, and TIME-OF-DAY.

### Punctuation

Because of the use of reserved words in COBOL, punctuation is a minor concern—provided that a few simple rules are followed. Punctuation rules that are specific to a particular division of a COBOL program are covered when that division is presented in detail. A key point is that the space character, the comma, the semicolon, and the period are used in the same way they would be used in the English language. The general rules are:

1. When a period, semicolon, or comma is used, it must not be preceded by a space but must be followed by a space.
2. A left parenthesis must not be followed immediately by a space and a right parenthesis must not be preceded immediately by a space.
3. Two or more successive spaces are treated as a single space—except in nonnumeric literals.
4. At least one space must appear between two successive words, nouns, or parenthetical clauses.
5. An operator, including the equals sign denoting replacement, must be preceded and followed by a space.
6. A comma may be used between successive operands in a statement. A comma followed by a space is equivalent to a space.
7. A comma or a semicolon may be used to separate a series of clauses. (Successive clauses are frequently used in the environment and data divisions to specify the attributes of a data item, file, or hardware name.)
8. A comma or semicolon may be used to separate a series of statements—although the only punctuation needed between successive statements is a single space.

9. Sentences, paragraphs, sections, and divisions must always end with a period.

The flexibility of the punctuation rules in COBOL permits many installations to adopt fairly rigid but useful documentation standards. For example, a frequently used convention in many installations is to separate successive clauses and operands with a comma and to end each statement with a semicolon. Presumably, effective documentation is an installation management problem and this is a case where the versatility of a programming language has partially solved a nonprogramming problem.

### Data Reference

The reserved words IN and OF were mentioned previously as qualifier connectives. A name must be qualified when it does not, by itself, provide a unique reference to the data item or paragraph that it names. Qualification is achieved by following a data name or a paragraph name by one or more phrases composed of a qualifier preceded by IN or OF. (IN and OF may be used interchangeably.) The general form for qualification is:[5]

$$\begin{Bmatrix} \text{data-name} \\ \text{condition-name} \end{Bmatrix} \begin{bmatrix} \begin{Bmatrix} \underline{\text{OF}} \\ \underline{\text{IN}} \end{Bmatrix} \text{data-name} \end{bmatrix} \dots$$

for data and condition names, and

$$\text{paragraph-name} \begin{bmatrix} \begin{Bmatrix} \underline{\text{OF}} \\ \underline{\text{IN}} \end{Bmatrix} \text{section-name} \end{bmatrix}$$

for paragraph names. For example, in the structures

```
01  BIGA        01  BIGB
    02  A ...        02  HIGH
    02  B ....           03  A ...
                         03  C ...
                     02  LOW
                         03  B ...
                         03  D ...
```

[5] Format notation is reviewed later in this chapter.

qualification is needed for the compiler to distinguish between the data items A and B in records BIGA and BIGB. Thus, a reference to A and B in record BIGA must be written A IN BIGA and B IN BIGA, respectively. Similarly, data item A in record BIGB must be qualified and can be referred to as A IN HIGH IN BIGB. Only enough qualification is needed to make a reference unique. Thus, provided that no other conflict exists, the reference B IN BIGB is equivalent to B IN LOW IN BIGB.

A paragraph name cannot be duplicated within a section of the procedure division. Therefore, at most, one level of qualification is needed for a paragraph name. The statements:

```
BIG SECTION.
FAST-PAR.
     MOVE A TO B,...
     .
     .
     .

LITTLE SECTION.
FAST-PAR.
     ADD A TO B,...
     .
     .
     .

OTHER SECTION.
SLOW-PAR.
     .
     .
     .
     GO TO FAST-PAR IN LITTLE.
     .
     .
     .
```

depict an example of a case where qualification is needed for a paragraph name. When a section name is used as a qualifier, the word SECTION must not appear. When a paragraph name is referred to from within its own section, it need not be qualified; that is, for example,

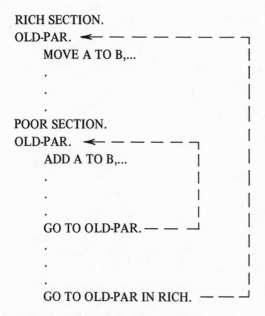

```
RICH SECTION.
OLD-PAR. ←— — — — — — — ┐
      MOVE A TO B,...            |
      .                          |
      .                          |
      .                          |
POOR SECTION.                    |
OLD-PAR. ←— — — — — ┐            |
      ADD A TO B,...     |       |
      .                  |       |
      .                  |       |
      .                  |       |
      GO TO OLD-PAR. — — ┘       |
      .                          |
      .                          |
      .                          |
      GO TO OLD-PAR IN RICH. — — ┘
```

The following rules apply to qualification:

1. Each qualifier must be of successively higher level and must be within the same hierarchy (record or section) as the name that it qualifies. (However, as mentioned, only enough qualification is needed to make a name unique.)
2. The same name must not appear at two levels in the same hierarchy so that name would appear to qualify itself.
3. If a name requires qualification, then it must be qualified each time it is used in a program.
4. A data name used as a qualifier cannot be subscripted. However, the complete data reference can be subscripted.
5. A name can be qualified even though it is unique and qualification is not needed.

Another form of data reference requires subscripting wherein an element of an array is selected. An array is defined with the OCCURS clause in the data division, as in the following example:

```
01  BIG-REC.
    02  TABLE OCCURS 50 TIMES.
        03  SYMBOL PICTURE X(8).
        03  VALUE PICTURE S9(5).
```

that defines a one-dimensional array of structures (a single level table, as it is called) of the form:

| Index | Symbol | Value |
|-------|--------|-------|
| 1 | XXXXXXXX | S99999 |
| 2 | XXXXXXXX | S99999 |
| 3 | XXXXXXXX | S99999 |
| . | . | . |
| . | . | . |
| . | . | . |
| 50 | XXXXXXXX | S99999 |

An individual element of an array is selected with a subscript, represented either by a numeric literal with an integral value, by the special register TALLY, or by a data name. A subscript is enclosed in parentheses following the array name or following a subelement of the array. Thus, the reference TABLE (I) selects the *I*th structure in the array of structures named TABLE and the reference SYMBOL IN TABLE (I) selects the data item SYMBOL in the *I*th structure of TABLE. If SYMBOL in TABLE is unique, then the last reference can be simplified as SYMBOL (I).

Up to three dimensions are permitted for arrays such that more than one subscript, in an array reference, must be separated by commas. In general, a reference to an array variable takes the form:

$$\text{data-name} \left[ \left\{ \begin{matrix} \underline{\text{OF}} \\ \underline{\text{IN}} \end{matrix} \right\} \text{data-name} \right] \ldots \left[ (\text{subscript[,subscript[,subscript]]}) \right]$$

COBOL also includes a table-handling facility that permits an index variable along with SEARCH and SET statements to be used. This topic is discussed further in Chapter 12.

### Comment Lines

The programmer may insert commentary information into the identification and procedure divisions of a COBOL program. In the identification division, the REMARKS clause is used and the commentary information can take the form of a set of sentences that ends with the beginning of the environment division.

In the procedure division, the keyword NOTE is used to mark the beginning of commentary information. If the NOTE sentence is the first sentence in a paragraph, then the entire paragraph is considered to be commentary information. If the NOTE sentence appears other than as the first sentence of a paragraph, then the comment ends with the first period followed by a space.

## 9.4 FORMAT NOTATION

The format notation used to describe the COBOL language is a variation to the syntax notation used to describe BASIC and FORTRAN. The variation is caused by the fact that COBOL utilizes reserved words, which, in some cases, are optional in the sense that they can be included or elided at the discretion of the programmer. The COBOL format notation is described as follows:

1. All words printed entirely in capital letters are reserved words, which have preassigned meaning in COBOL and may not be used as user-defined names. These words must be used in the exact position and form that they are shown in the format.
2. All underlined reserved words are required unless the syntactical unit of which they are a part is optional. A reserved word that is not underlined may be included or omitted by the programmer in writing the clause or statement of which it is a part.
3. Operators, such as + or =, and punctuation characters must be used where indicated in the format. Additional punctuation may be added in line within the rules given previously for punctuation.
4. Words represented by lower-case letters or lower- and upper-case words separated by a hyphen denote information that must be supplied by the programmer.
5. Square brackets ([]) denote optional items. When a choice may be made among optional items, they are stacked with brackets, for example, $\begin{bmatrix} \underline{RIGHT} \\ \underline{LEFT} \end{bmatrix}$.
6. Braces ({ }) denote that a choice *must* be made among the items stacked vertically within the braces, for example, $\begin{Bmatrix} \underline{REEL} \\ \underline{UNIT} \end{Bmatrix}$.
7. The ellipsis (...) denotes that the immediately preceding syntactical unit may occur one or more times in succession. (A unit is defined as a single lower-case word or a collection of syntactical units enclosed in brackets or braces.)

For example, the statement

$$\underline{\text{DIVIDE}} \left\{ \begin{array}{l} \text{identifier} \\ \text{literal} \end{array} \right\} \underline{\text{INTO}} \text{ identifier } [\underline{\text{ROUNDED}}]$$
$$[\text{ON } \underline{\text{SIZE ERROR}} \text{ imperative-statement}]$$

exhibits required elements (such as $\underline{\text{DIVIDE}}$ and $\underline{\text{INTO}}$), alternate elements (such as identifier or literal), a simple optional element (such as $\underline{\text{ROUNDED}}$), and an optional unit (such as ON $\underline{\text{SIZE ERROR}}$ imperative-statement) that includes both required and optional elements.

## 9.5   COMMENTS

At this point the reader should have a conceptual idea of what COBOL is all about along with a diverse collection of facts and rules. A quick review of section 9.2, "Overview of the COBOL Language," would be appropriate at this point since many of the details are now more meaningful. The data and procedure divisions are relatively long and are covered in Chapters 10 and 11, respectively. Chapter 12 covers miscellaneous topics such as the identification and environment divisions, library facilities, random-access processing, table handling, and editing.

## EXERCISES

1. What is meant by the remark that "COBOL programs are self-documenting"?
2. What is the difference between a data name and a constant?
3. In what margins (A or B) do each of the following start:

   | | |
   |---|---|
   | Division | Sentence |
   | Section | Statement |
   | Paragraph | Continuation line |

4. In your own words (and without reviewing the text), state the role of each of the divisions in a COBOL program.
5. What purpose does a "PICTURE clause" serve?
6. List all of the COBOL rules, formal and informal, that are given in the chapter. (The list will be a handy reference later in the book.)
7. Why is qualification necessary? What kinds of qualification are there?

8. Give three figurative constants.
9. Can you think of any reason why the length of a nonnumeric literal is from 1 to 120 characters?
10. Give errors in the following constants (if any):

    123.456     89.9–
    –9.14       63192283764192004
    5,143.00    +123.

11. Which of the following are valid data names?

    JONES    PL/I     ZERO
    K-25     SIX      15–M
    12BLOT   A+B+C    ADD

12. True or false. Data names and paragraph names are constructed using the same COBOL rules.
13. Which of the following nonnumeric literals are invalid and give the reason why?

    "TEA FOR TWO"    "COMMON BUSINESS ORIENTED LANGUAGE
    "12+.+AB"        "THE ANS="F3.4" DOLLARS"
    SPACES

14. What is a literal?
15. The following format notation defines a class of valid ADD statements:

$$\underline{\text{ADD}} \begin{Bmatrix} \text{identifier-1} \\ \text{literal-1} \end{Bmatrix} \begin{bmatrix} \text{,identifier-2} \\ \text{,literal-2} \end{bmatrix} ...\underline{\text{TO}} \text{ identifier-}m \text{ [ROUNDED]}$$

Using this format notation, give five valid instances of the ADD statement.

# THE DATA
# DIVISION

## 10.1 INTRODUCTION

Most algorithms are relatively independent of the manner in which the data is stored. Obviously, a necessary distinction must be made between data with different type attributes, such as real and complex, but other than that, the majority of algorithms are practically insensitive to changes in data representation. Data description is of lesser concern in scientific applications than the procedure description and in languages like BASIC and FORTRAN, data declarations are intermingled with the procedure part of the program. In data processing, the form of data is of major concern and the data description is frequently a lengthy part of the program specification. Although the data and procedure divisions of a COBOL program, for example, are distinct, the object program is very sensitive to the precise nature of the data on which it operates. Another characteristic of data processing is that the output of one program is frequently used as input to another program. It is necessary, therefore, to have a data description that is completely independent of the procedure description. If the form of a data record, for example, changes then only the data description need be modified and the procedure description is left intact. Similarly, when a program change needs to be made, only the procedure description needs to be modified. Another consideration is that data and file descriptions that are needed for more than one application can be stored in a library and be retrieved when the program is compiled. (This subject, by the way, is covered in Chapter 12.)

The data division in COBOL is used to describe files and their associated records, working storage, and reports. The file and working storage sections are covered in detail. The report section is not covered at all. It is one of the least successful and infrequently used features of the COBOL language and at least one proposal has been made by a major organization to the COBOL language development group to remove the report-writer feature from the official COBOL language.

The structure of the data division is given as follows:

DATA DIVISION.
FILE SECTION.
{ file-description-entry
{ record-description-entry }...}...
WORKING-STORAGE SECTION.
[independent-storage-entry]...
[record-description-entry]...

Each of these sections is optional but must be presented to the compiler in the order given.

## 10.2  DATA DIVISION ELEMENTS

This section presents basic language elements that are used in writing data division entries. Most of the concepts are not discussed after this section because they are considered to be general knowledge. The reader is directed to Murach (reference [7], p. 47) for additional introductory information .

### File Concepts

The concept of a data file is introduced in Chapter 1 where a distinction is made between a block (sometimes referred to as a physical record) and a data record (sometimes referred to as a logical record). The BASIC and FORTRAN languages do not utilize these concepts except through facilities of the operating system. Because data processing frequently deals with large amounts of data and because storage density is important, the use of blocked records is regarded as an integral part of the COBOL language. Blocked records are necessary in COBOL, from a practical point of view, regardless of whether an operating system is used or not.

In COBOL, the user denotes blocked records in the file description and is permitted to specify the recording mode (fixed-length, variable-length, or undefined-length records), block size (in terms of the number of records or as a block length), and record size.

As shown in the example of Chapter 9, the description of a data record is not restricted to a file description. Data items can be grouped to form a data record in the working storage section. Records defined in the working storage section can be used solely for working storage or can be used in conjunction with records defined in the file section for input and output.

### Levels and Data Categorization

The concept of levels is necessary for structuring a data record and is the means by which elements contained in a structure are categorized. A data record is the most inclusive category and the level number for a record starts at 1 or 01. Less inclusive structures are assigned higher-level numbers but level numbers need not be successive. Thus, the following structures are equivalent:

```
01  A                    01  A
    02  B                    07  B
        03  C                    18  C
        03  D                    18  D
    02  E                    07  E
```

Level numbers greater than 49 are not permitted within record descriptions, except for 88-level items that denote condition names. Independent working storage data items are denoted by a level number of 77 in the working storage section.[1]

A *group item* is an item having further subdivisions; for example, in the structure

```
01  A
    03  B
        06  C
        06  D
    03  E
        05  F
```

A, B, and E are group items. More specifically, an item is a group item if its level number is less than the level number of the immediately succeeding item, unless

---

[1] A 66-level item is also defined in the full COBOL language. It is used to RENAME a data item or a set of data items.

the immediately succeeding item is an 88-level item. In a record description, an item that is not a group item must be an elementary item or a condition name.

An *elementary item* is a data item that contains no subordinate items. In the preceding example, C, D, and F are elementary items. The distinction between a group item and an elementary item is important because certain attributes and operations can only be applied to data items in one of the two categories.

A data item is further classified by the information that it contains. An *alphabetic item* contains only the letters A through Z and the space character. A *numeric item* contains only numeric digits in either an external or an internal representation. An *alphanumeric item* can contain any character in the COBOL alphabet, including characters relevant to a particular implementation of COBOL. A *numeric edited item* is an alphanumeric item containing only digits and numeric editing characters, such as $, ., *, and so forth. An *alphanumeric edited item* is an edited version of an alphanumeric field. (Limited editing facilities are defined on alphanumeric fields.)

Recall the previous comment that certain operations are permitted on group items and others are permitted only on elementary items. The class of a group item is treated as alphanumeric, regardless of the class of the subordinate elementary items. In general, therefore, an operation defined on alphanumeric data is permitted on a group item, whereas an operation that is not defined on alphanumeric data is *not* permitted on a group item. Table 10.1 depicts the relationship between level, class, and category of COBOL data.

Table 10.1

Relationship between Level and the Class and Category of COBOL Data

| Level | Class | Category |
|-------|-------|----------|
| Elementary | { Alphabetic<br>Numeric | Alphabetic<br>Numeric |
| | Alphanumeric | Numeric edited<br>Alphanumeric edited<br>Alphanumeric |
| Group | Alphanumeric | Alphabetic<br>Numeric<br>Numeric edited<br>Alphanumeric edited<br>Alphanumeric |

### Data Representation

Although the representation of data in a COBOL program is implementation dependent, certain general guidelines exist to permit programs to be written in a machine independent fashion. First, alphabetic and alphanumeric information is stored in an external representation, usually taken to be binary coded decimal. Expressed in another way, alphabetic and alphanumeric information is not considered to be "coded data" in the sense that the manner in which the data is stored is dependent on a particular model of computer or implementation of the language. (It is recognized here that certain coding methods exist for information interchange, such as card code, punched tape code, ASCII, and EBCDIC.[2] The above discussion refers to internal coding other than for information interchange.)

Numeric data, on the other hand, can be stored in decimal form or in a computational form such as binary. There can be more than one form of decimal; for example, there can be external form, such as with alphanumeric information, and there can be packed decimal. Similarly, a computational form can be fixed point or floating point and utilize short precision or long precision. In fact, computational form need not be binary—depending on the computer equipment used. In this book only two forms of numeric data representation are identified: computational and display. A numeric data item in computational form can be used in an arithmetic operation without requiring conversion; however, it cannot be printed (or displayed) without conversion and/or editing. A numeric data item stored in display form, that is, an external form such as binary coded decimal, can be printed (or displayed) without conversion; however, it cannot be used in an arithmetic operation without being converted to a computational form. A numeric data item stored in display form may still require editing before printing, depending on the needs of a particular application.[3]

### Format and Punctuation

Each entry in the data division begins with a "level indicator" or a level number, followed by at least one space, followed by a data name, optionally followed by one or more clauses that give the attributes of the data item. *The last clause for each entry must always be terminated with a period.*

The *level indicator* takes the form FD and denotes the start of a file descrip-

---

[2] ASCII stands for "American Standard Code for Information Interchange." EBCDIC stands for "Extended Binary Code Decimal Interchange Code."

[3] Such as zero suppression or check protection.

tion in the file section. (Similarly, the level indicator for the report description is written RD.) The level indicator is always written in area A, of the reference format, followed in area B by its data name and descriptive clauses. For example,

| A | B |
|---|---|
| FD | MFILE; RECORDING MODE IS F;<br>BLOCK CONTAINS 10 RECORDS;<br>LABEL RECORDS ARE STANDARD;<br>DATA RECORDS ARE A-REC, B-REC, C-REC. |

In the data division, clauses must be separated by at least one space. Clauses may optionally be separated by a semicolon followed by a space or a comma followed by a space.

Data division entries that begin with a *level number* are referred to as data description entries. Data description entries with level numbers of 01 or 77 must begin in area A, followed in area B by the associated data name and descriptive clauses. Successive data description entries may have the same format as the 01 level entry or may be indented according to level number. Indentation does not affect the magnitude of the level number and all successive level numbers need not be indented. However, at least one space must separate the level number from the word following the level number. For example, the structures of the following records are equivalent:

```
01  ALPHA              1 ALPHA
    02  BETA           2 BETA
    02  GAMMA          2 GAMMA
        03 A           3 A
        03 B           3 B
```

Single-digit level numbers are written as a space followed by a digit or a zero followed by a digit.

## 10.3  FILE SECTION

The *file section* supplies the attributes of files used in a COBOL program and a description of data records contained in those files. The general format of the file section is:

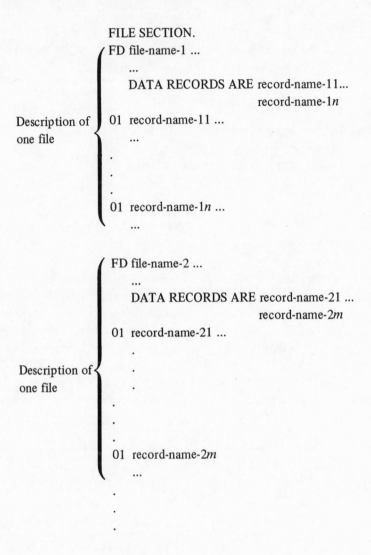

In other words, the description of a file includes:

1. The attributes of that file
2. A complete description of *all* of the data records that can be used with that file

The complete skeleton of an FD entry is given in Figure 10.1. The various entries are presented in the following paragraphs.

FD file-name [;RECORDING MODE IS mode]

$$
\left[ \text{;BLOCK CONTAINS [integer-1 \underline{TO}] integer-2} \begin{Bmatrix} \text{\underline{RECORDS}} \\ \text{\underline{CHARACTERS}} \end{Bmatrix} \right]
$$

$$
\left[ \text{;DATA} \begin{Bmatrix} \text{\underline{RECORD} IS} \\ \text{\underline{RECORDS} ARE} \end{Bmatrix} \text{data-name-1 [,data-name-2] ...} \right]
$$

[; RECORD CONTAINS [integer-3 TO] integer-4 CHARACTERS]

$$
\text{;LABEL} \begin{Bmatrix} \text{\underline{RECORD} IS} \\ \text{\underline{RECORDS} ARE} \end{Bmatrix} \begin{Bmatrix} \text{\underline{STANDARD}} \\ \text{\underline{OMITTED}} \\ \text{data-name-3 [,data-name-4] ...} \end{Bmatrix}
$$

$$
\left[ \text{; VALUE OF data-name-5 IS} \begin{Bmatrix} \text{data-name-6} \\ \text{literal-1} \end{Bmatrix} \right.
$$

$$
\left. \left[ \text{, data-name-7 IS} \begin{Bmatrix} \text{data-name-8} \\ \text{literal-2} \end{Bmatrix} \right] ... \right].
$$

Fig. 10.1. Format of the FD entry for a file description.

**File Name**

The *file name* is a user-defined word that contains at least one alphabetic character. The named file must correspond to a file with the same name in a SELECT statement in the environment division. Many implementations of COBOL restrict the length of file names to a much smaller size than the 30-character limit on names.

**Recording Mode**

The recording mode clause is used to specify the format of logical records in a block. It has the following format:

    RECORDING MODE IS mode

where "mode" is an implementation defined value. Typical "modes" are F, V, and U for fixed-length, variable-length, and undefined-length records, respectively. For example, the clause

    RECORDING MODE IS V

specifies variable-length records.

### Block Size

The BLOCK clause specifies the size of a physical record and takes the form:

$$
\text{\underline{BLOCK} CONTAINS [integer-1 \underline{TO}] integer-2} \left\{ \begin{array}{l} \text{\underline{RECORDS}} \\ \text{\underline{CHARACTERS}} \end{array} \right\}
$$

where "integer-1" and "integer-2" are positive integers. This clause is required when blocked records are used.

When the CHARACTERS option is used, integer-1 and integer-2 refer to the minimum and maximum size, respectively, of the physical record. If only integer-2 is written, then it refers to the exact size of the physical record.

When the RECORDS option is used, integer-1 and integer-2 refer to the minimum and maximum number of data records in a block, respectively, and is intended for use with mass storage files. Examples,

BLOCK CONTAINS 5 TO 10 RECORDS

BLOCK CONTAINS 4096 CHARACTERS

### Data Records Clause

The DATA RECORDS clause associates a set of data records with a data file and takes the form:

$$
\text{\underline{DATA}} \left\{ \begin{array}{l} \text{\underline{RECORD} IS} \\ \text{\underline{RECORDS} ARE} \end{array} \right\} \text{data-name-1 [,data-name-2]...}
$$

where "data-name-*i*" is the name of a record description that follows the FD entry. Only one record storage area is assigned to a file and the record description effectively serves as a template so that fields in a record can be accessed. Examples:

DATA RECORD IS ABC-REC

DATA RECORDS ARE A-REC, B-REC, BIGGY

### Record Size

The RECORD size clause gives the size of a data record and takes the form:

RECORD CONTAINS [integer-3 TO] integer-4 CHARACTERS

where "integer-3" and "integer-4" are positive integers. This clause is not required since the size of data records can be determined by the compiler from succeeding record descriptions.

When integer-3 and integer-4 are both used, then integer-3 denotes the minimum number of characters in the smallest size data record and integer-4 denotes the maximum number of characters in the largest size data record. When integer-4 is used alone, all data records in the file have the same size. Examples:

RECORD CONTAINS 133 CHARACTERS

RECORD CONTAINS 80 TO 192 CHARACTERS

**Data File Labels**

Descriptive file labels can be used with data files depending on the needs of a particular application. File labels are useful for insuring that the correct file is being accessed, to protect against a file being inadvertently "scratched," and to facilitate the use of multivolume files. The LABEL clause allows the type of labels to be specified and takes the form:

$$\text{LABEL} \begin{Bmatrix} \underline{\text{RECORD IS}} \\ \underline{\text{RECORDS ARE}} \end{Bmatrix} \begin{Bmatrix} \underline{\text{STANDARD}} \\ \underline{\text{OMITTED}} \\ \text{data-name-3 [,data-name-4]...} \end{Bmatrix}$$

The OMITTED option specifies that no labels exist for the associated file. The STANDARD option specifies that standard implementation-defined labels are to be used.

"Data-name-*i*" refers to a record specified with the file as a record description but not included in the DATA RECORDS clause. This option permits the user to specify his own labels.

The VALUE OF clause specifies additional label checking and takes the form:

$$\text{VALUE OF data-name-5 IS} \begin{Bmatrix} \text{data-name-6} \\ \text{literal-1} \end{Bmatrix}$$
$$\begin{bmatrix} \text{,data-name-7 IS} \begin{Bmatrix} \text{data-name-8} \\ \text{literal-2} \end{Bmatrix} \end{bmatrix} ...$$

where "data-name-5, data-name-7," and so on, are label records and "data-name-6, data-name-8," and so on, are items defined in the working storage section.

For input, the label-checking routine verifies that data-name-5 is equal to data-name-6 or literal-1, whichever is specified. For output, the value of data-name-5 is made equal to data-name-6 or literal-1, whichever is specified, when the user-defined label is written. Examples:

LABEL RECORDS ARE STANDARD

LABEL RECORD IS LBL-REC; VALUE OF
  LBL-REC IS CHECK-VALUE

The VALUE OF clause is an infrequently used facility and is interpreted as a comment by some compilers.

### Comments on the File Section

A major part of the file section is a description of the data records associated with a file. Record description in the file section is the same as record description in the working storage section and is given the name "Data Description." Data description is covered in the next section.

### 10.4 DATA DESCRIPTION

The *data description entry* specifies the attributes of a particular data item. The format of a complete data description entry is given as Figure 10.2. The various clauses are described in the following paragraphs.

General rules for writing the data description are:

1. All semicolons and commas are optional.
2. The level number may be any number from 1 to 49 or be 77. (The 88-level item is presented separately.)
3. The clauses may be written in any order except for the data name or the FILLER clause, which must immediately follow the level number.
4. The REDEFINES clause, when used, must follow the data name.
5. A data description entry must always be terminated with a period.
6. The PICTURE clause must be specified for each elementary item (except for an index data item which is presented in Chapter 12).

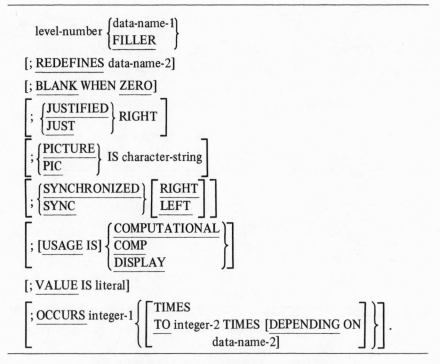

Fig. 10.2. Format of the data description entry.

7. The clauses SYNCHRONIZED, PICTURE, JUSTIFIED, and BLANK WHEN ZERO may only be specified at the elementary item level.

### Data Name or FILLER Clause

The data name clause takes the form:

$$\text{level-number} \begin{Bmatrix} \text{data-name-1} \\ \text{FILLER} \end{Bmatrix}$$

where "data-name-1" is a user-defined COBOL word that contains at least one alphabetic character. Data-name-1 may have a length of 1 to 30 characters.

The reserved word FILLER specifies a group item or an elementary item that is never referred to and need not be named.

Level-77 and level-01 entries must always be given unique data names since they cannot be qualified.

## The REDEFINES Clause

The REDEFINES clause provides a means of specifying an alternate description of a storage area. The form of the REDEFINES clause is:

> level-number data-name-1 REDEFINES data-name-2

where "data-name-1" is the alternate name for the storage area previously described as "data-name-2." The level numbers of data-name-1 and data-name-2 must be the same. Example:

```
03 NAME.
   04 FIRST PICTURE X(12).
   04 MI      PICTURE A(1).
   04 LAST  PICTURE X(20).
03 IDENT REDEFINES NAME PICTURE X(33).
```

In this example, IDENT is data-name-1 and NAME is data-name-2. The redefinition of data-name-2 includes all data items subordinate to it. Moreover, data-name-2 may not contain an OCCURS clause or be subordinate to a data item that contains an OCCURS clause. However, data-name-1 may include an OCCURS clause as depicted in the following example:

```
02 CARD PICTURE X(80).
02 C-ARRAY REDEFINES CARD PICTURE X(1)
   OCCURS 80 TIMES.
```

In the file section, redefinition at the 01 level is not permitted. In fact, redefinition is implicitly provided when more than one level-01 entry follows an FD entry.

## The BLANK WHEN ZERO Clause

The BLANK WHEN ZERO clause causes a field to be set to spaces (that is, blank characters) when the value of the data item is zero; the clause has the form

> BLANK WHEN ZERO

The BLANK WHEN ZERO applies only to elementary items specified as numeric or numeric edited.

### The JUSTIFIED Clause

The JUSTIFIED clause is used to depart from normal positioning rules when the receiving field is alphabetic or alphanumeric. Normally, alphabetic or alphanumeric information is moved to a receiving field on a left-to-right basis. If the sending field is shorter than the receiving field, then the receiving field is padded on the right with spaces. If the sending field is longer than the receiving field, then the sending field is truncated on the right during replacement. The normal mode is depicted as follows:

> 77 A PICTURE X(5) VALUE IS "QRSTU".
> 77 B PICTURE X(3).
> 77 C PICTURE X(8).
>
> .
> .
> .
>
> MOVE A TO B
>
> A $\boxed{\text{QRSTU}}$ →B $\boxed{\text{QRS}}$
>
> MOVE A TO C
>
> A $\boxed{\text{QRSTU}}$ →C $\boxed{\text{QRSTU}\not{b}\not{b}\not{b}}$

The JUSTIFIED clause takes the form:

$$\boxed{\left\{ \begin{array}{l} \underline{\text{JUSTIFIED}} \\ \underline{\text{JUST}} \end{array} \right\} \text{RIGHT}}$$

and affects the positioning of data in the *receiving* field as follows:

1. When the sending field is larger than the receiving field, truncation occurs on the left.
2. When the receiving field is larger than the sending field, it is padded on the left with spaces.

The use of the JUSTIFIED clause is depicted as follows:

77 A PICTURE X(5) VALUE IS "QRSTU".
77 B PICTURE X(3) JUSTIFIED RIGHT.
77 C PICTURE X(8) JUSTIFIED RIGHT.

.
.
.

MOVE A TO B

A | QRSTU |  →B | STU |

MOVE A TO C

A | QRSTU |  →C | bbbQRSTU |

The JUSTIFIED clause may only be used with elementary items.

### The PICTURE Clause

The PICTURE clause is used to specify the attributes and editing requirements of an elementary item. The form of the PICTURE clause is:

$$\left\{ \begin{array}{l} \underline{\text{PICTURE}} \\ \underline{\text{PIC}} \end{array} \right\} \text{ IS character-string}$$

where "character string" is a series of picture characters, the maximum length of which is 30 characters.[4] The PICTURE clause effectively specifies one of the five categories of data, that is, alphabetic, numeric, alphanumeric, alphanumeric edited, and numeric edited. The picture characters permitted for each of these categories are given in the following list:

| Category | Permitted Picture Characters |
|----------|------------------------------|
| Alphabetic | "A" |
| Numeric | "9", "P", "S", and "V" |
| Alphanumeric | "A", "X", and "9" |
| Alphanumeric edited | "A", "X", "9", "B", and "0" |
| Numeric edited | "B", "P", "V", "Z", "0", "9", ",", ".", "*", "+", "−", "CR", "DB", and "$" |

[4]The size of the data item being described is not restricted in length.

(The enclosing quotation marks are not written when a picture character is used.) The functions performed by each of the above picture characters are summarized in Table 10.2. Picture editing is presented in detail in Chapter 12.

Table 10.2

Function and Use of Characters Used in the Picture Clause

| | |
|---|---|
| A | Represents a character position that can contain only a letter or a space. |
| B | Represents a character position into which the space character will be inserted. |
| P | Represents a decimal scaling position and is used to denote the location of the implied decimal point when it is not inside the numeric data item. |
| S | Represents the presence of an operational sign. |
| V | Indicates the location of the implied decimal point in a numeric data item. |
| X | Represents a character position that can contain any character in the COBOL alphabet or in the allowable character set. |
| Z | Represents a leading numeric character position used for zero suppression; leading zeros denoted by a Z item are replaced by a space character during editing. |
| 9 | Represents a character position that can contain only a digit character. |
| 0 | Represents a character position into which the digit character zero will be inserted. |
| , | Represents a character position into which a comma will be inserted. |
| . | Represents a character position into which a decimal point will be inserted, *and* also represents the decimal point for alignment purposes. |
| + − CR DB | Represent character positions into which sign control characters will be inserted. |
| * | Represents a leading numeric character position into which an asterisk will be placed during editing when that position contains a zero. |
| $ | Represents a character position into which a dollar sign will be placed. |

As far as the nonedited data categories are concerned, the allowable picture characters specify the size of the data item, the type of characters it can contain, and the implied decimal point.

Several instances of PICTURE clauses have been given in previous examples.

## The SYNCHRONIZED Clause

The SYNCHRONIZED clause is used to align an elementary data item on a natural boundary in main storage—such as the beginning of a computer word. The form of the SYNCHRONIZED clause is:

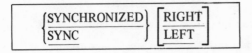

SYNCHRONIZED LEFT and SYNCHRONIZED RIGHT specify that the data item is to be aligned on the left and right boundary, respectively, of the main storage unit in which the data item is placed. If neither LEFT nor RIGHT is specified, then the data item is placed so as to effect efficient use of the data item.

If the SYNCHRONIZED clause is used in conjunction with the OCCURS clause, each occurrence of the item is synchronized.

## The USAGE Clause

The USAGE clause specifies the representation of a data item in main storage. The form of the USAGE clause is:

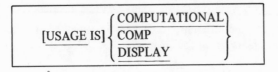

where COMP is an abbreviation for COMPUTATIONAL. The USAGE clause can appear at the elementary or group level. If the clause is used at the group level, it applies to all subordinate entries.

The PICTURE of a computational data item may contain only the following picture characters: 9, S, and V.

The USAGE clause specifies the manner in which a data item is stored and does not affect the manner in which the data item is used.

A data item specified as being computational cannot be displayed without conversion and/or editing.

If the USAGE clause is not specified, the usage of a data item is assumed to be DISPLAY.

## The VALUE Clause

The VALUE clause gives the initial value of working storage items or the values associated with a condition name. The form of the VALUE clause is:

VALUE IS  literal

where "literal" is a numeric constant, nonnumeric constant, or figurative constant in the domain of the data item being described. Example:

77 PERCENT; PICTURE S99V99; USAGE IS COMPUTATIONAL;
VALUE IS 07.25.

The VALUE clause cannot be used in the file section, except as the value associated with a condition name, and must not be used in a data description entry that uses the OCCURS clause.

## The OCCURS Clause

The OCCURS clause is used to define an array (or a table as it is called in COBOL) and has the form:

$$\underline{\text{OCCURS}}\ \text{integer-1}\left\{\left[\begin{array}{l}\text{TIMES}\\ \underline{\text{TO}}\ \text{integer-2 TIMES}\ [\underline{\text{DEPENDING}}\ \text{ON data-name-1}]\end{array}\right]\right\}$$

where "integer-1" and "integer-2" must be positive integers, and if integer-2 is used, then integer-1 must be less than integer-2. If integer-1 is used alone, it specifies a fixed-size array. If integer-1 and integer-2 are both used, integer-1 specifies the minimum number of occurrences and integer-2 specifies the maximum number of occurrences of each array element. If the DEPENDING ON clause is used, the "data-name-1" contains the count of the number of occurrences, which cannot exceed integer-2.

The following data description entry defines a one-dimensional array of alphabetic data items each with a size of 8 characters:

03  SYMBOL-LIST PICTURE A(8) OCCURS 150 TIMES.

A two-dimensional array is specified by defining an array of arrays, as follows:

03  A OCCURS 10 TIMES.
    04  B PICTURE S999V99 OCCURS 15 TIMES.

Variable-length arrays of up to three dimensions are permitted in COBOL.

The OCCURS clause cannot be used with a 01-level or a 77-level entry.

An element of an array can be a structure—that is, an array of structures—as defined in Chapter 1. Thus, in the array specification:

    02  SYMTAB OCCURS 100 TIMES.
        03  SYMBOL PICTURE X(8).
        03  VALUE PICTURE 9(5) COMPUTATIONAL.

each element of SYMTAB is composed of a SYMBOL and a VALUE.

If a data item has an OCCURS clause or is subordinate to a data item with an OCCURS clause, it must be subscripted (or indexed) each time that it is referenced. (Indexing and table handling are covered in Chapter 12.)

A subscript is a positive nonzero integer expressed as a data name or a numeric literal. When a two- or three-dimensional array is defined by describing a group item with an OCCURS clause, which contains data items also described with OCCURS clauses, multilevel subscripting is required. Multilevel subscripts are always written from left to right, in decreasing order to the hierarchy of the groupings in the structure. For example, consider the three-dimensional array defined as follows:

    01  ALPHA.
        02  OUTSIDE OCCURS 2 TIMES.
            03  MIDDLE OCCURS 3 TIMES.
                04  INSIDE OCCURS 2 TIMES PICTURE 9(3).

It is represented and accessed in storage as follows:

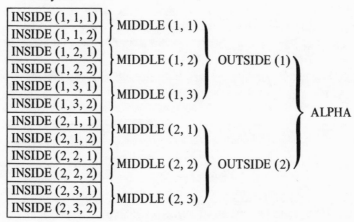

When a data name in an array definition is not unique, qualification is required. Only enough qualification to make a name unique is necessary; however, additional qualification is permitted. When subscripting a qualified name, the subscript is moved to the right of the qualified name. For example, the following references to the first element (INSIDE) of the third MIDDLE of the second OUTSIDE are equivalent:

    INSIDE (2, 3, 1)
    INSIDE IN MIDDLE (2, 3, 1)
    INSIDE IN OUTSIDE (2, 3, 1)
    INSIDE IN MIDDLE IN OUTSIDE (2, 3, 1)

A reference to the group array item MIDDLE (1, 3) would include elements INSIDE (1, 3, 1) and INSIDE (1, 3, 2); similarly, a reference to OUTSIDE (2) would include elements INSIDE (2, 1, 1), INSIDE (2, 1, 2), INSIDE (2, 2, 1), INSIDE (2, 2, 2), INSIDE (2, 3, 1), and INSIDE (2, 3, 2).

**Condition Name**

The definition of a condition name (88-level item) uses the following data description entry:

```
88 condition-name
     ⎧ VALUE IS   ⎫
   ; ⎨            ⎬  literal-1 [THRU literal-2]
     ⎩ VALUES ARE ⎭
   [, literal-3 [THRU literal-4]]...
```

where "condition-name" is a user-defined COBOL word with at least one alphabetic character and possessing a length less than 31 characters. When the THRU options are specified, literal-1 must be less than literal-2, literal-3 must be less than literal-4, etc.

The above format states that the VALUE clause is required in the specification of a condition name and specifies a value or a range of value to be associated with the named condition. Examples:

    03  MARITAL-STATUS PICTURE A.
        88  MARRIED VALUE IS "M".
        88  SINGLE VALUE IS "S".

07 TEMP PICTURE 99 USAGE IS COMPUTATIONAL.
  88 COLD VALUES ARE 0 THRU 32.
  88 MODERATE VALUES ARE 33 THRU 50.
  88 HOT VALUES ARE 51 THRU 100.

The use of condition names is discussed further in Chapter 11, "The Procedure Division."

## 10.5 WORKING STORAGE SECTION

The working storage section describes noncontiguous working storage and working storage records. It has the general form:

WORKING-STORAGE SECTION.
77 DATA-DESCRIPTION ENTRY
  .
  .
  .
77 data-description entry
01 data-description entry
  02 data-description entry
  .
  .
  .
01 data-description entry
  02 data-description entry
    03 data-description entry

Data items in noncontiguous working storage have a level number 77 and have no hierarchic relationship to one another and are not grouped into records. The following clauses are required for each 77-level entry:

1. A level-number 77.
2. A data-name.
3. The PICTURE clause.

Other data description clauses for 77-level data items are optional.

Working storage records describe data items with a hierarchic relationship to one another. The description of working storage records uses the conventions for

"Data Description" given in the previous section, with the exception that the VALUE clause can be used in the working storage section whereas it cannot be used in the file section—except for condition names.

## 10.6  OTHER DATA DIVISION FACILITIES

Other COBOL facilities are reflected in the data division: the report section for the report writer, a sort description facility, a saved area description for program segmentation, a linkage section for using subprograms, and even an obsolete constant section. The structure of the data division in COBOL is given in this chapter and these additional topics are "frosting on the cake." In fact, they are rarely covered in introductory textbooks on the COBOL language. The reader is directed to the COBOL standard or the reference manual for a particular implementation of COBOL.

## EXERCISES

1. Give errors (if any) in the following COBOL entries:

   a.  03 16M-1 PICTURE IS 999 USAGE IS DISPLAY.
   b.  WORKING STORAGE SECTION.
   c.  04 X OCCURS 10 TO 15 TIMES DEPENDING ON N.
   d.  15 TIMES PICTURE 999V99.
   e.  02 COW PIC 99 COMP.
   f.  01 BIG PICTURE IS X(45).
   g.  07 LITTLE PICTURE 99999 USAGE IS DISPLAY.

2. Does an FD entry denote whether a file is to be used for input or output?
3. Does a decimal point take up storage space? Be specific.
4. Why can the RECORD CONTAINS clause be omitted?
5. Is it necessary that the level number of a record be 01 or can it be the lowest level number in a structure?
6. When can the VALUE clause be used in the file section?
7. Write record descriptions for the following structures:

| PERSONNEL-RECORD | | | | | | | | | |
|---|---|---|---|---|---|---|---|---|---|
| MAN NUMBER | NAME | | ADDRESS | | | | JOB | | |
| | LAST | INITIALS | STREET | CITY | STATE | ZIP | DEPT | CLASSIFICATION | RATING |
| | | FIRST MIDDLE | | | | | | | |

where:

| | |
|---|---|
| MAN NUMBER | is 6 digits |
| LAST | is 20 letters |
| FIRST | is 1 letter |
| MIDDLE | is 1 letter |
| STREET | is 15 characters |
| CITY | is 10 letters |
| STATE | is 3 letters |
| ZIP | is 5 digits |
| DEPT | is 4 characters |
| CLASSIFICATION | is 5 digits |
| RATING | is 7 characters |

| PAYROLL | | | | | | | | |
|---|---|---|---|---|---|---|---|---|
| MAN NUMBER | NAME | | SOCIAL SECURITY NO | RATE | DEPT | YEAR TO DATE | | |
| | LAST | INITIALS | | | | GROSS | FICA | TAX |
| | | FIRST / MIDDLE | | | | REGULAR / OVERTIME | | |

where:

| | |
|---|---|
| MAN NUMBER | is 6 digits |
| LAST | is 20 letters |
| FIRST | is 1 letter |
| MIDDLE | is 1 letter |
| SOCIAL SEC NO | is 9 digits |
| RATE | is 6 digits |
| DEPT | is 4 characters |
| REGULAR | is 8 digits |
| OVERTIME | is 8 digits |
| FICA | is 6 digits |
| TAX | is 8 digits |

Add other specifications, as required.

8. Obviously, the records for personnel and payroll in exercise 7 are not complete for most applications. Extend and/or modify both descriptions to your satisfaction.

9. Combine the records of exercise 7 into one complete "data base" record.

10. Write data description entries for the following:

   a. A one-dimensional array of signed five digit integers to be used in arithmetic operations. Let the size of the array be 75 elements.

   b. A symbol table that will contain 100 entries. Each entry contains a symbol that is 8 characters long and a value that is an unsigned 3-digit integer.

c. A three-dimensional array of values of the form ±XXXX.XXX; let the dimensions be 11 rows, 16 columns, and 9 planes.

# 11

# THE PROCEDURE DIVISION

## 11.1 STRUCTURE OF THE PROCEDURE DIVISION

The procedure division specifies the computer processing to be performed and must be included in every COBOL source program. Statements in the procedure division are grouped into two general categories: declaratives and procedures. The *declarative section* allows the programmer to include procedures that are invoked asynchronously as a result of conditions that normally cannot be tested by the programmer. The *procedure section* allows the programmer to write sequential coding (that is, statements that are executed sequentially) to solve a given problem.

The general format of the procedure division is:

PROCEDURE DIVISION.
[DECLARATIVES.
{ section-name SECTION. declarative-sentence.
{ paragraph-name { sentence }...}...}...
END DECLARATIVES.]
{ section-name SECTION.
{ paragraph-name. { sentence }...}...}...

or

PROCEDURE DIVISION.
{ paragraph-name. { sentence }...}...

The second format simply implies that if one paragraph is in a section, then all paragraphs must be in sections. The declaratives must be grouped at the beginning of the procedure division.

## Procedures

The term *procedure* refers to a paragraph or a group of successive paragraphs, or a section or a group of successive sections. The term *procedure name* refers to a paragraph name or a section name.

A *section* consists of a section header, that is,

    section-name SECTION.

followed by one or more successive paragraphs. The section ends at the next section header or the end of the procedure division.

A *paragraph* consists of a paragraph name followed by one or more sentences. A paragraph ends at the next paragraph name or the end of the procedure division.

A *sentence* consists of one or more statements and ends with a period. A *statement* begins with a COBOL verb and is a syntactically valid combination of words and symbols.

## Statements

Statements are grouped into three classes: imperative, conditional, and compiler directing. A *conditional statement* establishes a condition with a truth value of true or false; the action of the object program is dependent on this condition. Sample conditional statements are IF and READ. A *compiler directing statement* provides information to the compiler and does not result in the generation of object code, per se. Sample compiler directing statements are COPY and NOTE. An *imperative statement* is any statement that is neither a conditional nor a compiler directing statement; it causes a specific action to be taken in the object program. Sample imperative statements are ADD and OPEN.

## Format

The *division header* takes the form:

> PROCEDURE DIVISION.

It starts in area A of the reference format. A *section header,* that is,

    section-name SECTION.

also starts in area A of the reference format. No text may follow either the division or section header statements until another header statement is written.

The *paragraph header* starts in area A and terminates with a period followed by a space. A sentence may appear on the same line as the paragraph header.

Sentences must be written in area B of the reference format.

### Declaratives

Declaratives can be associated with the following types of procedures:

1. Input/output label handling
2. Input/output error-checking procedures
3. Report writing procedures

The format of the declaratives section is repeated here:

```
DECLARATIVES.
{ section-name SECTION. declarative-sentence.
{ paragraph-name. { sentence }...}...}...
END DECLARATIVES.
```

Each section is associated with a specific condition and is *only* invoked when that condition arises and not during normal execution of the program.

Input/output label handling procedures use the following declarative sentence:

$$\text{USE} \left\{ \begin{array}{c} \underline{\text{BEFORE}} \\ \underline{\text{AFTER}} \end{array} \right\} \text{STANDARD} \left[ \begin{array}{c} \underline{\text{BEGINNING}} \\ \underline{\text{ENDING}} \end{array} \right] \left[ \begin{array}{c} \underline{\text{REEL}} \\ \underline{\text{FILE}} \\ \underline{\text{UNIT}} \end{array} \right] \text{LABEL PROCEDURE ON}$$

$$\left\{ \begin{array}{l} \text{file-name-1 [, file-name-2]} ... \\ \underline{\text{INPUT}} \\ \underline{\text{OUTPUT}} \\ \underline{\text{I-O}} \end{array} \right\}$$

where "file-name-$i$" denotes the files to which the declarative applies. INPUT denotes all input files; OUTPUT denotes all output files; and I-O denotes all input and output files. BEFORE and AFTER denote that nonstandard user file labels are to be processed. BEGINNING and ENDING refer to header and trailer labels, respectively. If neither BEGINNING nor ENDING is used, the procedures are executed for both header and trailer labels. REEL, UNIT, and FILE specify when the procedures should be applied. If neither is specified, the procedures are executed for each reel or unit, whichever is appropriate.

When the condition specified in the USE statement arises, the procedure declared with it is executed. An exit is made from a declarative section when the last statement in the section is executed. After a declarative procedure is executed, the execution of the program is continued from where it was interrupted—figuratively speaking, as if the declarative procedure did not exist.

Input/output error-handling procedures use the following declarative sentence:

$$\underline{\text{USE AFTER STANDARD ERROR PROCEDURE}}$$

$$\text{ON} \left\{ \begin{array}{l} \text{file-name-1 [, file-name-2]} ... \\ \underline{\text{INPUT}} \\ \underline{\text{OUTPUT}} \\ \underline{\text{I-O}} \end{array} \right\}$$

where "file-name-$i$," INPUT, OUTPUT, and I-O exist as defined above. The declarative procedure is invoked after the standard error procedure, defined by the operating system, is executed. A declarative procedure for input/output error handling is terminated in the same manner as the declarative procedure for label processing.

INPUT, OUTPUT, and I-O need further clarification. They refer to files that are *opened* for input, output, and input and output, respectively. A file may be opened for input and for output at different times during the execution of a program.

Within a declarative procedure, no reference must be made to a nondeclarative procedure. Similarly, a nondeclarative procedure may not refer to a declarative procedure.

Report-writing declarative procedures are not covered. The reader is referred to the COBOL standard (reference [9], p. 2-239).

### Execution of the Procedure Division

The execution of the procedure division begins with the first nondeclarative sentence following the procedure division header. The execution continues as governed by the execution time behavior of the program until either a STOP RUN statement is encountered, in a nondeclarative or declarative procedure, or a situation is encountered that prevents further execution of the program.

## 11.2  DATA MANIPULATION

Data manipulation statements are used to transfer data from one area of main storage to another and to perform a limited amount of character manipulation. During a data movement operation, conversion and/or editing may be performed on the data being moved as governed by the characteristics of the sending and receiving fields.

### The MOVE Statement

The MOVE statement causes data to be transferred from one area of main storage to one or more other areas. The form of the most elementary form of the MOVE statement is:

$$\underline{\text{MOVE}} \begin{Bmatrix} \text{identifier-1} \\ \text{literal} \end{Bmatrix} \underline{\text{TO}} \text{ identifier-2 [identifier-3]} \dots$$

"Identifier-1" and "literal" are referred to as the sending area; "identifier-2," "identifier-3," and so forth, represent the receiving areas. The data specified by identifier-1 or literal is moved first to identifier-2, then to identifier-3, and so on, such that the statement:

    MOVE A TO B, C

is equivalent to the statements:

    MOVE A TO B
    MOVE A TO C

Any subscripting associated with the receiving areas is evaluated immediately before the data is moved to the respective data item.

A move in which both the sending and receiving areas are elementary is defined with respect to elementary items and extended to group items in a systematic manner. Each elementary item belongs to one of the following categories: numeric, alphabetic, alphanumeric, numeric edited, and alphanumeric edited. (Recall here that the category into which an elementary item is classed is specified in its PICTURE clause.) The figurative constant ZERO, and its equivalent forms ZEROS and ZEROES, is categorized as numeric. The figurative constant SPACE, or SPACES, belongs to the alphabetic category. All other figurative constants are regarded as alphanumeric.

The execution of the move operation is governed by several rules:

1. Any required conversion from one internal form to another is performed automatically during the move operation, including editing specified for the receiving item.
2. When the receiving item is numeric or numeric edited:
    a. Alignment is made by decimal point. Excess character positions in the sending area are truncated. Unused character positions in the receiving area are filled with zeros, except when editing is specified.
    b. If the receiving item has no operational sign, the absolute value of the sending item is used.
    c. The sending item may not be numeric edited, alphanumeric edited, or alphabetic. When the sending area is alphanumeric, it is moved as though it were an unsigned numeric integer data item.
3. When the receiving item is alphabetic, alphanumeric, or alphanumeric edited:
    a. When the sending item is larger than the receiving item, the sending characters are truncated after the receiving area is filled. Movement is from left to right.
    b. When the sending item is smaller than the receiving item, unused character positions are padded with spaces. Movement is from left to right.
    c. The case where the receiving field is justified is covered under the JUSTIFIED clause in Chapter 10.
    d. A noninteger numeric data item cannot be moved to an alphabetic or alphanumeric edited data item.
4. When the sending and receiving fields overlap, the results are formally defined as being unpredictable. However, good common sense usually applies here for most implementations of COBOL. (Data movement is always from left to right, except for a numeric receiving item, and the user can easily determine if the sending item is being "clobbered" during the move operation.)
5. Any move that is not an elementary move (that is, at least one operand is not elementary) is treated as though it were an alphanumeric-to-alphanumeric elementary move. With a group move, however, there is *no* conversion from one internal form to another.
6. The legality of moves is summarized in Table 11.1.
7. In a MOVE operation, the sending item remains unchanged unless the fields overlap.

Table 11.1

Legal Operands for the MOVE Operation

| *Category of Sending Data Item* | *Category of Receiving Data Item* | | | | | | |
|---|---|---|---|---|---|---|---|
| | *GR* | *A* | *AN* | *ANE* | *NI* | *N* | *NE* |
| Group (GR) | Y | Y | Y | $Y^a$ | $Y^a$ | $Y^a$ | $Y^a$ |
| Alphabetic (A) | Y | Y | Y | Y | N | N | N |
| Alphanumeric (AN) | Y | Y | Y | Y | $Y^b$ | $Y^b$ | $Y^b$ |
| Alphanumeric edited (ANE) | Y | Y | Y | Y | N | N | N |
| Numeric integer (NI) | Y | N | Y | Y | Y | Y | Y |
| Numeric noninteger (N) | Y | N | N | N | Y | Y | Y |
| Numeric edited (NE) | Y | N | Y | Y | N | N | N |

Key: Y—permitted; N—not permitted
$^a$No conversion is performed.
$^b$The sending field is moved as though it were an unsigned numeric integer data item; no conversion is performed.

Editing that is performed during data movement is generally expected as a matter of course. Conversion is not but is also performed automatically. If, for example, the data item A has the characteristics PICTURE 9(3) COMPUTATIONAL and data item B has the characteristics PICTURE 9(3) DISPLAY, then the statement:

MOVE A TO B

converts the value stored in A from a computational form (usually binary) to a display form (usually BCD). In this case, B could be printed without further editing or conversion; A could *not* be printed without editing or conversion.

### The MOVE CORRESPONDING Statement

The MOVE CORRESPONDING statement applies to group level moves and has the form:

MOVE $\left\{ \dfrac{\text{CORRESPONDING}}{\underline{\text{CORR}}} \right\}$ identifier-1 TO identifier-2

where "identifier-*i*" refers to group items and at least one data item in identifier-1 has the same name and qualification as a data item in identifier-2. Data items in identifier-1 are moved to data items in identifier-2 if the names agree. Thus, for the structures:

```
01 A               01 W
   02 B               02 B
   02 C               02 M
      03 D               03 R
      03 E               03 E
```

the statement:

MOVE CORRESPONDING A TO W

is equivalent to writing:

MOVE B IN A TO B IN W
MOVE E IN C IN A TO E IN M IN W

## The EXAMINE Statement

The EXAMINE statement can be used to count the number of times a single character appears in a data item, to replace a character with another character, or both. The form of the EXAMINE statement with the TALLYING option is:

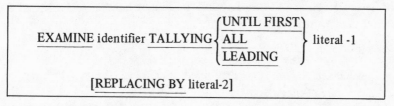

The characteristics of "identifier" must be such that its usage is DISPLAY. The scan is always left to right. When "identifier" represents a numeric data item with an operational sign, the sign is ignored by the EXAMINE statement.

The EXAMINE statement operates on a character basis. The operand "identifier" is examined character by character. "Literal-1" and "literal-2" must be nonnumeric literals, each containing a single character from the COBOL alphabet, or must be an unsigned numeric literal containing a single digit. The literal must belong to a class consistent with the identifier. Each literal may also be a figurative constant, except ALL.

The above form of the EXAMINE statement operates as follows:

1. An integral count is created that replaces the contents of the special register TALLY.

2. The count represents the occurrences of literal-1 when the ALL option in the EXAMINE statement is used.
3. The count represents the occurrences of literal-1 prior to encountering a character other than literal-1 when the LEADING option is used.
4. The count represents the number of characters not equal to literal-1 that are encountered before the first occurrence of literal-1 when the UNTIL FIRST option is used.

The REPLACING option permits a character replacement to be made during the scan. It operates in precisely the same manner as the second form of the EXAMINE statement (given below)—except for the fact that a count is made as given above.

The second form of the EXAMINE statement is given as follows:

$$\text{EXAMINE identifier REPLACING} \left\{ \begin{array}{l} \text{ALL} \\ \text{LEADING} \\ \text{FIRST} \\ \text{UNTIL FIRST} \end{array} \right\} \text{literal-1}$$

$$\text{BY literal-2}$$

"Identifier" and "literal-*i*" are the same as defined for the first form of the EXAMINE statement.

The "replacement" form of the EXAMINE statement operates as follows:

1. When the ALL option is specified, literal-2 is substituted for each occurrence of literal-1.
2. When the LEADING option is specified, each leading occurrence of literal-1 is replaced with literal-2. The scan terminates with the first character that is not equal to literal-1 or when the data item represented by identifier is exhausted.
3. When the FIRST option is specified, the first occurrence of literal-1 is replaced with literal-2.
4. When the UNTIL FIRST option is specified, the leading characters of identifier are replaced by literal-2. The process terminates when literal-1 is encountered during the scan or when the data item represented by identifier is exhausted.

The examples in Table 11.2 demonstrate the use of both forms of the EXAMINE statement.

Table 11.2

Examples of the Use of the EXAMINE Statement

| EXAMINE Statement | OPND (Before) | OPND (After) | Contents of TALLY |
|---|---|---|---|
| EXAMINE OPND TALLYING ALL SPACE | TEAþFORþTWO | TEAþFORþTWO | 2 |
| EXAMINE OPND TALLYING LEADING "0" | 000123 | 000123 | 3 |
| EXAMINE OPND TALLYING UNTIL FIRST "=" | ALOG=B+C | ALOG=B+C | 4 |
| EXAMINE OPND TALLYING LEADING "0" REPLACING BY SPACES | 000123 | þþþ123 | 3 |
| EXAMINE OPND REPLACING LEADING "0" BY "*" | 000123 | ***123 | Unchanged |
| EXAMINE OPND REPLACING FIRST "*" BY "$" | ***123 | $**123 | Unchanged |

### Comments on Data Manipulation

The use of the MOVE statement is practically necessary in COBOL. In FORTRAN, for example, a statement to move B to A is written:

$$A = B$$

which is simply an application of the assignment statement. COBOL also allows an assignment statement of the form (to be covered later):

$$COMPUTE \ v = e$$

where $v$ is a variable and $e$ is an expression. However, operands in the COMPUTE

statement are limited to numeric data items. Therefore, the COMPUTE statement cannot be used to move nonnumeric data items and use of the MOVE
statement is necessary.

The EXAMINE statement, on the other hand, is a useful convenience that can
be substituted for laborious programming. For example, consider the data declaration:

```
02  OPND PICTURE 9(6) USAGE IS DISPLAY.
02  STRING REDEFINES OPND PICTURE X(1) OCCURS 6 TIMES.
     .
     .
     .

77  I PICTURE 9(5) USAGE IS COMPUTATIONAL.
```

The EXAMINE statement:

```
EXAMINE OPND REPLACING LEADING "0" BY "*"
```

can also be programmed as:

```
        MOVE 1 TO I.
AGAIN.  IF STRING (I) NOT = "0" NEXT SENTENCE;
        ELSE MOVE "*" TO STRING (I); ADD 1 TO I;
        IF I < 7 GO TO AGAIN.
            .
            .
            .
```

Use of the EXAMINE statement for editing and character manipulation is more
convenient and more efficient (as far as execution time is concerned) than using
the "programmed" method.

## 11.3  ARITHMETIC STATEMENTS

The COBOL language includes two types of arithmetic statements: the COM-
PUTE statement, which is analogous to the assignment statement in languages
like BASIC or FORTRAN, and those such as the ADD statement that perform a

single arithmetic operation. Statements that perform a single arithmetic operation are not actually necessary since the same functions can be specified with the COMPUTE statement. In general, however, the same amount of computation is executed regardless of whether the programmer writes:

ADD A, B GIVING C

or

COMPUTE C = A + B

The ADD statement, for example, is more readable and practically allows a COBOL program to be "read" as a prose description of an algorithm.

### Arithmetic Expression

An arithmetic expression can be used in the COMPUTE statement and in a relational condition, covered later. An arithmetic expression is one of the following constructs:

1. An identifier that names a numeric elementary data item.
2. A numeric literal (including the numeric figurative constant).
3. Two identifiers and/or literals separated by an arithmetic operator.
4. Two arithmetic expressions separated by an arithmetic operator.
5. An arithmetic expression enclosed in parentheses.
6. An arithmetic expression preceded by a minus sign (for unary minus).

A necessary restriction is that two operators may not appear in succession, except that the unary minus that may follow a left parenthesis (for an expression enclosed in parentheses), may appear at the beginning of an expression, or may follow a binary operator. The following arithmetic operators are defined:

| Arithmetic Operator | Meaning |
|---|---|
| ** | Exponentiation |
| * | Multiplication |
| / | Division |
| + | Addition |
| - | Subtraction or unary minus |

Parentheses are used for grouping to specify the order in which arithmetic operators are executed. An expression within parentheses is executed before the arithmetic operator of which it is an operand.

When parentheses are not used to completely specify the order in which operators are executed, the following hierarchy of operator execution is used:

| Operator | Hierarchy |
|----------|-----------|
| Unary – | Highest |
| ** | |
| *,/ | ↓ |
| +,– | Lowest |

Operators at the same hierarchical level are executed from left to right. The fact that a unary minus has the highest priority permits an expression such as A*–B to have meaning. If unary minus had a lower priority, it could not follow a binary operator in an expression.

The manner in which a simple operand[1] (identifier or literal), an operator and parentheses can be combined is summarized in Table 11.3. An arithmetic expression must begin with one of the symbols "(" and "–" or a simple operand; it must end with a right parenthesis or a simple operand.

Table 11.3

Permissible Combinations of Symbol Pairs in Arithmetic Expressions

| 1st Symbol \ 2nd Symbol | Simple Operand | Binary Operator | Unary – | ( | ) |
|---|---|---|---|---|---|
| Simple Operand[a] | N | P | N | N | P |
| Binary Operator (**, *, /, +, –) | P | N | P | P | N |
| Unary minus (–) | P | N | N | P | N |
| ( | P | N | P | P | N |
| ) | N | P | N | N | P |

Key: P–Permitted
  N–Not Permitted

[a] A simple operand is defined as an identifier or a literal, for the purposes of this table.

[1] Use of the term "simple operand" to refer to an identifier or a literal is admittedly vague. However, the COBOL standard uses the term "variable" that is clearly misleading.

## Statement Options

Most arithmetic statements allow one or more options that govern how the statement is executed under special conditions.

The CORRESPONDING option is used in the same manner for arithmetic statements as it is for the MOVE statement. The CORRESPONDING option permits group items to be used as operands; the operation applies to subordinate data items with the same name and structure.

The GIVING option specifies that the identifier following the word GIVING is to be set equal to the computed result. This identifier (the one following GIVING) may contain editing symbols, provided that it is not used as an operand in the calculations.

The ROUNDED option adds a one to the low-order digit of a computed result if the excess digit to the right of the low-order digit is greater than or equal to five. The ROUNDED option operates as follows: (1) After decimal point alignment, the number of places to the right of the decimal point (that is, the fraction) in the computed result is compared with the number of places provided in the destination field. (2) When the size of the fraction of the computed result exceeds the size of the fraction in the destination field, the computed result is normally truncated. (3) When the ROUNDED option is specified, the computed result is rounded as specified above.

The ON SIZE ERROR option specifies an action to be taken when the size of the integral part of the computed result, after decimal point alignment, exceeds the space provided for it in the destination field. In general, division by zero causes a size error condition. If the ON SIZE ERROR option is not used and a size error condition arises, the results are defined to be unpredictable.

## The ADD Statement

The ADD statement causes two or more operands to be added and the result to be stored as specified in one of the three statement formats:

---

*Format 1:*

ADD $\begin{Bmatrix} \text{identifier-1} \\ \text{literal-1} \end{Bmatrix}$ $\begin{bmatrix} , \text{identifier-2} \\ , \text{literal-2} \end{bmatrix}$ ... TO identifier-*m* [ROUNDED]

[, identifier-*n* [ROUNDED]]... [; ON SIZE ERROR imperative-
statement]

---

*Format 2:*

$$\underline{\text{ADD}} \begin{Bmatrix} \text{identifier-1} \\ \text{literal-1} \end{Bmatrix} , \begin{Bmatrix} \text{identifier-2} \\ \text{literal-2} \end{Bmatrix} \begin{bmatrix} , \text{identifier-3} \\ , \text{literal-3} \end{bmatrix} \cdots$$

$$\underline{\text{GIVING}} \text{ identifier-}m \text{ [\underline{ROUNDED}] [; ON \underline{SIZE ERROR}}$$
$$\text{imperative-statement]}$$

*Format 3:*

$$\underline{\text{ADD}} \begin{Bmatrix} \underline{\text{CORRESPONDING}} \\ \underline{\text{CORR}} \end{Bmatrix} \text{ identifier-1 } \underline{\text{TO}} \text{ identifier-2[\underline{ROUNDED}]}$$

$$\text{[; ON \underline{SIZE ERROR} imperative-statement]}$$

The identifiers in formats 1 and 2 must name numeric elementary data items, except for the identifier after the GIVING option that may contain editing symbols. The literals must be numeric literals or the figurative constant ZERO or one of its variations. The maximum size of each operand and the computed result is 18 digits.

In format 1, the operands preceding the word TO are added together; the sum is then added to the current value of the identifiers following TO and the respective identifier is replaced with the result. Thus, for example, the statement:

ADD A, B, C TO B, D

is equivalent to:

COMPUTE TEMP = A + B + C
COMPUTE B = B + TEMP
COMPUTE D = D + TEMP

and is also equivalent to:

ADD A, B, C GIVING TEMP
ADD TEMP TO B
ADD TEMP TO D

where TEMP is a temporary variable.

In format 2, the operands preceding the word GIVING are added together and the identifier following the word GIVING is replaced with the result. Thus, the statement:

ADD A, B, C GIVING D

is equivalent to:

COMPUTE TEMP = A + B + C
MOVE TEMP TO D

where TEMP is again a temporary variable.

In format 3, the numeric elementary data items in identifier-1 are added to corresponding numeric elementary data items in identifier-2.

The "imperative statement" used with the ON SIZE ERROR option is an imperative statement, as defined previously.

## The COMPUTE Statement

The COMPUTE statement is the ordinary assignment statement prefixed with the key word COMPUTE. The COMPUTE statement has the form:

$$\underline{\text{COMPUTE}} \text{ identifier-1 } [\underline{\text{ROUNDED}}] = \begin{cases} \text{identifier-2} \\ \text{literal-1} \\ \text{arithmetic-expression} \end{cases}$$

where:

"literal-1" is a numeric literal or the ZERO figurative constant.
"identifier-2" is a numeric elementary data item.
"arithmetic-expression" is an arithmetic expression, defined previously.
"identifier-1" is an elementary data item that may contain editing symbols.

The maximum size of each operand and the computed result in the COMPUTE statement is 18 digits; however, there is no restriction on the size of intermediate results. A sample COMPUTE statement is:

COMPUTE GROSS = RATE * (40 + (HOURS – 40) * 1.5)

The COMPUTE statement is the only means by which the exponentiation operator can be executed.

### The DIVIDE Statement

The DIVIDE statement is used to divide one operand by another and replace the value of an identifier with the result. The two formats of the DIVIDE statement are:

---

*Format 1:*

DIVIDE $\begin{Bmatrix} \text{identifier-1} \\ \text{literal-1} \end{Bmatrix}$ INTO identifier-2 [ROUNDED]

[; ON SIZE ERROR imperative-statement]

*Format 2:*

DIVIDE $\begin{Bmatrix} \text{identifier-1} \\ \text{literal-1} \end{Bmatrix}$ $\begin{Bmatrix} \text{INTO} \\ \text{BY} \end{Bmatrix}$ $\begin{Bmatrix} \text{identifier-2} \\ \text{literal-2} \end{Bmatrix}$ GIVING identifier-3

[ROUNDED] [REMAINDER identifier-4]

[; ON SIZE ERROR imperative-statement]

---

In format 1, the value of the first operand (either "identifier-1" or "literal-1") is divided into "identifier-2"; the value of the quotient replaces the value of the dividend.[2]

In format 2, the first operand (either "identifier-1" or "literal-1") is divided *into* or *by* the second operand (either "identifier-2" or "literal-2") and the quotient is stored in "identifier-3." The remainder from the division operation is optionally stored as "identifier-4." The remainder is defined as the result obtained from subtracting the product of the quotient and the divisor from the dividend. When the ROUNDED option is used, the quotient is rounded after the remainder, if specified, is computed.

Each *identifier* must name a numeric elementary data item; only the identifier following the word GIVING in format 2 may contain editing symbols. Each *literal* must be a numeric literal.

The maximum size of each operand and the quotient is 18 digits and division by zero results in a size error condition. Thus, the statement:

DIVIDE A BY B GIVING C

is equivalent to:

DIVIDE B INTO A GIVING C

[2] The terminology is QUOTIENT = DIVIDEND ÷ DIVISOR.

Both statements are equivalent to the following assignment statement:

COMPUTE C = A / B

Although the remainder of a division operation is easily computed, COBOL is one of few programming languages that allows the remainder to be stored as an adjunct to the divide operation. Moreover, the option of storing the remainder is not available with the COMPUTE statement and must be computed in a separate statement.

### The MULTIPLY Statement

The MULTIPLY statement is used to multiply two numeric data items and set the value of an identifier equal to the result. There are two forms of the MULTIPLY statement:

---

*Format 1:*

MULTIPLY $\begin{Bmatrix} \text{identifier-1} \\ \text{literal-1} \end{Bmatrix}$ BY identifier-2 [ROUNDED]

      [; ON SIZE ERROR imperative-statement]

*Format 2:*

MULTIPLY $\begin{Bmatrix} \text{identifier-1} \\ \text{literal-1} \end{Bmatrix}$ BY $\begin{Bmatrix} \text{identifier-2} \\ \text{literal-2} \end{Bmatrix}$ GIVING identifier-3

      [ROUNDED] [; ON SIZE ERROR imperative-statement]

---

Each "identifier-*i*" must refer to a numeric elementary data item except "identifier-3" in format 2 which may contain editing symbols. Each literal must be a numeric literal or the ZERO figurative constant.

In format 1, the value of the first operand ("identifier-1" or "literal-1") is multiplied by the value of "identifier-2"; the product replaces "identifier-2." In format 2, the first operand ("identifier-1" or "literal-1") is multiplied by the second operand ("identifier-2" or "literal-2"); the product replaces "identifier-3." In both formats, the value of "identifier-1" remains unchanged by the multiply operation. In format 2, the values of "identifier-1" and "identifier-2" are unchanged by the operation.

As in other arithmetic statements, the maximum size of each operand is 18 digits.

The statement:

MULTIPLY 2 BY COUNT

for example, is equivalent to:

MULTIPLY 2 BY COUNT GIVING COUNT

An equivalent assignment statement is:

COMPUTE COUNT = 2 * COUNT

(The operands seem to be reversed here. It would seem that MULTIPLY A BY B should be equivalent to A = A * B, but it is not.)

### The SUBTRACT Statement

The SUBTRACT statement is used to subtract the value of one or more data items from one or more data items and set the value of one or more data items equal to the result. There are three formats for the SUBTRACT statement:

*Format 1:*

SUBTRACT $\begin{Bmatrix} \text{identifier-1} \\ \text{literal-1} \end{Bmatrix}$ $\begin{bmatrix} \text{, identifier-2} \\ \text{, literal-2} \end{bmatrix}$ ...

FROM identifier-*m* [ROUNDED] [, identifier-*n* [ROUNDED]] ...

[; ON SIZE ERROR imperative-statement]

*Format 2:*

SUBTRACT $\begin{Bmatrix} \text{identifier-1} \\ \text{literal-1} \end{Bmatrix}$ $\begin{bmatrix} \text{, identifier-2} \\ \text{, literal-2} \end{bmatrix}$ ...

FROM $\begin{Bmatrix} \text{identifier-}m \\ \text{literal-}m \end{Bmatrix}$ GIVING identifier-*n* [ROUNDED]

[; ON SIZE ERROR imperative-statement]

*Format 3:*

SUBTRACT $\begin{Bmatrix} \text{CORRESPONDING} \\ \text{CORR} \end{Bmatrix}$ identifier-1

FROM identifier-2 [ROUNDED]

[; ON SIZE ERROR imperative-statement]

Each "identifier-$i$" must refer to a numeric elementary data item except for "identifier-$n$" in format 2 which may contain editing symbols. "Literal" must be a numeric literal and the maximum size of each operand is limited to 18 digits or less. CORR is an abbreviation for CORRESPONDING.

In format 1, all operands preceding the word FROM are added together and the sum is subtracted from "identifier-$m$," which participates in the operation and must be a numeric elementary data item. If more than one identifier follows the keyword FROM, the sum is subtracted from the value of each additional identifier, as well. "Identifier-$n$" must also name a numeric elementary data item. Thus, the statement:

    SUBTRACT A, B, C FROM C, E

is equivalent to:

    COMPUTE TEMP = A + B + C
    COMPUTE C = C - TEMP
    COMPUTE E = E - TEMP

where TEMP is a temporary variable.

In format 2, the operands preceding FROM are added together; the sum is subtracted from "identifier-$m$" or "literal-$m$" and the result replaces the value of "identifier-$n$." Thus, the statement:

    SUBTRACT A, B, C FROM D GIVING E

is equivalent to:

    COMPUTE TEMP = A + B + C
    COMPUTE E = D - TEMP

where TEMP is again a temporary variable.

In format 3, the numeric elementary data items in "identifier-1" are subtracted from corresponding numeric elementary data items in "identifier-2." The results are stored as new values for "identifier-2." (Recall here that two data items correspond if they have the same name and structure.) Given the following structures:

```
02 A                    02 X
   03 B                    03 B
   03 C                    03 T
      04 D                    04 D
      04 E                    04 P
```

the statement:

SUBTRACT CORRESPONDING A FROM X

is equivalent to:

SUBTRACT B IN A FROM B IN X
SUBTRACT D IN C IN A FROM D IN T IN X

The SUBTRACT statement is a convenience over the assignment statement in many cases. In programming, it is frequently necessary to decrement two or more index values by the same amount, that is, for example:

I=I-1
J=J-1

With the SUBTRACT statement, both operations can be executed with a single statement, such as:

SUBTRACT 1 FROM I, J

A similar argument could be made for the ADD statement.


## Comments

It is frequently stated that the only arithmetic statement needed is the COMPUTE statement. Perhaps that is so. On the other hand, the ADD, SUBTRACT, MULTIPLY, and DIVIDE statements in COBOL allow the programmer to express his program in a form analogous to the way that he thinks about his problem. If he thinks, "Add one to I," then he should use the ADD statement. If he thinks of the operation as a mathematical statement, then he should use the COMPUTE statement. The programming standards in a given installation frequently influence the statements that a programmer is permitted to use.

## 11.4 PROGRAM CONTROL

Program control statements control the order in which the statements of a program are executed. Statements are normally executed sequentially; program control statements permit the sequential flow of execution to be altered on a conditional or an unconditional basis.

This section describes four statements: IF, GO TO, and STOP. Each of these statements has been mentioned or used previously and the objective here is to present the material in a more detailed manner.

### Conditions

A *condition* is an expression that has the value true or false when it is evaluated as part of the IF statement.[3] COBOL does not permit logical variables so that logical expressions cannot be used in other statements. The conditional facilities in COBOL include options not available with other programming languages and as a result it is a topic of interest in its own right.

A *simple condition* is one of the following: a class condition, a condition-name condition, a relation condition, or a sign condition. Simple conditions may be grouped using parentheses and logical operators to form compound conditions. Logical operators include AND, OR, and NOT.

The *class condition* is used to determine whether a data item is alphabetic or numeric. The general form of a class test is:

$$\text{identifier IS [NOT]} \left\{ \begin{array}{l} \underline{\text{NUMERIC}} \\ \underline{\text{ALPHABETIC}} \end{array} \right\}$$

where "identifier" names a data item declared, explicitly or implicitly, with a usage of DISPLAY. Table 11.4 lists the value forms of the class test. For example, an alphabetic data item cannot be tested for NUMERIC; it can only be tested as being ALPHABETIC or NOT ALPHABETIC. A *numeric data item* consists of the digits 0 through 9 with an optional operational sign. An *alphabetic data item* consists of the space characters and the letters A through Z. The "identifier," frequently referred to as the "subject," is not constrained to be an elementary data item.

The *condition-name condition* causes a variable to be tested to determine if

---

[3] A *limited* form of the condition in COBOL is also permitted in PERFORM and SEARCH statements.

its value is equal to one or more values declared with an 88-level condition name. The form of a condition-name test is the name of the condition itself, that is:

> condition-name

as shown in the following example:

```
02 SEX PICTURE X.
   88 MALE VALUE "M".
   88 FEMALE VALUE "F".
   88 UNKNOWN VALUE "-".
```

One of the above condition names would be used as follows:

    IF FEMALE GO TO FEMALE-PAR.

The use of a condition name is an abbreviation for a relation condition, such as:

    IF SEX = "F" GO TO FEMALE-PAR.

Table 11.4

Valid Forms of the Class Test

| Type of Identifier[a] | Valid Forms of the Class Test | |
|---|---|---|
| Alphabetic | ALPHABETIC | NOT ALPHABETIC |
| Alphanumeric | ALPHABETIC<br>NUMERIC | NOT ALPHABETIC<br>NOT NUMERIC |
| Numeric | NUMERIC | NOT NUMERIC |

[a]USAGE must be DISPLAY.

A *relation condition* is simply a comparison operation that takes the form:

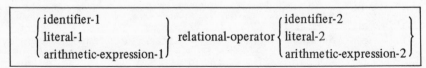

where the first operand is called the *subject* of the condition and the second operand is called the *object* of the condition. The subject and the object cannot both be literals. The relational operators (frequently referred to as comparison operators) are summarized in Table 11.5 and are used in the conventional manner. The use of relational operators is governed by the following rules:

1. The subject and object must have the same usage, except when numeric operands are being compared.
2. Unsigned numeric operands are considered to be positive.
3. Numeric operands are compared with respect to algebraic value.
4. Nonnumeric operands are compared with respect to the collating sequence of the constituent characters. If the operands are of unequal length, the shorter operand is extended with spaces.

Table 11.5

Relational Operators

| Operator | Meaning |
| --- | --- |
| IS [NOT] GREATER THAN<br>IS [NOT] > | Greater than or not greater than |
| IS [NOT] LESS THAN<br>IS [NOT] < | Less than or not less than |
| IS [NOT] EQUAL TO<br>IS [NOT] = | Equal to or not equal to |

5. The comparison of a nonnumeric data item and a numeric data item with display usage (see rule 1) is permitted; they are compared as two nonnumeric operands.
6. Group items are treated as nonnumeric operands.

For example, if nonnumeric variables A and B contain the characters "ABLE" and "BAKER," respectively, then the relation A IS GREATER THAN B has the logical value false. Similarly, if the numeric variable DELTA has the value –123.45, then the relation DELTA < 59.41 has the logical value true. The key word NOT in a relation serves to complement the meaning of the relational operator. For example, using the above definition for A and B, the relation A NOT > B has the logical value true.

The *sign condition* is used to determine whether a numeric elementary data item is less than, greater than, or equal to zero. The sign condition has the form:

$$\left\{\begin{array}{l}\text{identifier}\\\text{arithmetic-expression}\end{array}\right\}\text{ IS [\underline{NOT}]}\left\{\begin{array}{l}\text{POSITIVE}\\\text{NEGATIVE}\\\text{ZERO}\end{array}\right\}$$

where "identifier" is a numeric data item and "arithmetic expression" is an arithmetic expression as defined in section 11.3. An operand is positive if its value is greater than zero, negative if its value is less than zero, and zero if its value is equal to zero. An unsigned data item is *always* positive.

The logical operators, along with parentheses if necessary, can be used to construct *compound conditions.* The operands to the logical operators are the four conditions previously defined. Thus, for example, the expression:

MALE AND AGE = 34

is a valid compound condition provided that MALE is a condition name. Parentheses are used for grouping as in arithmetic expressions. Table 11.6 lists the most frequently used compound conditions. When parentheses are not used to specify the order of evaluation, the following order is assumed:

1. arithmetic expressions;
2. relational operations (relation conditions);
3. class, condition name, and sign conditions, including the NOT option;
4. the logical operator NOT;
5. the logical operator AND;
6. the logical operator OR.

Table 11.6

Frequently Used Compound Conditions

| $A$ | $B$ | $A$ AND $B$ | $A$ OR $B$ | NOT $A$ | NOT ($A$ AND $B$) | NOT $A$ AND $B$ | NOT ($A$ OR $B$) | NOT $A$ OR $B$ |
|---|---|---|---|---|---|---|---|---|
| T | T | T | T | F | F | F | F | T |
| T | F | F | T | F | T | F | F | F |
| F | T | F | T | T | T | T | F | T |
| F | F | F | F | T | T | F | T | T |

Key: T–True, F–False

A and B are simple conditions.

For example, the compound condition

A – B * C < 100 OR MALE AND C + D IS POSITIVE

is evaluated as though the following fully parenthesized expression were used:

(((A – (B * C)) < 100) OR ((MALE) AND ((C+D) IS POSITIVE)))

COBOL also permits the use of implied subjects and implied relational operators. For example, when writing a compound conditional expression such as:

A GREATER THAN B AND A LESS THAN C

it is more convenient to write:

A GREATER THAN B AND LESS THAN C

as it is stated in ordinary English. This is the use of an implied subject. Similarly, an expression such as:

A LESS THAN B AND A LESS THAN C

is more succinctly expressed as:

A LESS THAN B AND C

This is the use of an implied subject *and* an implied relational operator. The form of an *implied subject* is:

```
subject relational-operator object {AND}
                                    {OR }
        [NOT] relational-operator object
```

where "subject" and "object" are identifiers, literals, or arithmetic expressions. The NOT operator is interpreted as being part of the logical operator and *not* a part of the relational operator. For example, the expression:

A < B OR NOT > C

is equivalent to:

$$A < B \text{ OR NOT } A > C$$

The form of the implied subject and relational operator is:

$$\text{subject relational-operator object} \left\{ \begin{matrix} \text{AND} \\ \text{OR} \end{matrix} \right\} \text{ [\underline{NOT}] object}$$

where "subject," "object," and NOT assume the same meaning and interpretation as given above. For example, the expression:

$$A < B \text{ AND NOT } C$$

is equivalent to:

$$A < B \text{ AND NOT } A < C$$

When using implied subjects and relational operators, the following rules are used:

1. The omitted subject is taken as the most recently stated subject.
2. The omitted relational operator is taken as the most recently stated relational operator.

For example, the expression:

$$A < B \text{ OR } > C \text{ AND } D$$

is equivalent to:

$$A < B \text{ OR } A > C \text{ AND } A > D$$

using the two rules.

### The IF Statement

The form of the IF statement is:

where "condition" is a simple or a compound condition and "statement-$i$" represents one or more statements. If the condition is true, the statements represented by statement-1 are executed and program control flows to the next sentence. If the NEXT SENTENCE option is selected, then program control flows directly to the next sentence. If the condition is false, program control flows to the next sentence unless the ELSE clause is used. If ELSE is used in this case, the statements represented by statement-2 are executed. The statements represented by statement-1 in the above format terminate with the key word ELSE or the first period encountered. The statements represented by statement-2 in the above format terminate with the first period encountered. For example, the statement:

IF C1 S1.

is equivalent to the following flow diagram:

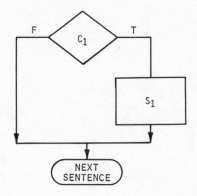

whereas the statement

IF C1 S1 ELSE S2.

is equivalent to:

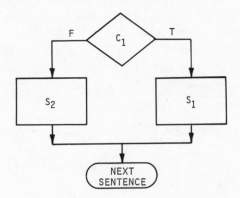

(Here C1 is a simple or compound condition and S1 and S2 are sets of imperative statements. If either S1 or S2 contains a GO TO procedure name statement,
then program control is directed to that procedure.)

The series of statements represented by statement-1 or statement-2 may include additional IF statements. In this case, the nested IF statement(s) are interpreted as IF-ELSE pairs and executed from left to right. For example, the statement:

IF C1 IF C2 S1 ELSE S2.

is equivalent to the following flow diagram:

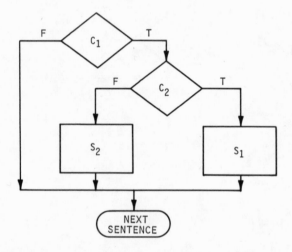

The ELSE statement is always paired with the IF statement to its immediate left.

The NEXT SENTENCE option always means that program control should
pass to the next sentence, regardless of the level of nesting of IF statements.

The IF statement is the first statement in COBOL for which the concept of a
sentence has a functional meaning. With the other procedure division statements
covered thus far, the use of punctuation is optional. With the IF statement, the
use of the period is necessary.

### The GO TO and ALTER Statements

The execution of the GO TO statement causes program control to be passed
unconditionally to the specified procedure. The formats for the GO TO statement are:

THE PROCEDURE DIVISION 341

---

*Format 1:*

GO TO [procedure-name-1]

*Format 2:*

GO TO procedure-name-1 [, procedure-name-2] ...
  DEPENDING ON identifier

---

where "procedure-name-*i*" is the name of a paragraph or a section in the procedure division of the program, and "identifier" is an integer data item.

In format 1, program control is passed to "procedure-name-1"; if the procedure name is not written, then a branch point must be established with the
ALTER statement, prior to execution of the GO TO statement. (When the
GO TO statement is referenced in an ALTER statement, the GO TO statement
must be the only statement in the paragraph.)

In format 2, program control is passed to "procedure-name-*i*," depending on
the value of the integer variable. If the value of the identifier is one, then program control is passed to the first procedure name in the list; if the value of the
identifier is two, then program control is passed to the second procedure name
in the list, and so forth.

The GO TO ... DEPENDING ON statement in COBOL is analogous to the
computed GO TO statement in FORTRAN.

The ALTER statement is used to change the branch point in a GO TO statement; it has the form:

---

ALTER procedure-name-1 TO [PROCEED TO] procedure-name-2
[, procedure-name-3 TO [PROCEED TO] procedure-name-4] ...

---

When the ALTER statement is executed, the GO TO statement in the named
paragraph (that is, "procedure-name-1") is altered so that program control is
passed to "procedure-name-2" when the GO TO is executed. The same interpretation applies to "procedure-name-3" and "procedure-name-4," and so on. The
keywords PROCEED TO in the statement format are included for readability.

The GO TO/ALTER statements in COBOL can be used in a similar manner to
the way the GOSUB/RETURN statements are used in BASIC and the ASSIGN/
GO TO statements are used in FORTRAN. For example, the statements can be
used to define a subprogram, that is,

```
        ALTER GOBACK TO PROCEED TO PAR-1 GO TO BIG-BOY.
    PAR-1. ...
            .
            .
            .
        ALTER GOBACK TO PROCEED TO PAR-2 GO TO BIG-BOY.
    PAR-2. ...
            .
            .
            .
    BIG-BOY. ...
            .
            . (Body of subroutine)
            .
    GOBACK. GO TO.
```

Another use of the ALTER statement is to change the execution time behavior of a program on a dynamic basis, for example:

```
    ENTRY-POINT. GO TO INIT-PAR.
    PROG-BODY. ...
            .
            .
            .
    INIT-PAR. ...
            .
            .
            .
        ALTER ENTRY-POINT TO PROCEED TO PROG-BODY
        GO TO PROG-BODY.
```

The first time through this program segment, program control goes to INIT-PAR, perhaps for initialization. After INIT-PAR is executed, the GO TO statement in ENTRY-PAR is altered so that INIT-PAR is not executed for subsequent passes through the program segment.

The preceding comment on the use of the GO TO/ALTER statements to cause a subroutine-type procedure to be executed is given for pedagogical purposes only. Section 11.5 describes the PERFORM statement that can be used to achieve the same results.

## The STOP Statement

The STOP statement is used to halt the execution of a program permanently or temporarily. The form of the STOP statement is:

$$\text{STOP} \begin{Bmatrix} \text{RUN} \\ \text{literal} \end{Bmatrix}$$

where "literal" is a numeric or nonnumeric literal or a figurative constant (excluding ALL). STOP RUN terminates execution of the program permanently and returns control to the compute operating system (if one exists). Use of the literal option causes the value of the literal to be displayed on the operator's console and the execution of the program is suspended. If the program is restarted by the operator, execution continues with the statement following the STOP statement.

The STOP statement can appear anywhere in the procedure division of a program.

## 11.5 CONTROLLED EXECUTION AND LOOPING

As was mentioned in an earlier chapter, a program loop in data processing is most frequently used to repeat a procedure or a set of procedures with different data, as compared to scientific computing where iterative procedures are frequently used.[4] Data processing frequently utilizes procedures that perform a relatively simple task, such as to print a page title, that are "called" from different points in a program.

### Controlled Execution

A program loop coded as a DO loop in a programming language such as FORTRAN is a set of statements through which program control flows. In other words, the *main* flow of control of the program actually passes into the DO loop and later it exits from the loop when the required number of iterations has been completed. The process is depicted as follows:

---

[4] This statement is not intended to be a definitive comparison of data processing and scientific computing; its purpose is to introduce the difference between a DO loop, as in FORTRAN, and the PERFORM statement in COBOL.

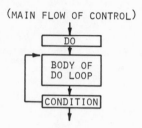

(MAIN FLOW OF CONTROL)

In this case, the DO loop is "normally" a major constituent of the program.

In data processing where iterative procedures are not as prevalent, program segments analogous to a DO loop are developed that perform either relatively minor tasks, such as the printing of a page title, or tasks that are utilized from several places in a program, similar to the way a subroutine is used. Another kind of execution control statement is needed; one with the following general structure:

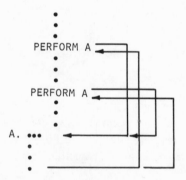

with the added provisions that "A" could be a paragraph, set of consecutive paragraphs, a section, or a set of consecutive sections, and that execution could be controlled with some sort of indexing and control parameters.

The latter case describes the PERFORM statement in COBOL that is used to invoke a set of statements in a manner similar to an internal subroutine or an "out-of-line" DO loop.

### The Basic PERFORM Statement

The PERFORM statement has four different but related formats. In all cases, the PERFORM statement causes program control to flow to an out-of-line procedure; when the execution of the procedure is completed, program control returns to the statement immediately following the PERFORM statement. It should be emphasized that the PERFORM statements and the procedure being "performed" are both contained in the procedure division of the same program. The most basic form of the PERFORM statement is given as follows:

---

*Format 1:*

PERFORM procedure-name-1 [THRU procedure-name-2]

---

where "procedure-name-1" and "procedure-name-2" are the names of the paragraph or section in the procedure division. When this format is used, the specified procedure(s) is executed once. The *range* of the PERFORM statement is determined as follows:

1. If procedure-name-1 is a paragraph name and procedure-name-2 is not specified, then the range of the PERFORM statement ends with the last statement of procedure-name-1 and program control is returned to the statement immediately following the PERFORM statement.
2. If procedure-name-1 is a section name and procedure-name-2 is not specified, then the range of the PERFORM statement ends with the last statement of the last paragraph in procedure-name-1.
3. If procedure-name-2 is specified and exists as a paragraph name, then the range of the PERFORM statement ends with the last statement of procedure-name-2.
4. If procedure-name-2 is specified and exists as a section name, then the range of the PERFORM statement ends with the last statement of the last paragraph of procedure-name-1.

The range of the PERFORM statement must be a set of *consecutive* statements specified by procedure-name-1 and procedure-name-2.

A PERFORM statement can be used in the range of another PERFORM statement. However, the range of the nested PERFORM statement must be entirely within or entirely outside the range of the outer PERFORM statement. The following program segment depicts the use of a basic PERFORM statement:

```
PROCEDURE DIVISION.
INIT SECTION.
TITLE-PAR. WRITE PRINT-LINE FROM TITLE AFTER
    ADVANCING 0 LINES; MOVE SPACES TO PRINT-LINE;
    WRITE PRINT-LINE; MOVE 2 TO LINE-COUNT.
```

NEXT-PAR. ...

.
.
.

OTHER-PAR. IF LINE-COUNT NOT LESS THAN 56 PERFORM
    TITLE-PAR.

.
.
.

This example depicts two important points: (1) A PERFORM statement is an imperative statement that can be used wherever the use of an imperative statement is permitted; and (2) a paragraph can be "flowed through" and *also* "performed."

The general specifications defined for the basic PERFORM statement apply to the other formats, as well.

### The Repetitive and Conditional PERFORM Statements

A second general class of PERFORM statements causes a procedure to be executed a specified number of times or until a specified condition is met. Formats 2 and 3 are given as:

---

*Format 2:*

PERFORM procedure-name-1 [THRU procedure-name-2] $\begin{Bmatrix} \text{identifier} \\ \text{integer} \end{Bmatrix}$

    TIMES

*Format 3:*

PERFORM procedure-name-1 [THRU procedure-name-2]

    UNTIL condition

---

where "identifier" is a positive integer variable, "integer" is a positive integer constant, and "condition" is a logical expression as defined in section 11.4, "Program Control."

When the TIMES option (format 2) is used, the procedure is performed the number of times specified by the initial value of "identifier" or "integer." If the initial value of "identifier" is negative or zero, the specified procedure is not executed and program control passes to the next statement following the PERFORM. Changing the value of "identifier" from within the range of the PERFORM statement does not alter the number of times the procedure is executed.

When the UNTIL option (format 3) is used, the range of the PERFORM statement is executed repetitively until the value of the specified condition is "true." If the value of the condition is "true" initially, then the specified procedure is not executed, as in the TIMES option.

### The Varying PERFORM Statement

The fourth form of the PERFORM statement permits the use of control variables, control parameters, and logical conditions. It has the form:

---

*Format 4:*

$\underline{\text{PERFORM}}$ procedure-name-1 [$\underline{\text{THRU}}$ procedure-name-2]

$\underline{\text{VARYING}} \begin{Bmatrix} \text{index-name-1} \\ \text{identifier-1} \end{Bmatrix} \underline{\text{FROM}} \begin{Bmatrix} \text{index-name-2} \\ \text{literal-2} \\ \text{identifier-2} \end{Bmatrix}$

$\underline{\text{BY}} \begin{Bmatrix} \text{literal-3} \\ \text{identifier-3} \end{Bmatrix} \underline{\text{UNTIL}} \text{ condition-1}$

$\left[ \underline{\text{AFTER}} \begin{Bmatrix} \text{index-name-4} \\ \text{identifier-4} \end{Bmatrix} \underline{\text{FROM}} \begin{Bmatrix} \text{index-name-5} \\ \text{literal-5} \\ \text{identifier-5} \end{Bmatrix} \right.$

$\underline{\text{BY}} \begin{Bmatrix} \text{literal-6} \\ \text{identifier-6} \end{Bmatrix} \underline{\text{UNTIL}} \text{ condition-2}$

$\left[ \underline{\text{AFTER}} \begin{Bmatrix} \text{index-name-7} \\ \text{identifier-7} \end{Bmatrix} \underline{\text{FROM}} \begin{Bmatrix} \text{index-name-8} \\ \text{literal-8} \\ \text{identifier-8} \end{Bmatrix} \right.$

$\underline{\text{BY}} \begin{Bmatrix} \text{literal-9} \\ \text{identifier-9} \end{Bmatrix} \underline{\text{UNTIL}} \text{ condition-3} \Big] \Big]$

---

where the specified procedure is executed repetitively as the specified control variables assume the specified values. The *initial value* for each control variable must be positive; the *step* (increment or decrement) may be positive or negative; and the "perform cycle" continues until the specified condition is true. Each time program control passes through the specified procedure, the control variable is incremented (or decremented) by the specified increment (or decrement). The statement format is self-explanatory; each of the three options available with the VARYING option is described separately.

When one identifier is varied, the PERFORM statement is expressed symbolically as:

> PERFORM $p$ VARYING $v$ FROM $i$
> BY $d$ UNTIL $c$

where $p$ is the procedure, $v$ is the control variable, $i$ is the initial value, $d$ is the increment or decrement, and $c$ is the condition that specifies when the procedure has been executed the required number of times. The functional structure of this option is depicted in Figure 11.1. This form of the PERFORM statement is analogous to a single DO statement (in FORTRAN) or FOR statement (in

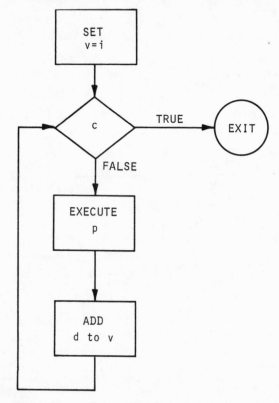

Fig. 11.1. Functional structure of the PERFORM statement with the VARYING option when one variable is varied.

BASIC). After the execution of the PERFORM statement with the VARYING option is complete, the control variable has a value that exceeds the last used value by the increment (or decrement), unless the condition was true when the PERFORM statement was entered. In the latter case, the control variable contains its initial value. This fact is inherent in the flow diagram of Figure 11.1.

When two identifiers are varied, the PERFORM statement is expressed symbolically as:

PERFORM $p$ VARYING $v_1$ FROM $i_1$
    BY $d_1$ UNTIL $c_1$
    AFTER $v_2$ FROM $i_2$
    BY $d_2$ UNTIL $c_2$

This form is analogous to a doubly nested DO loop or FOR loop, where $v_1$ corresponds to the outer control variable and $v_2$ corresponds to the inner control variable as follows:

FOR $v_1 = i_1$ TO ... STEP $d_1$
    FOR $v_2 = i_2$ TO ... STEP $d_2$

        $\left. \begin{array}{l} . \\ . \\ . \end{array} \right\}$ Body of the procedure $p$

    NEXT $v_2$
NEXT $v_1$

The functional structure of the PERFORM statement when two identifiers are varied is depicted in Figure 11.2. When the execution of the PERFORM statement is complete, the inner control variable $v_2$ contains its initial value while the outer control variable $v_1$ has a value that exceeds the last value used by the increment (or decrement), unless condition $c_1$ was true when the PERFORM statement was entered. In the latter case, both control variables contain their initial values. These facts are inherent in the flow diagram of Figure 11.2.

When three identifiers are varied, the PERFORM statement is expressed symbolically as:

PERFORM $p$ VARYING $v_1$ FROM $i_1$
    BY $d_1$ UNTIL $c_1$
    AFTER $v_2$ FROM $i_2$
    BY $d_2$ UNTIL $c_2$
    AFTER $v_3$ FROM $i_3$
    BY $d_3$ UNTIL $c_3$

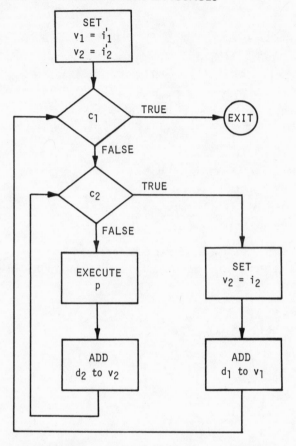

Fig. 11.2. Functional structure of the PERFORM statement with the VARYING option when two variables are varied.

This form is analogous to a triply nested DO loop or FOR loop, where $v_1$, $v_2$, and $v_3$ correspond to the outer, middle, and inner control variables, respectively; a triply nested FOR loop is given as follows:

FOR $v_1 = i_1$ TO ... STEP $d_1$
    FOR $v_2 = i_2$ TO ... STEP $d_2$
        FOR $v_3 = i_3$ TO ... STEP $d_3$

            $\left.\begin{array}{c} \cdot \\ \cdot \\ \cdot \end{array}\right\}$ Body of the procedure $p$

        NEXT $v_3$
    NEXT $v_2$
NEXT $v_1$

The functional structure of the PERFORM statement when three identifiers are varied is depicted in Figure 11.3. Determination of the values assumed by each of the control variables when the execution of the PERFORM statement is complete is left as an exercise for the student.

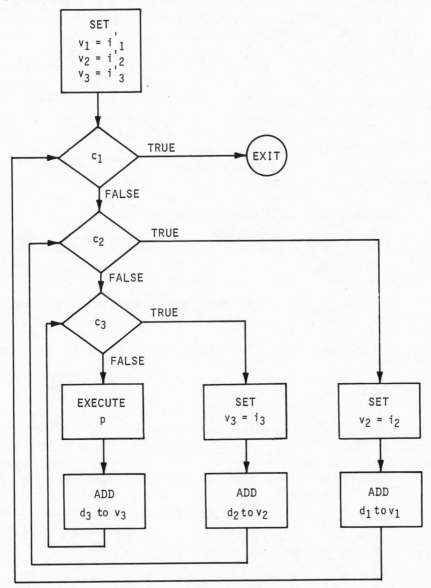

Fig. 11.3. Functional structure of the PERFORM statement with the VARYING option when three variables are varied.

## The EXIT Statement

The EXIT statement is used as a common end point to a procedure, analogous to the CONTINUE statement in FORTRAN. The form of the EXIT statement is:

> paragraph-name. EXIT.

The EXIT statement must be preceded by a paragraph name and be the only statement in that paragraph. An example of the use of the EXIT statement is given as follows:

        PERFORM JABBER THRU CLOCK VARYING I
            FROM 1 BY 1 UNTIL I > 10.
            .
            .
            .

        JABBER.   IF A (I) NOT > 0 GO TO CLOCK.
                  MOVE A (I) TO TEMP; COMPUTE A (I) = B (I) ** 2 + 1;
                  B (I) = TEMP.
        CLOCK. EXIT.

If a procedure is being "flowed through" and no associated PERFORM statement is active, then program control passes through the EXIT statement to the first sentence of the next paragraph.

## 11.6   INPUT AND OUTPUT

The input and output facilities in COBOL permit the processing of both sequential and random-access files, as well as input from low-volume input and output to low-volume output devices. This section presents an overview of input and output operations; details specific to random-access processing are given in Chapter 12.

### Open and Close Processing

An input or an output file, in COBOL, must be "opened" before it can be accessed and must be "closed" after the processing of that file is complete. The *open* operation logically connects a file, defined in the data division, to the program during execution. Open effectively results in volume mounting and positioning, label processing, the priming of input buffers, and attaches the COBOL program to an input/output routine (called an *access method*) that handles the input or output operations. The *close* operation logically disconnects a file from the program. Close effectively results in the emptying of output buffers, volume dismounting, file positioning, and release of the access method routine.

The OPEN statement performs the open operation and the CLOSE statement performs the close operation. Both statements are presented in a general fashion in this chapter.

The form of the OPEN statement is:

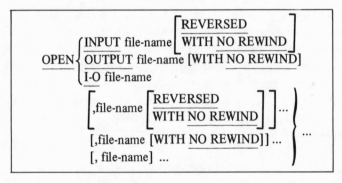

where "file name" specifies the name of a data file defined in the data division. Several files may be opened with a single OPEN statement; however, the keywords INPUT, OUTPUT, and I-O must only appear once. The following statement shows how the OPEN statement can be used:

```
OPEN INPUT MAST-FILE, TRANS-FILE
     OUTPUT PRINT-FILE, NEW-MAST
     I-O SCRATCH
```

OPEN and CLOSE statements for the same file must be paired such that a second OPEN for a file cannot be executed prior to the execution of a CLOSE statement for that file. The options for this statement are listed as follows:

| Option | Meaning |
|--------|---------|
| INPUT | File may be read only |
| OUTPUT | File may be written only |
| I-O | File may be read or written (referred to as an update file) |

Although the OPEN statement may cause input buffers to be primed, it does not obtain or release the first data record. A READ or a WRITE statement must be executed to obtain or release, respectively, the first data record for a file. During label processing, the user's label processing routines are invoked only if an appropriate USE statement has been specified.

The form of the CLOSE statement is:

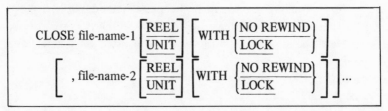

where "file-name-*i*" is the name of the file to be closed. The keyword LOCK refers to an implementation-defined technique for insuring that the current reel or unit cannot be processed again. REWIND refers to positioning the file at its initial point, an option that is generally assumed by default. For input files, normal label and USE processing is performed only if the file is positioned at its beginning. For output, close causes normal label and USE processing to be performed in all cases. An example of the CLOSE statement is:

> CLOSE MAST-FILE REEL WITH LOCK, NEW-MAST REEL WITH
> LOCK, PRINT-FILE

In general, the term "unit" refers to all input-output devices; the term "reel" refers to tape devices only. Therefore, rewind for a unit denotes that the file is to be positioned at its beginning, while for a reel, rewind denotes that the reel is to be physically rewound.

### Read and Write Processing

The read and write operations were introduced in Chapter 9. In COBOL, the program reads "files" and writes "records." Each file that is read or written must be defined in the data division with an FD entry and must be opened for the appropriate input and output operation.

The form of the READ statement is:

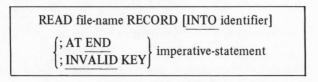

where "file name" is a defined file and "identifier" is a record description defined in the working storage section. Associated with each input file is an input area. Execution of the READ statement causes the next record to be read from the specified file and placed into the input area for that file. If the INTO option is specified, the input record is additionally moved to the storage area occupied by the named identifier, so that the input record is available in both areas. (Recall here that when a record, defined for a file, is addressed, the record description is "effectively" used as a template for referencing specific data fields in the input area.) The AT END option must be specified for sequential files; the "imperative-statement" is executed when an end-of-data condition is recognized for the input file. The INVALID KEY option is used only for random-access files; the "imperative-statement" is executed when the contents of the ACTUAL KEY field are invalid. (This topic is covered in Chapter 12; for the moment, however, a random-access file is accessed by a data key specified in the environment division.) A sample READ statement is:

READ MAST-FILE INTO WORK-RECORD
    AT END GO TO CLOSE-PAR

In this statement, MAST-FILE is a sequential file since the AT END option is used. After the READ statement is executed, the next data record from MAST-FILE is available in the input area associated with MAST-FILE and as the record WORK-RECORD in working storage.

The form of the WRITE statement is:

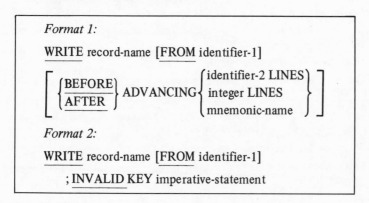

where "record-name" is the name of a data record specified in the DATA RECORDS clause of a file description. The WRITE statement causes the specified record to be written to the data file associated with "record-name." After the execution of the WRITE statement is completed, the data record in "record-name" is no longer accessible to the program. If the FROM option is specified, the data record specified by "identifier-1" is moved to the storage assigned to "record-name" and the WRITE operation is executed. The data record written by the WRITE statement is no longer available in "record-name" but *is* available as "identifier-1," which must be a record description defined in the working storage section or as another FD entry. The ADVANCING clause in format 1 refers to spacing on the printed page. In general, this option is self-explanatory, except for "mnemonic name" that specifies a particular feature defined by the implementor. The INVALID KEY option in format 2 is used when an invalid key exists during random-access processing. A sample WRITE statement is:

> WRITE M-REC FROM WORK-RECORD

This statement causes the data record stored as WORK-RECORD to be moved to the storage area associated with M-REC. (The information is still available as WORK-RECORD.) The data, now stored as M-REC, is written to the file associated with M-REC in an FD entry. (After the WRITE statement is complete, the information in M-REC is released for output and is no longer available to the program.)

**Low-Volume Input and Output**

The READ and WRITE statements are designed and are usually implemented to handle large amounts of input and output data effectively and efficiently. Because the programmer is required to open, close, and define each file that is used, the process is sometimes viewed as being cumbersome—especially when a few data items are to be entered or displayed.

The COBOL language permits a special low-volume input or output device to be specified in the environment division. In the following formats, the device is called "mnemonic name." It is usually an on-line console, card reader, or low-speed printer, but can also be specified as the system input device (SYSIN) or the system output device (SYSOUT), as well.

The ACCEPT statement causes the transfer of data from the specified input device and has the form:

> ACCEPT identifier [FROM mnemonic-name]

The input data replaces the contents of the data item named by the identifier. The size of the data transfer is implementation defined. If the FROM option is not used, an implementation-defined standard input device is used.

The DISPLAY statement displays the specified data items on the low-speed output device specified by "mnemonic name." The DISPLAY statement has the form:

$$\underline{\text{DISPLAY}} \begin{Bmatrix} \text{literal-1} \\ \text{identifier-1} \end{Bmatrix} \begin{bmatrix} \text{, literal-2} \\ \text{, identifier-2} \end{bmatrix} \dots [\underline{\text{UPON}} \text{ mnemonic-name}]$$

where "literal-$i$" and "identifier-$i$" assume their usual definitions. The size and manner of the output operation is implementation defined as is the output device when the UPON option is not used.

One implementation of COBOL refers to the system output device as SYSOUT and permits a DISPLAY statement of the form:

$$\text{DISPLAY} \begin{Bmatrix} \text{literal-1} \\ \text{identifier-1} \end{Bmatrix} \begin{bmatrix} \text{, literal-2} \\ \text{, identifier-2} \end{bmatrix} \dots \text{UPON SYSOUT}$$

The programmer can conveniently write commentary information to the printed page with a DISPLAY statement, such as:

DISPLAY "END OF JOB" UPON SYSOUT

without having to define an output file, data records, and commentary information in the data division of the program.


## 11.7  COMMENTS ON OTHER PROCEDURE DIVISION FACILITIES

Compared with the BASIC and FORTRAN languages, COBOL is a more extensive language. As a statement of fact, languages designed by committee usually are. The facilities presented in this chapter are the "nucleus" of the COBOL language; this nucleus can be augmented by operational facilities for: table handling, sorting, report writing, random-access processing, program segmentation, library management, and the use of subprograms. Table handling, random-access processing, library management, and subprograms are presented briefly in the next chapter, in addition to some details of the language that have been left until last.

The objective is to promote a general knowledge of COBOL, rather than present a language primer. Toward that end, only items of the most general interest are covered.

## EXERCISES

1.  Complete the following table:

| Statement | Value after execution of statement | | | |
|---|---|---|---|---|
| | A | B | C | D |
| Initial values | 16 | 8 | 4 | 100 |
| ADD A TO B | | | | |
| ADD A,B TO C | | | | |
| ADD A,B,C GIVING D | | | | |
| ADD 10.1, B TO A | | | | |
| SUBTRACT B FROM A | | | | |
| SUBTRACT B,C FROM A | | | | |
| SUBTRACT A,B,C GIVING D | | | | |
| MULTIPLY A BY B | | | | |
| MULTIPLY A BY B GIVING C | | | | |
| DIVIDE B INTO A | | | | |
| DIVIDE B INTO A GIVING D | | | | |
| COMPUTE C = A + B | | | | |
| COMPUTE C = A − B | | | | |
| COMPUTE D = A * B − C | | | | |
| COMPUTE C = A / B | | | | |
| COMPUTE A = A / B | | | | |

2.  For the statement MOVE A TO B, complete the following:

(The caret (∧) denotes the location of the decimal point.)

3. Complete the following table:

| Sending Field | Receiving Field | Legal | Illegal |
|---|---|---|---|
| Group item | Alphanumeric item | | |
| Alphabetic item | Numeric integer item | | |
| Numeric integer item | Alphabetic item | | |
| Alphabetic item | Noninteger numeric item | | |
| Alphanumeric item | Numeric integer item | | |
| Alphabetic item | Numeric edited item | | |
| Numeric edited item | Alphabetic item | | |

4.  For the statement

> IF $A > B$ GO TO X ELSE GO TO Y.

determine the statement branched to for each pair of (A,B) values:

| A | B | Branch To? | |
|---|---|---|---|
| 10 | 5 | X | (example) |
| J O N E S | J O H N | | |
| –123.45 | –167.932 | | |
| ⎵ ⎵ D O G | D O G ⎵ ⎵ | | |
| 639.1 | 639.123 | | |
| A D A M | A D A M ⎵ | | |

5.  For the statement

> GO TO APAR, BPAR, CPAR DEPENDING ON ITEM.

complete the table for various values of ITEM:

| Value of ITEM | Statement Branched To | |
|---|---|---|
| 1 | APAR | (example) |
| 3 | | |
| 2 | | |
| 0 | | |
| 4 | | |

6. Give the COBOL equivalent of the following DO loop:

   DO 50 I=1,10
   50 A(I)=I

7. Give the COBOL equivalent of the following logical IF statement:

   IF (A+B.GT.10) A=13

8. Write COBOL statements to exchange the contents of fields ALPHA and BETA.
9. Write COBOL statements that execute the following computational tasks:

   a. Subtract .10 from NEW-BALANCE.
   b. Calculate TAX as 5% of TOTAL.
   c. Add BASE-PAY and BONUS to give TOTAL-PAY.
   d. Compute AVERAGE as SUM divided by N.
   e. Multiply HOURS over 40 by 1.5 giving OVERTIME.
   f. Place the remainder from dividing A by B into C.
   g. Decrease COUNTER by 1.

10. Write COBOL statements to do the following data transfer operations:

   a. Replace A with spaces.
   b. Make field XONE zero.
   c. Make LIMIT-VALUE the highest value in the COBOL collating sequence.
   d. Make the value of A-VALUE equal to 63.
   e. Make the value of TRICK equal to the value of CAT; leave CAT unchanged.

11. Write COBOL program segments (i.e., one or more COBOL statements) to perform the following tasks:

    a. Prepare the file MFILE for subsequent input processing.
    b. Print the last record on file MFILE.
    c. If BALANCE is negative, set it equal to zero.
    d. Write the contents of record A to file B using the storage area C. Do not use the MOVE verb.
    e. Branch to paragraph A-PAR if field LIST contains only letters.
    f. Given a list of 100 values stored in array A, find the largest value and place it in B.
    g. Write "END OF PAYROLL JOB" on the computer system's console.
    h. Perform the following calculation:

$$\frac{b^2 - 4ac}{2a}$$

    and replace $x$ with the result.
    i. Given the following record definition:

```
01  BIGGY.
    02  CODE PIC 999.
    02  REST PIC X(77).
```

    for records stored on file MFILE. Print all records for which CODE is equal to VAL but less than LIMIT.
    j. Copy file MASTER-COPY to file SAVE-COPY; each file contains record TIME-DATA.

12. Draw a flowchart giving the functional structure of the following PERFORM statement:

```
PERFORM BIG-PAR VARYING ID FROM 1 BY JL
    UNTIL A (I) > BAKER AFTER COUNT FROM
    LEAST BY INCR UNTIL COUNT < 100 AND LIMIT.
```

13. Give an example of each of the following conditions:

    a. class condition
    b. condition-name condition
    c. relation condition
    d. sign condition
    e. compound condition

and the use of

    f.  implied subject
    g.  implied relational operator
    h.  implied subject and implied relational operator

14.  A FORTRAN program segment that multiplies two matrices A and B is given as follows:

```
REAL A(15,10), B(10,7), C(15,7)
...
DO 50 I=1,15
DO 50 J=1,7
SUM=0.0
DO 30 K=1,10
30 SUM=SUM+A(I,K)*B(K,J)
50 C(I,J)=SUM
```

Write a COBOL version of the same program segment. Also, write the data division entries that describe A, B, and C.

15.  Describe what the following statement does:

```
EXAMINE BIG-NAME TALLYING ALL "A"
     REPLACING BY "LA".
```

# ADDITIONAL COBOL FACILITIES

## 12.1 INTRODUCTION

The objective of this chapter is to cover details of COBOL that are necessary for a comprehensive understanding of the language in addition to extended features of widespread interest. Items that fall into the first category are the identification and environment divisions, random-access processing, and picture editing. Extended features include table handling, library management, the use of subprograms, and a short comment on the various computational forms.

## 12.2 THE IDENTIFICATION DIVISION

The general format of the identification division is:

```
IDENTIFICATION DIVISION.
PROGRAM-ID. program-name.
[AUTHOR. [comment-entry] ...]
[INSTALLATION. [comment-entry] ...]
[DATE-WRITTEN. [comment-entry] ...]
[DATE-COMPILED. [comment-entry] ...]
[SECURITY. [comment-entry] ...]
[REMARKS. [comment-entry] ...]
```

where all entries begin in area A of the reference format. The division header and the program identification are the only required entries. The "program-name" is an ordinary COBOL name. However, most COBOL compilers use only the first few characters (for example, the first six or eight) of the name because of restrictions on program names by the computer operating system.

If the DATE-COMPILED entry is used, it is replaced by the compiler with an entry of the form:

DATE-COMPILED. current-date.

so that the correct date can be placed on the program listing.

Comment entries and remarks are continued in area B of the reference format.

## 12.3 THE ENVIRONMENT DIVISION

The Environment Division relates a COBOL program to the physical characteristics of a specific computer system. The environment division consists of a configuration section and an input-output section; the environment division must be included in every COBOL program. The overall format for the environment division is given as follows:

```
ENVIRONMENT DIVISION.
CONFIGURATION SECTION.
SOURCE-COMPUTER. source-computer-entry.
OBJECT-COMPUTER. object-computer-entry.
[SPECIAL-NAMES. special-names-entry.]
[INPUT-OUTPUT SECTION.
FILE CONTROL. { file-control-entry }...
[I-O-CONTROL. input-output-control-entry.]]
```

### The Configuration Section

The configuration section specifies the characteristics of the source and object computers. This section is divided into three paragraphs: the source-computer paragraph, the object-computer paragraph, and the special-names paragraph. The special-names paragraph relates implementation-defined names, used by the compiler, to the mnemonic names used in the source program. The formats of the three paragraphs are given as follows:

*Source-computer paragraph:*

SOURCE-COMPUTER. computer-name.

*Object-computer paragraph:*

OBJECT-COMPUTER. computer-name.

$$\left[ , \underline{\text{MEMORY SIZE}} \text{ integer} \left\{ \begin{array}{l} \underline{\text{WORDS}} \\ \underline{\text{CHARACTERS}} \\ \underline{\text{MODULES}} \end{array} \right\} \right]$$

*Special-names paragraph:*

SPECIAL-NAMES. [implementor-defined-name

$$\left\{ \begin{array}{l} \underline{\text{IS}} \text{ mnemonic-name } [, \underline{\text{ON STATUS IS}} \text{ condition-name-1} \\ \underline{\text{IS}} \text{ mnemonic-name } [, \underline{\text{OFF STATUS IS}} \text{ condition-name-2} \\ \underline{\text{ON STATUS IS}} \text{ condition-name-1} \\ \underline{\text{OFF STATUS IS}} \text{ condition-name-2} \end{array} \right.$$

$$\left. \begin{array}{l} [, \underline{\text{OFF STATUS IS}} \text{ condition-name-2}]] \\ [, \underline{\text{ON STATUS IS}} \text{ condition-name-1}]] \\ [, \underline{\text{OFF STATUS IS}} \text{ condition-name-2}] \\ [, \underline{\text{ON STATUS IS}} \text{ condition-name-1}] \end{array} \right\} \ldots$$

[, CURRENCY SIGN IS literal] [, DECIMAL-POINT IS COMMA] .

The above formats suggest the flexibility inherent in the configuration section. Although the implementor is generally permitted to use this section as he sees fit, it is evident that most hardware devices or computing conventions specified to a given computer system can be utilized in a COBOL program.

### The Input-Output Section

The input-output section is used to specify information necessary for controlling the transmission of data between external media and the computer. The file-control paragraph associates data files, defined in the data division, with an input/output device external to the computer. The input/output control paragraph gives specific control techniques to be used during the execution of the program. The formats of the *file-control paragraph* are given as follows:

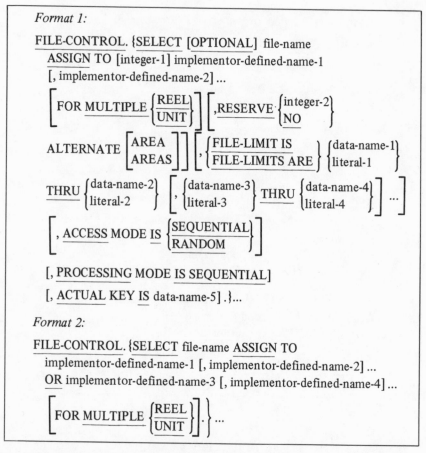

A complete discussion of the format of the file-control paragraph is of marginal value by itself since it necessarily relates to a given operational environment. From an overall point of view, however, the above formats give a general "flavor" for what can be specified in the input/output section.

The ACTUAL KEY clause is of special concern since it is used to read or write a data record to a randomly accessed file. The format of the ACTUAL KEY clause is:

ACTUAL KEY IS data-name

where "data-name" is a data item, defined in the file or working storage sections of the data division, composed of two components:

1. A *track identifier* that contains the relative track number at which a

search is to begin for the new record (in case of a read) or at which a
search is to begin for an unused space (in the case of a write)

2. A *record identifier* which is a symbolic identifier for the record itself

The ACTUAL KEY *must* be used for a random-access file; before each READ or
WRITE to that file, the "data-name" field must be set to a desired value.

The optional *input/output control paragraph* specifies points in a program
where checkpoints are to be taken, the main storage that can be shared among
files, information for multiple-reel files, and other input/output control information. The format of the input/output control paragraph is:

$$
\begin{aligned}
&\underline{\text{I-O-CONTROL.}} \left[\ ;\ \underline{\text{RERUN}} \left[\underline{\text{ON}}\ \begin{Bmatrix} \text{file-name-1} \\ \text{implementor-defined-name} \end{Bmatrix}\right]\right. \\[2ex]
&\underline{\text{EVERY}} \left.\begin{Bmatrix} \left[\underline{\text{END OF}}\right] \begin{Bmatrix} \underline{\text{REEL}} \\ \underline{\text{UNIT}} \end{Bmatrix} \right\} \text{OF file-name-2} \\ \text{integer-1}\ \underline{\text{RECORDS}} \\ \text{integer-2}\ \underline{\text{CLOCK-UNITS}} \\ \text{condition-name} \end{Bmatrix} \right] \ldots \\[2ex]
&\left[\ ;\ \underline{\text{SAME}} \left[\begin{Bmatrix} \underline{\text{RECORD}} \\ \underline{\text{SORT}} \end{Bmatrix}\right]\ \text{AREA FOR file-name-3}\ \{,\ \text{file-name-4}\}\ldots\right]\ \ldots \\[2ex]
&\left[\ ;\ \underline{\text{MULTIPLE FILE TAPE}}\ \text{CONTAINS file-name-5}\left[\underline{\text{POSITION}}\ \text{integer-3}\right]\right. \\
&\left[,\ \text{file-name-6}\ \left[\underline{\text{POSITION}}\ \text{integer-4}\right]\right]\ \ldots]\ \ldots
\end{aligned}
$$

The RERUN clause specifies a "checkpoint" that records the state of the computer system so that a program need not be completely rerun in the event of a
serious hardware malfunction. Checkpoint information can be read back into
main storage and a program can be restarted from the point that the checkpoint
was taken. The SAME ... clause specifies that the same storage area can be used
for two or more files, and the MULTIPLE FILE ... clause is used when more than
one file occupies the same magnetic tape reel.

### Comments on the Environment Division

The environment division as defined in the COBOL standard provides a general language structure that can be used by a given implementor to utilize the
features of a computer system or an operating system. In some cases, environment division entries can be treated as comments by the compiler if a particular

hardware or software feature does not exist. In other cases, the COBOL standard requires that the implementor actually implement a given facility.

The COBOL standard for the environment division is general and inclusive so that the language can meet the needs of a great many implementors and users. This is good. However, the reader who is interested in specific details is required to consult the reference manual for a particular implementation to gain the information he needs.

## 12.4 TABLE HANDLING

The table-handling feature of COBOL is used to facilitate the searching of tables and the management of associated indexes. Four COBOL clauses or statements are involved: the OCCURS clause, the USAGE clause, and the SET and SEARCH statements. (The "full" table-handling feature in COBOL also includes a KEY option that allows a data key, stored as part of the table, to be used during the search operation. This extension is not covered here and the reader is directed to reference [4] or [9].)

### The OCCURS Clause

The OCCURS clause is augmented by an INDEXED option that supplies information required for the application of subscripts or indexes. If "normal" subscripts are used and the table-handling feature is not used, then the INDEXED option need not be specified. However, normal subscripts and array handling procedures *can* still be utilized if the INDEXED option is specified. The extended form of the OCCURS clause is:[1]

$$\underline{\text{OCCURS}} \text{ integer-1} \begin{bmatrix} \text{TIMES} \\ \text{TO integer-2 TIMES } [\underline{\text{DEPENDING}} \text{ ON data-name-1}] \end{bmatrix}$$
$$[\underline{\text{INDEXED}} \text{ BY index-name-1 } [, \text{index-name-2}]...]$$

where the syntactical elements in the format are the same as defined in Chapter 10 and "index-name-*i*," which is new, is a data name that can be used for indexing and may appear only in SET, SEARCH, or PERFORM statements.

_____

[1]The KEY option is omitted in this format.

## Indexing

An index is a data item associated with a table (usually referred to as an array) or a data name with a usage of INDEX. (The manner in which an index is handled internally to the computer is usually implementation defined.) An index-name specified in an INDEXED BY clause may not appear in other data division entries since its attributes have been implicitly specified. An indexed data name takes the form:

```
data-name (index-name [{ ± } integer]
   [, index-name [{ ± } integer] [, index-name [{ ± } integer]]])
```

A simple index, such as DATA (IND), is referred to as a *direct index*. An index incremented or decremented by an integer, such as DATA (IND + 3), is referred to as a *relative index*. An indexed data name may be qualified, as with subscripted arrays covered in Chapter 10, and the indexes, enclosed in parentheses, are always moved to the extreme right of the array reference, for example,

DATA IN M-REC (IND + 3)

## Usage Clause

A data item may be defined as an index name without binding it to a specific table. The usage clause takes the form:

```
[USAGE IS] INDEX
```

The usage clause can be written at any level, for example,

77  IND USAGE IS INDEX.

## The SET Statement

The SET statement is used to assign a reference point in a table to an index name; that is, it is used to give the index an initial value. Since an index name cannot be used in conventional arithmetic and data manipulation statements, an index name must be initialized with the SET statement before a SEARCH statement is executed. The format of the SET statement is:

*Format 1:*

$$\underline{\text{SET}} \begin{Bmatrix} \text{index-name-1 [, index-name-2] ...} \\ \text{identifier-1 [, identifier-2] ...} \end{Bmatrix} \underline{\text{TO}} \begin{Bmatrix} \text{index-name-3} \\ \text{identifier-3} \\ \text{literal-1} \end{Bmatrix}$$

*Format 2:*

$$\underline{\text{SET}} \text{ index-name-4 [, index-name-5] ...} \begin{Bmatrix} \underline{\text{UP BY}} \\ \underline{\text{DOWN BY}} \end{Bmatrix} \begin{Bmatrix} \text{identifier-4} \\ \text{literal-2} \end{Bmatrix}$$

Each "identifier" must name either an index data item or an elementary integer data item; "identifier-4" must be an elementary integer data item. The "literal" must be a positive integer.

It is necessary to emphasize here that an index is not simply a number, but it is a displacement into a table, which may contain a complex combination of table elements. This fact causes an obvious restriction. If "identifier-1" names an index data item, defined with the USAGE clause, then the "literal-1" option cannot be used since the table for which the identifier is used is not known and an appropriate displacement cannot be computed.

### The SEARCH Statement

The SEARCH statement is used to search a table for a table element that satisfies one or more conditions that are part of the SEARCH statement. The SEARCH statement has the form:

$$\underline{\text{SEARCH}} \text{ identifier-1} \left[ \underline{\text{VARYING}} \begin{Bmatrix} \text{index-name-1} \\ \text{identifier-2} \end{Bmatrix} \right]$$

$$[; \underline{\text{AT END}} \text{ imperative-statement-1}]$$

$$; \underline{\text{WHEN}} \text{ condition-1} \begin{Bmatrix} \text{imperative-statement-2} \\ \underline{\text{NEXT SENTENCE}} \end{Bmatrix}$$

$$\left[ ; \underline{\text{WHEN}} \text{ condition-2} \begin{Bmatrix} \text{imperative-statement-3} \\ \underline{\text{NEXT SENTENCE}} \end{Bmatrix} \right] ...$$

where "identifier-1," which is the table, must not be subscripted and must be defined in the data division with the OCCURS and INDEXED clauses. "Identifier-2" must be an index name or an elementary integer data item. The "conditions" and "imperative-statement" are the same as defined previously.

The SEARCH statement steps through the specified table sequentially until one of the conditions is met or the end of the table is reached. The conditions are evaluated in the order they are specified. The SEARCH statement, specifying two conditions, is expressed symbolically as:

SEARCH $t$ VARYING $i$; AT END $s_1$;
    WHEN $c_1$ $s_2$;
    WHEN $c_2$ $s_3$

where $t$ is the name of the table, $i$ is the index name, $c_1$ and $c_2$ are conditions, and $s_1$, $s_2$, and $s_3$ are imperative statements. The functional structure of the search operation is depicted in Figure 12.1.

If the VARYING option is not used, then the first index defined with the table is used in the search operation.

### Example

A simple example is given to illustrate the preceding concepts. A symbol table is defined in the data division as follows:

    02  SYMTAB OCCURS 100 TIMES INDEXED BY PILL.
        03  NAME PICTURE X(8).
        03  VALUE PICTURE 9(5) COMPUTATIONAL.
        .
        .
        .
    77  SYMBOL PICTURE X(8).

A symbol to be "looked up" is stored in SYMBOL. A simple example to search the table for the first occurrence of SYMBOL as a NAME entry is given as follows:

    SET PILL TO 1.
    SEARCH SYMTAB VARYING PILL; AT END GO TO NOT-FOUND;
        WHEN NAME IN SYMTAB (PILL) = SYMBOL
        MOVE VALUE IN SYMTAB (PILL) TO NEWVAL GO TO FOUND.

This process makes available the table value associated with SYMBOL as the data

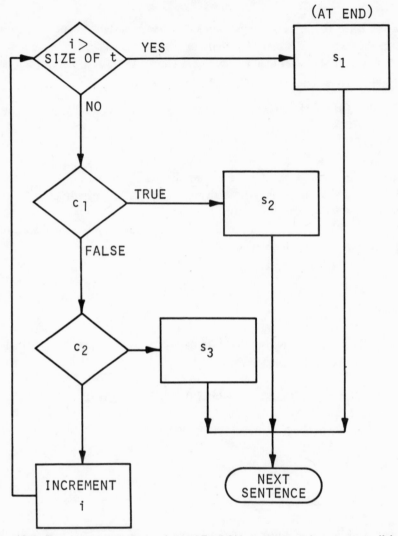

Fig. 12.1. Functional structure of the SEARCH statement when two conditions are used.

item named NEWVAL. If the search value is not found in the table, the AT END exit is taken. The search terminates when the value of the index exceeds the size of the table as defined in the OCCURS clause.

The search operation need not begin with the first table entry. The search is initiated with the current value of the index specified in the SEARCH statement, and the SET statement can be used to initialize the index to a desired value.

## 12.5 RANDOM-ACCESS INPUT AND OUTPUT PROCESSING

One of the major disadvantages of a serial input/output device, such as magnetic tape, is that it is necessary to pass over the $(i-1)$th record to access the $i$th record. In many file-processing applications, serial devices are not satisfactory because master records and transaction records are sorted and processed in order. For nonfile-processing applications, it is frequently desirable to retrieve a record directly from a direct-access device, such as magnetic disk or drum. (The reader is expected to know the general characteristics of these devices.) Magnetic disk is the more frequently used direct-access device and is discussed briefly in the next paragraph; it is used as a conceptual model for random-access input and output processing.

### Basic Concepts

A magnetic disk unit is depicted in Figure 12.2. Information is recorded serially by bit on the concentric tracks. A specific track is located by read-write head number and by track number. Information is recorded on a track as blocks, separated by gaps. A single data record is recorded as a series of three blocks: a count block, a key block, and a data block. Track format is suggested by Figure 12.3. The *count block* identifies the data record, gives the length of the data block, and denotes the presence or absence and the length of the key block. The optional *key block* contains a key that can be used to locate a specific record. A nominal length of the key is 1 to 256 bytes. The *data block* contains the data portion of the record.

A disk record is accessed as follows:

1. The read/write heads are moved to the specified track position. (In most disk systems, the read/write heads are a comblike arrangement that moves in and out together.) This is called the *seek operation*.
2. During a read operation, the specified read/write head is activated (electronically) and the disk control unit locates the requested record by comparing the key portion of the record identification contained in the read operation to the record identification contained in the key subblock. During a write operation, the specified read/write head is activated (electronically) and the record is written in the first unused space on the track.

The read/write head number, the track number, and a record identification and a

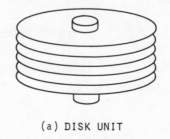

(a) DISK UNIT

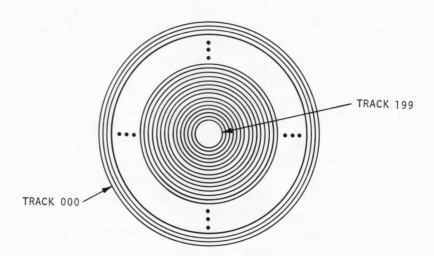

TRACK 199

TRACK 000

(b) DISK SURFACE (200 CONCENTRIC TRACKS SEE FIG.12.3)

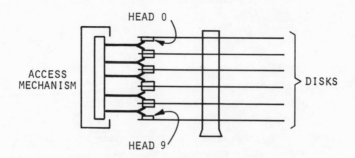

HEAD 0

ACCESS
MECHANISM

DISKS

HEAD 9

(c) ACCESS MECHANISM AND READ/WRITE HEADS

Fig. 12.2. A magnetic disk unit.

data key comprise the "actual key" mentioned in section 12.3, "The Environment Division." The key block is normally used in COBOL random-access input/output processing to locate a desired record. The reader is directed to Chapin [2],

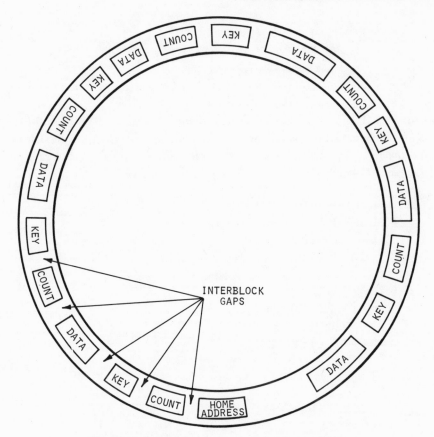

Fig. 12.3. Record format on a direct-access device.

Flores [3], or Murach [7] for additional information on the subject of direct-access input/output device utilization.

### "Direct" Random-Access Processing

A typical read operation of a direct random file is described first. (The term "direct" refers to a record that is accessed by its physical location on the direct-access medium.) The environment division would contain an entry such as:

ENVIRONMENT DIVISION.
.
.
.

FILE CONTROL.
    SELECT IN-DISK-FILE ASSIGN TO SYSDISK-2314
    ACCESS IS RANDOM
    ACTUAL KEY IS LOCATE-KEY.

IN-DISK-FILE is the file name assigned by the programmer. SYSDISK-2314 is an implementor-defined name for a specific kind of disk unit. LOCATE-KEY is the name of a key defined in the data division—but not in the data record being read. A corresponding set of data division entries might be:

DATA DIVISION.
FILE SECTION.
FD IN-DISK-FILE
    LABEL RECORDS ARE STANDARD.
    DATA RECORD IS DUM-REC.
01 DUM-REC.
    02 A PICTURE X(20).
    02 B PICTURE X(30).
    02 C PICTURE X(30).
    .
    .
    .

WORKING-STORAGE SECTION.
01 LOCATE-KEY.
    02 DISK-PACK-NO PICTURE 9(3).
    02 FILLER      PICTURE 9(2).
    02 TRACK-NO   PICTURE 9(3).
    02 RECORD-NO  PICTURE X.
    02 DATA-KEY   PICTURE X(20).
01 NEEDED-KEY.
    .
    .
    .

Using the above definitions, a hypothetical program segment to read a record from the named file would exist as follows:

PROCEDURE DIVISION.
    .
    .

OPEN INPUT IN-DISK-FILE

.
.  } Obtain needed key to read record.
.

MOVE NEEDED-KEY TO LOCATE-KEY.

.

.

.

READ IN-DISK-FILE; INVALID KEY GO TO BAD-KEY-PAR.

.

.

.

CLOSE IN-DISK-FILE.

which makes available the record with the specified key as the input record DUM-REC.

Programs that utilize random-access processing usually employ a table lookup technique or a sophisticated algorithm to locate data records on the direct-access medium. The key point is that the location of a record must be known and the read/write head must be moved to its track position before it can be read. For that reason, the COBOL standard defines a SEEK statement that has the form:

<u>SEEK</u> file-name RECORD

where "file-name" specifies the file to be read and the data name specified in the ACTUAL KEY clause (environment division) contains a record identification that includes the physical position to which the read/write head should be moved. The SEEK statement is included so that a user can initiate a "seek" for a given record that would execute in parallel with the execution of his program. The SEEK statement would be executed prior to the execution of a READ or WRITE statement and is intended to compensate for the seek time inherent in random-access processing. The manner in which the SEEK statement is implemented may be specified by the implementor.

The "direct" WRITE statement can be used to create a new file or to update an old file. A new file is opened for OUTPUT; an update file is opened for I-O. For update, a WRITE statement follows a READ statement for a particular record and the old data block is simply "written over." The ACTUAL KEY field remains the same. For a new file, the programmer supplies a new ACTUAL KEY field, containing the record identification and a new data key. For an update file, the INVALID KEY exit should never be taken by the computer since the "old data record" exists, and so on. For a new file, the INVALID KEY exit is taken if insufficient space exists for the record to be written.

This section augments section 11.6, "Input and Output," and should give the reader an idea of how and why random-access processing is used. Before actually using these concepts, the reader should consult the COBOL reference manual for the computer system he is using.

### Indexed Sequential

An indexed sequential file allows records to be accessed sequentially or randomly. Records are written and read with a "key field" that is part of the data record. Associated with each indexed sequential file is an index that gives the highest key (in collating sequence) of the records on that track or cylinder of the file. The program requests the read (for example) of a data record with a specific key. The input/output routine, through the index, finds the track or cylinder on which the record is found. A search for the particular record is made from there. A file of this type can be read randomly, by supplying a desired key, or sequentially by following down the index of keys. Indexed sequential files are always created sequentially, for obvious reasons, but can be updated in place. The index of an indexed sequential file is stored with the file. Before an indexed sequential file is accessed, the index is read into main storage so that the index can be searched for a specified key.

An extension to the COBOL language permits the use of indexed sequential files. The concepts are presented through an example that creates an indexed sequential file.

In the environment division, the ACTUAL KEY clause is replaced by a NOMINAL KEY and a RECORD KEY. The RECORD KEY clause specifies a field in the data record associated with a file, as follows:

```
ENVIRONMENT DIVISION.
        .
        .
        .
    FILE CONTROL.
        SELECT OUT-DISK-FILE ASSIGN TO SYSDISK-2314-I
            ACCESS IS SEQUENTIAL
            RECORD KEY IS REC-KEY.
```

OUT-DISK-FILE is the name of the file; SYSDISK-2314-I is an implementor-defined name for an indexed sequential file; and REC-KEY is the name of the key field in the record. ACCESS IS SEQUENTIAL specifies that the file is created sequentially; the index is created automatically. (The NOMINAL KEY clause is used for input or update; it specifies a field in working storage that is used in the search of the index.)

Corresponding data division entries are:

```
DATA DIVISION.
FILE SECTION.
FD   OUT-DISK-FILE
       LABEL RECORDS ARE STANDARD
       DATA RECORD IS OUT-REC.
01   OUT-REC.
       02  FILLER      PICTURE X.
       02  REC-KEY     PICTURE 9(7).
       02  REST        PICTURE X(72).
     .
     .
     .
```

Since an indexed sequential file is created sequentially, it is the user's responsibility to write the records to the file with the "record keys" in an ordered sequence. As mentioned, the index is created automatically. A sample program segment to create the indexed sequential file is given as follows:

```
PROCEDURE DIVISION.
     .
     .
     .

       OPEN OUTPUT OUT-DISK-FILE.

     .  ⎫
     .  ⎬  Obtain record to be written.
     .  ⎭

WRITE OUT-REC; INVALID KEY GO TO TROUBLE
     .
     .
     .

CLOSE OUT-DISK-FILE.
```

In reading or updating an indexed file, the NOMINAL KEY clause is required as shown in the following environment division entries:

ENVIRONMENT DIVISION.
        .
        .
        .

FILE CONTROL.
        SELECT INDEX-FILE ASSIGN TO SYSDISK-2314-I
                ACCESS IS RANDOM
                RECORD KEY IS REC-KEY
                NOMINAL KEY IS FIND-KEY.

where FIND-KEY gives the key of the record to be read. Data division entries are:

DATA DIVISION.
FILE SECTION.
FD INDEX-FILE
        LABEL RECORDS ARE STANDARD
        DATA RECORD IS IN-REC.
01    IN-REC.
        02    FILLER        PICTURE X.
        02    REC-KEY      PICTURE 9(7).
        02    REST          PICTURE X(72).
        .
        .
        .

WORKING-STORAGE SECTION.
77  FIND-KEY PICTURE 9(7).

For an ordinary read operation, the key of the record to be read is moved to FIND-KEY, which is the nominal key. The record is read and placed in the storage area corresponding to file INDEX-FILE so that it can be accessed as record IN-REC. A program segment to read a record from an indexed sequential file is:

PROCEDURE DIVISION.
        .
        .
        .
        OPEN INPUT INDEX-FILE.

.
. } Move key of desired record to FIND-KEY.
.

READ INDEX-FILE; INVALID KEY GO TO ERROR.

.

.

.

CLOSE INDEX-FILE.

The invalid key exit is taken when a record with the specified key does not exist in the file.

The update operation uses a new statement:

```
REWRITE record-name [FROM identifier]
       [; INVALID KEY imperative statement]
```

that is designed for use with an indexed sequential file. The statement is functionally the same as the WRITE statement, except that the file must be opened for I-O and the RECORD KEY and NOMINAL KEY fields *must* contain the same value; otherwise, the INVALID KEY exit is taken in most implementations of COBOL. Using the last environment and data division entries given, a program segment to update a record is given as follows:

PROCEDURE DIVISION.

.

.

.

OPEN I-O INDEX-FILE.

.
. } Move key of desired record to FIND-KEY.
.

READ INDEX-FILE; INVALID KEY GO TO ERR-COND-1.

.
. } Update record IN-REC.
.

REWRITE IN-REC; INVALID KEY GO TO ERR-COND-2.

.

.

.

CLOSE INDEX-FILE.

The preceding presentation of indexed sequential input and output is not intended to be a definitive treatment of the subject—only an introduction. This area of data processing is currently going through a period of great change, and of all the COBOL language facilities, this area will probably change the most. More than likely, the changes will not be in language structure but in the interpretation of the language features by the COBOL language development committee.

## 12.6 LIBRARY FACILITIES

In COBOL programming, sequences of statements or clauses are frequently repeated in different programs. Typical examples are record- and file-description entries in the data division and file-control entries in the environment division. This is so because the output of one program is frequently used as input to another program. Although the names of some of the constituents may vary, the structure of the entries is frequently the same. A similar need exists in the procedure and identification divisions and entire paragraphs or sections are copied for use in another program. A typical example is a single input/output error-processing routine that is used in several different programs. Some of the names, such as the file name, may change but the structure of error processing remains the same.

The library facility in COBOL allows a program text to be placed in a library and assigned a name. (A utility program is used to create a library of this type.) Then during compilation, the programmer can use a COPY statement to copy a named body of text from the library to his program. The program is then compiled as though the library text were actually part of his program. The COPY statement is one of the "compiler-directing" statements that were mentioned previously.

### The COPY Statement

The form of the COPY statement is:

COPY library-name

[REPLACING word-1 BY $\begin{Bmatrix} \text{word-2} \\ \text{literal-1} \\ \text{identifier-1} \end{Bmatrix}$

[, word-3 BY $\begin{Bmatrix} \text{word-4} \\ \text{literal-2} \\ \text{identifier-2} \end{Bmatrix}$ ] ...] .

where "library-name" specifies the name of the text to be copied into the source program at the point that the COPY statement is written and "word-*i*" is one of the following: data name, procedure name, condition name, mnemonic name, or file name. The constructs "literal-*i*" and "identifier-*i*" conform to previous definitions.

When the REPLACING option is not used, a direct copy from librrry to source program is made. If, for example, the library entry named A-REC is:

```
  02 S-S-NO       PICTURE 9(9).
  02 NAME         PICTURE X(35).
  02 ADDRESS.
        03 STREET  PICTURE X(20).
        03 CITY    PICTURE A(15).
        03 STATE   PICTURE A(3).
        03 ZIP     PICTURE 9(5).
  02 PAY-DATA.
        03 GROSS   PICTURE 99999V99.
        03 M-RATE  PICTURE 9999V99.
        03 TAX     PICTURE 99999V99.
```

then the record specification:

```
  01 PAY-REC COPY A-REC.
```

causes A-REC to be copied such that PAY-REC is defined as:

```
        01 PAY-REC.
  c         02 S-S-NO       PICTURE 9(9).
  c         02 NAME         PICTURE X(35).
  c         02 ADDRESS.
  c              03 STREET  PICTURE X(20).
  c              03 CITY    PICTURE A(15).
  c              03 STATE   PICTURE A(3).
  c              03 ZIP     PICTURE 9(5).
  c         02 PAY-DATA.
  c              03 GROSS   PICTURE 99999V99.
  c              03 M-RATE  PICTURE 9999V99.
  c              03 TAX     PICTURE 99999V99.
```

where "c" denotes entries that are copied from the library.

When the REPLACING option is used, specified words are replaced by the given replacement. For example, if the copy library contained an entry name FILE-SPEC composed of the following text:

```
SELECT A-FILE ASSIGN TO A-UNIT
    ACCESS IS RANDOM
    RANDOM KEY IS KEY-1
    RECORD KEY IS KEY-2.
```

then the file-control paragraph written as:

```
FILE CONTROL.
    COPY FILE-SPEC REPLACING A-FILE
    BY IN-DISK-FILE, A-UNIT BY SYSDISK-2314-I,
    KEY-1 BY NEEDLE, KEY-2 BY KNEL.
```

causes the following source code to be compiled:

```
FILE CONTROL.
    SELECT IN-DISK-FILE ASSIGN TO SYSDISK-2314-I
    ACCESS IS RANDOM
    NOMINAL KEY IS NEEDLE
    RECORD KEY IS KNEL.
```

The COPY statement is used for standardization, for programmer efficiency, and to minimize programmer errors.

### Use of the COPY Statement

The places in a COBOL program that the COPY statement can be used are well defined and specified as follows:

In the configuration section:

| | |
|---|---|
| SOURCE-COMPUTER. | COPY-statement. |
| OBJECT-COMPUTER. | COPY-statement. |
| SPECIAL-NAMES. | COPY-statement. |

In the input-output section:

FILE-CONTROL. COPY-statement.

I-O-CONTROL.   COPY-statement.

In the file section:[2]

FD file-name COPY-statement.

In a record description:

01  data-name COPY-statement.

In the procedure division:

$$\left\{ \begin{array}{l} \text{section-name SECTION.} \\ \text{paragraph-name} \end{array} \right\} \text{COPY-statement.}$$

The REPLACING option can be used in all cases where the COPY statement can be used.

## 12.7  SUBROUTINE FACILITIES

One of the features that is noticeably absent from the COBOL language is facilities for defining and calling subroutines. Subroutines are not defined in COBOL. However, most operating environments allow subroutines as a normal function of the loading phase of program execution. The COBOL language does, on the other hand, include an ENTER statement that allows statements from another language to be used in a COBOL program. This is the means by which subroutines *can be* implemented in COBOL.

### The ENTER Statement

The ENTER statement permits the use of a programming language other than COBOL in a COBOL program. The form of the ENTER statement is:

---

[2]The COPY statement is also permitted in the sort description and the report section not covered in this book.

---

ENTER language-name [routine-name].

---

where "language-name" is the name of a programming language defined by the implementor that can be entered through COBOL. "Routine-name" is used to identify statements in the entered language that cannot be written in line. A liberal flexibility is permitted with the ENTER statement and the use of "language name" and "routine name" is implementation defined. The ENTER statement is a compiler-directing statement.

The ENTER statement is normally used in somewhat the following manner:

```
ENTER LINKAGE.
CALL "TRYIT" USING A-REC, TVAR.
ENTER COBOL.
```

where TRYIT is the name of the subroutine being called and A-REC and TVAR are arguments. The CALL statement demonstrates the use of a subroutine in the procedure division of a COBOL program.

It follows from the above discussion that a subroutine definition, which is also an operational function, is related to the procedure division of the subprogram. A sample subroutine definition might exist as follows:

```
PROCEDURE DIVISION.
     .
     .
     .

ENTER LINKAGE.
ENTRY "TRYIT" USING CAT, DOG.
ENTER COBOL.
     .
     .
     .



     .
     .
     .

ENTER LINKAGE
GOBACK.
ENTER COBOL.
     .
```

where TRYIT is the name of the subroutine entry point and CAT and DOG are parameters. The GOBACK statement causes a return to the calling program.

As in other programming languages, parameters and arguments must agree in number, order, and type.

### Sample Subroutine Statements

Although subroutine statements are implementor defined, some statements have been used by several implementors and are worthy of note. The formats of these statements are given as follows and briefly described in succeeding paragraphs:

```
CALL literal [USING identifier-1 [identifier-2] ...]
ENTRY literal [USING identifier-1 [identifier-2] ...]
PROCEDURE DIVISION [USING identifier-1 [identifier-2] ...] .
GOBACK.
```

where:

"Literal" is a nonnumeric literal specifying the subroutine name.
"Identifier-*i*" is a data name specifying an argument or parameter.
The CALL statement invokes the named subroutine.
The ENTRY statement defines a subroutine name and marks its entry point.
The USING option on the PROCEDURE DIVISION specifies subroutine parameters; the name of the program (that is, the PROGRAM-ID) is the name of the subroutine.
The GOBACK statement causes program control to be returned to the calling program.

The following program skeleton depicts the use of the CALL, ENTRY, and GOBACK statements:

*Calling Program*

IDENTIFICATION DIVISION.
PROGRAM-ID. ABLE.

```
        .
        .
        .
    ENVIRONMENT DIVISION.
        .
        .
        .
    DATA DIVISION.
        .
        .
        .
    WORKING-STORAGE SECTION.
    01  RECORD-A.
        02  A   PICTURE X(20).
        02  B   PICTURE 9(7).
        02  C   PICTURE A(30).
        .
        .
        .
    PROCEDURE DIVISION.
        .
        .
        .
    ENTER LINKAGE.
    CALL "TRBLE" USING RECORD-A.
    ENTER COBOL.
        .
        .
        .
    STOP RUN.
```

*Subroutine:*

```
    IDENTIFICATION DIVISION.
    PROGRAM-ID. BAKER.
        .
        .
        .
    ENVIRONMENT DIVISION.
        .
```

```
        .
        .
        .
    DATA DIVISION.
        .
        .
        .
    WORKING-STORAGE SECTION.
    01  PARAM-DATA.
            02  BIG1      PICTURE X(20).
            02  SEEP      PICTURE 9(7).
            02  COULD     PICTURE A(30).
        .
        .
        .
    PROCEDURE DIVISION.
        .
        .
        .
    ENTER LINKAGE.
    ENTRY "TRBLE" USING PARAM-DATA.
    ENTER COBOL.
        .
        .
        .
    ENTER LINKAGE.
    GOBACK.
    ENTER COBOL.
```

In the preceding examples, the word LINKAGE is an implementor-defined name that signals to the compiler that "linkage" (or subroutine) statements follow. Conventions differ between implementors, and in some cases the ENTER statements are not needed and the subroutine statements are implemented as extensions to a particular version of COBOL.

## 12.8  PICTURE EDITING

In Chapter 10, five categories of data are defined: alphabetic, alphanumeric, numeric, alphanumeric edited, and numeric edited. The categories relate to two areas:

1. How the data is stored
2. The characters that can be used in the PICTURE clause for a data item

## Categories of Data

An *alphabetic* data item may contain only alphabetic characters and the space; the only character permitted in the PICTURE clause of an alphabetic data item is the symbol "A". An *alphanumeric* data item may contain any character in the character set; the symbols "A", "9", and "X" are permitted in the PICTURE clause of an alphanumeric data item and the data item is treated as if the PICTURE clause contained all "X"s. A *numeric* data item may contain only digits and an operational sign; the symbols "9", "V", and "S" are permitted in the PICTURE clause for a numeric data item. Neither of these categories specifies editing. When a data item is moved to an alphabetic, alphanumeric, or numeric field, no editing is performed and the rules for data movement given in Chapter 11 apply.

An *alphanumeric-edited* data item is specified by a PICTURE clause that contains combinations of the symbols "A", "X", "9", "B", and "0" (that is, "zero"), in conjunction with the following conditions:

1. The PICTURE clause must contain at least one "B" and at least one "X";
2. The PICTURE clause must contain at least one "0" (that is, "zero") and at least one "X"; or
3. The PICTURE clause must contain at least one "0" (that is, "zero") and at least one "A".

The only type of editing that can be specified for an alphanumeric edited data item is "simple insertion," covered later.

A *numeric-edited* data item is specified by a PICTURE clause that contains combinations of the following symbols: "9", "V", ".", ",", "*", "+", "-", "B", "Z", "0", "$", "CR", and "DB". The source field during a data movement operation to a numeric edited field must be numeric with a size of 18 digits or less. *The editing is performed automatically as part of the data movement operation, and the result is a field with a DISPLAY usage, regardless of the type of the source field.*

Other than simple insertion, all editing applies to numeric data.

## Types of Editing

Editing is performed in one of two ways: by inserting characters into a field and by suppressing a digit and substituting a replacement character.

Four types of *insertion editing* exist: simple insertion, special insertion, fixed insertion, and floating insertion. Two types of *suppression and replacement editing* exist: zero suppression and replacement with spaces; and zero suppression and replacement with asterisks. Each type is presented as a separate topic.

### Simple Insertion

During simple insertion, a specified character is actually inserted into the resultant field. Three simple insertion symbols can be used in a PICTURE clause: "B", "0" (zero), and the comma. The "B" and "0" are used for alphanumeric editing, and the comma is used for numeric editing. Simple insertion is depicted in the following examples:

| Source Field | | Receiving Field | |
|---|---|---|---|
| *Picture* | *Data* | *Picture* | *Edited Result* |
| X(5) | ABCDE | XXBXX0X | AB CD0E |
| A(7) | HJJONES | ABABA(5) | H J JONES |
| S9(7)V99 | 123456789 | 9,999,999.99 | 1,234,567.89 |
| S9(4)V99 | 001234 | 9,999.99 | 0,012.34 |

The insertion characters are counted in the size of the receiving field.

### Special Insertion

Two of the preceding examples depicted special insertion, which uses the decimal point as an insertion character and performs decimal point alignment. The following examples depict other cases of special insertion:

| Source Field | | Receiving Field | |
|---|---|---|---|
| *Picture* | *Data* | *Picture* | *Edited Result* |
| S99 | 25 | 9(4).99 | 0025.00 |
| S9PPP | 3 | 9(4).99 | 3000.00 |
| S9V99 | 123 | 99.9 | 01.2 |
| S999 | 123 | 999. | 123. |
| SP(4)99 | 78 | 9(1).9(6) | 0.000078 |

## Fixed Insertion

Fixed insertion specifies the insertion of a currency symbol ($) or an editing sign control symbol (+, -, CR, or DB) in a fixed position in a numeric-edited field. The use of fixed-insertion symbols is governed by the following rules:

1. The currency symbol must be the leftmost character position in the field, unless preceded by a + or -.
2. The + or - must be the leftmost or rightmost character position in the field.
3. The CR and DB, representing credit and debit respectively, occupy two character positions in the rightmost positions in the field.

Table 12.1 gives the result of fixed-insertion editing depending on the operational sign of the source field. Fixed insertion is depicted in the following examples:

| Source Field | | Receiving Field | |
|---|---|---|---|
| *Picture* | *Data* | *Picture* | *Edited Result* |
| S9999V99 | 123456 | $9,999.99 | $1,234.56 |
| S999V99 | -12345 | $999.99CR | $123.45CR |
| S999V99 | 00025 | $999.99DB | $000.25 |
| S99V9 | 100 | +$999.99 | +$010.00 |
| S99V9 | -100 | +$999.99 | -$010.00 |
| S99V9 | 100 | -$999.99 | $010.00 |
| S99V99 | 2345 | 99.9+ | 23.4+ |

Fixed-insertion characters are counted in the size of the receiving field.

Table 12.1

Result of Fixed-Insertion Editing

| Editing Symbol in PICTURE Clause | Result When Source Field Is Positive or Zero | Result When Source Field Is Negative |
|---|---|---|
| + | + | - |
| - | space | - |
| CR | 2 spaces | CR |
| DB | 2 spaces | DB |

## Floating Insertion

Floating insertion specifies the insertion of the currency symbol ($) or one of the editing sign symbols (+ or -) into the character position immediately preceding the first nonzero digit in a numeric-edited field. Floating insertion is indicated in the PICTURE clause by using a string of at least two of the allowable floating-insertion characters to represent the leftmost numeric character positions into which the insertion character can be floated; that is, for example, a PICTURE such as $$.99. A simple insertion character (B, 0, or the comma) embedded in the string of floating-insertion characters or to the immediate right of the string of floating-insertion characters is a part of the floating string that is inserted if a digit appears to its left and right; that is, for example, a PICTURE such as $$,$$$.99.

The result of floating insertion depends on the position in which the floating-insertion characters are placed and on the value of the data. If the floating-insertion characters are placed only to the left of the decimal point, then a single floating-insertion character is placed into the character position immediately preceding the first nonzero digit that can be suppressed or the decimal point, whichever occurs first. If all numeric character positions in the PICTURE are represented by floating-insertion characters, then the result depends on the data. If the data is zero, then the field is filled with spaces. If the data is nonzero, then the result is the same as the case given above. Floating insertion is depicted in the following examples:

| Source Field | | Receiving Field | |
|---|---|---|---|
| Picture | Data | Picture | Edited Result |
| S9(4)V99 | 123456 | $$,$$$.99 | $1,234.56 |
| S9(4)V99 | 001234 | $$,$$$.99 | $12.34 |
| S9(4)V99 | 000012 | $$,$$$.99 | $.12 |
| S9(4)V99 | 000005 | $$,$$$.99 | $.05 |
| S9(7)V99 | 123456789 | $$,$$$,$$$.99 | $1,234,567.89 |
| S9(7)V99 | 001234567 | $$,$$$,$$$.99 | $12,345.67 |
| S9(4)V99 | 123456 | ++,+++.99 | +1,234.56 |
| S9(4)V99 | -123456 | ++,+++.99 | -1,234.56 |
| S9(4)V99 | 001234 | ++,+++.99 | +12.34 |
| S9(4)V99 | -001234 | ++,+++.99 | -12.34 |
| S9(4)V99 | 123456 | --,---.99 | 1,234.56 |
| S9(4)V99 | -123456 | --,---.99 | -1,234.56 |
| S9(4)V99 | 001234 | --,---.99 | 12.34 |
| S9(4)V99 | -001234 | --,---.99 | -12.34 |
| S9(4)V99 | 000123 | $$,$99.99 | $01.23 |

As shown, the + and – symbols are interpreted in the same manner as in fixed insertion.

## Zero Suppression and Replacement

The zero-suppression and -replacement symbols Z and * are used to suppress and replace leading zeros in numeric character positions in a field. The symbol Z denotes replacement with the space character. The symbol * denotes replacement with an asterisk; it is usually employed for check protection.

Zero suppression and replacement is indicated in a PICTURE by using a string of one or more of the symbols Z or * to represent leading numeric character positions. The symbols Z and * are mutually exclusive and cannot be used together. Simple insertion symbols are used in the same manner as in floating insertion.

Zero suppression applies only to numeric positions represented by zero-suppression characters. When zero-suppression symbols appear only to the left of the decimal point, zero suppression stops with the first nonzero digit or the decimal point—whichever occurs first. When all of the numeric character positions in the PICTURE clause are represented by zero-suppression symbols, the result depends on the data. If the value of the data is zero, the entire field is replaced with spaces if Z is used and with asterisks if * is used. If the value of the data is not zero, then the result is the same as in the case given above.

Zero suppression and replacement is depicted in the following examples:

| Source Field | | Receiving Field | |
|---|---|---|---|
| *Picture* | *Data* | *Picture* | *Edited Result* |
| S9(4)V99 | 123456 | $*,***.99 | $1,234.56 |
| S9(4)V99 | 012345 | $*,***.99 | $**123.45 |
| S9(4)V99 | 001234 | $*,***.99 | $***12.34 |
| S99V99 | 0012 | $**9.99 | $**0.12 |
| S999V99 | 00123 | $***.** | $**1.23 |
| S999V99 | 00000 | $***.** | $***.** |
| S999V99 | 12345 | ZZZ.99 | 123.45 |
| S999V99 | 01234 | ZZZ.99 | 12.34 |
| S999V99 | 00012 | ZZZ.99 | .12 |
| S999V99 | 00123 | ZZZ.ZZ | 1.23 |
| S999V99 | 00000 | ZZZ.ZZ | (spaces) |

## Comments on Picture Editing

The preceding discussion of picture editing satisfies the needs of most COBOL applications. As shown in many of the examples, many of the forms of editing can be used in combination. The forms that can or cannot be used together are fairly obvious. For example, fixed insertion and floating insertion or zero suppression and replacement can obviously be used together, whereas floating insertion and zero suppression and replacement cannot, in general, be used together.

When programming in COBOL, picture editing is the source of many reruns during the debugging process. Picture clauses are frequently adjusted to meet the needs of a particular application.

## 12.9  COMPUTATIONAL FORMS

One of the most frequently occurring extensions to the COBOL language is in the USAGE clause. The USAGE clause is used to specify the manner in which a data item is represented. Three options were given earlier: display, computational, and index. When a usage of DISPLAY is specified, a data item is stored in an external form, and a usage of INDEX is specified for data names used in table handling. The various computational forms are of interest here.

A usage of COMPUTATIONAL is implementor defined but usually denotes numeric data stored in fixed-point binary form. Most computers allow other forms for the representation and processing of numeric data. The IBM 360/370 implementation of COBOL, for example, allows four computational forms:

| *Usage* | *Representation* |
|---|---|
| COMPUTATIONAL | Fixed-point binary |
| COMPUTATIONAL-1 | Short precision floating-point binary |
| COMPUTATIONAL-2 | Long precision floating-point binary |
| COMPUTATIONAL-3 | Fixed-point packed decimal |

The various forms of data representation are covered in Chapter 1.

Although the structure of the procedure division is generally independent of the computational form used for numeric data, the choice of data representation can greatly affect the efficiency of the object program. When a sizable number of arithmetic operations are planned, it is frequently useful to consider the computational forms carefully to minimize the number of data conversions that are performed during the execution of a program.

## EXERCISES

1. Give applications where the following entries might be used:

   CURRENCY SIGN IS literal

   DECIMAL-POINT IS COMMA

2. Section 12.4 includes an example of table handling in which table SYMTAB is searched for the first occurrence of SYMBOL as a NAME entry. Write a COBOL program segment that executes the same function without the SET and SEARCH statements and indexing facilities.

3. Write a COBOL program segment to read a card deck and create an indexed sequential file. The card deck is formatted as follows:

   Col. 1-10:   Part name
   Col. 11-15: Part number
   Col. 16-80: Miscellaneous data

   The part number is the "record key". Include data and environment division entries.

4. Using the file created in exercise 3, read a set of cards, each containing a part number in columns 21-25. For each card (i.e., part number), fetch the master record from the indexed sequential file and print it. Include data and environment division entries.

5. Describe how COBOL library facilities might be used in a data processing installation.

6. Distinguish between and give examples of simple insertion, special insertion, fixed insertion, and floating insertion.

7. A form of zero suppression and replacement is the BLANK WHEN ZERO clause in the data division. What other similar clauses *might* be appropriate?

## SELECTED READINGS

1. Bernard, S. M. *System 360 COBOL*. Englewood Cliffs, N.J.: Prentice-Hall, Inc., 1968.

2. Chapin, N. *Computers: A System's Approach*. New York: Van Nostrand Reinhold Co., 1971.

3. Flores, I. *Data Structure and Management*. Englewood Cliffs, N.J.: Prentice-Hall, Inc., 1970.

4. IBM System/360 Operating System. *USA Standard COBOL*. New York: IBM Corporation, Form C28-6396.
5. Jones, R. L. *Fundamental COBOL for IBM System/360*. Englewood Cliffs, N.J.: Prentice-Hall, Inc., 1969.
6. McCracken, D. D., and U. Garbassi. *A Guide to COBOL Programming*. New York: John Wiley and Sons, Inc., 1970.
7. Murach, M. *Standard COBOL*. Chicago: Science Research Associates, 1971.
8. Saxon, J. A., and W. R. Englander. *ANSI COBOL Programming*. Englewood Cliffs, N.J.: Prentice-Hall, Inc., 1972.
9. *USA Standard COBOL*. New York: United States of America Standards Institute, X3.23-1968.

# INDEX